## Praise for *Transformative Learning*

The essays collected in *Transformative Learning* illustrate how incredibly successful Satish Kumar's inspired ideas have been in influencing individuals from around the world. It could not be published at a more opportune time as we emerge from the Covid-19 pandemic to face anew the existential threat of climate change. Creating the shift from a materialistic way of life to a new green economy will not be easy. This book provides some very valuable insights on how we might move in this direction.

— Jane Goodall, PhD, DBE, founder, the Jane Goodall Institute,
UN Messenger of Peace

This is how we begin again, even at this late hour. When the pandemic has pulled the plug on our global economy, when all the scientific reports, meetings, and treaties have not lowered by a hair our greenhouse gas emissions, and when the juggernaut of mass extinction threatens all that remains of our biodiversity, we can begin again. We can learn to trust our head and heart and hands, as Schumacher College has explored and proposed over the last thirty years. This book is a good guide as to how we can begin again.

— Joanna Macy, author, *A Wild Love for the World* and *Coming Back to Life*

Thank you, Satish Kumar, for this rich gift of powerful voices bringing forth an emergent, nature-centered learning essential to life itself. *Transformative Learning* should be essential reading for all educators and learners.

— Frances Moore Lappe, author, *Diet for Small Planet* and
18 other books, cofounder, Small Planet Institute

Thirty years ago, Schumacher College was founded, not just to teach radical economic and ecological ideas, but to teach them in a new way. Or rather, a very old way – one that unites the intellect with the rest of what makes us human. Hence, the title of this collection of essays: *Head, Heart, and Hands*. Today, with the dominant model of education in acute crisis, this book is an invaluable inspiration, transmitting the spirit of Schumacher and the possibility it holds to seed a new, holistic mode of education for the future.

— Charles Eisenstein, speaker and author,
*The More Beautiful World Our Heart Knows is Possible*

D1612776

Located among the rolling hills, woodlands and wild hedgerows of Devon, for thirty amazing years the convivial ethos of Schumacher College has attracted some of the finest educators, scientists, artists, and theorists from around the world, all eager to participate (even if just for a few weeks) in the small-scale, craft-centered, and place-based sanity that animates the college. Schumacher draws steady insight from its locale—from the unique biodiversity of the terrain that surrounds and sustains it—yet the ecological intelligence of its programs has spread out through its many international students to influence, deepen, and transform the practice of ecology on every continent. With its wide array of contributors, this book is a splendid testament to its thirty years carefully cultivating a full-bodied wisdom rooted in attentive reciprocity with the winds, the waters, and the soil underfoot.

— David Abram, author, *Becoming Animal* and *The Spell of the Sensuous*, and director, Alliance for Wild Ethics (AWE)

By beginning with rebuilding community and reconnecting with the natural world we are part of, Schumacher College cultivates the kind of imaginative thinking and transformative practice that can bring into being a better future for all of us. Schumacher College and its growing network of alumni around the world, many of whom have contributed to this book, are beacons of active hope whose time has come.

— Caroline Lucas, MP, Green Party Member of the British Parliament

The book describes the vision and reality of Schumacher College, which is a living example of a sustainable civilisation in the making. *Transformative Learning* brings together some of the leading voices of our time articulating the parameters of a regenerative culture, urgently needed for now and for the future. It is essential reading!

— Otto Scharmer, author, *Theory U*, founder, MITx u.lab and Presencing Institute

I have a prediction. As you read *Transformative Learning* the deep coherence of the ideas will ignite in you a profound trust. You will realize that things are going to work out. These authors are the architects of an entirely new civilization. By dwelling in their thinking, you become a pattern that connects our hard time to a vibrant new era of the Earth Community.

— Brian Thomas Swimme, professor, California Institute of Integral Studies

*For Emma, with love,*

*Satish*

*21/5/21*

# Transformative Learning

## Reflections on 30 Years of
## Head, Heart, and Hands
### at Schumacher College

Editors

**Satish Kumar** and **Pavel Cenkl**

Illustrations by Angéline Bichon
Photography by Delia Spatareanu

new society
PUBLISHERS

Cover Design by Diane McIntosh.
Cover Image Credits: Butterfly Illustration © Angéline Bichon.
Photograph is of Lilla Jessica Brokaw, Schumacher Graduate,
MSc in Holistic Science; Photograph © Delia Spatareanu.
All Interior Illustrations © Angéline Bichon. (unless otherwise noted).
All Interior Photographs courtesy of Delia Spatareanu.

Printed in Canada. First printing April, 2021.

Inquiries regarding requests to reprint all or part of *Transformative Learning*
should be addressed to New Society Publishers at the address below.
To order directly from the publishers, please call toll-free (North America)
1-800-567-6772, or order online at www.newsociety.com

Any other inquiries can be directed by mail to:

New Society Publishers
P.O. Box 189, Gabriola Island, BC V0R 1X0, Canada
(250) 247-9737

LIBRARY AND ARCHIVES CANADA CATALOGUING IN PUBLICATION

Title: Transformative learning : reflections on 30 years of head, heart, and
hands at Schumacher College / Satish Kumar and Pavel Cenkl.

Names: Satish Kumar, 1936- editor. | Cenkl, Pavel, 1971- editor.

Identifiers: Canadiana (print) 20200409581 | Canadiana (ebook) 20200409840
| ISBN 9780865719521 (softcover) | ISBN 9781550927450 (PDF) |
ISBN 9781771423410 (EPUB)

Subjects: LCSH: Schumacher College. | LCSH: Schumacher College—History.
| LCSH: Schumacher College—Anniversaries, etc. | LCSH: Ecology—Study and
teaching (Higher)—England—Devon. | LCSH: Holistic education—England—
Devon. | LCSH: Interdisciplinary approach in education—England—Devon.

Classification: LCC LF795.D48 S28 2021 | DDC 577.071/1423592—dc23

New Society Publishers' mission is to publish books that contribute in
fundamental ways to building an ecologically sustainable and just society,
and to do so with the least possible impact on the environment,
in a manner that models this vision.

*In nature nothing exists alone.*

*The human race is challenged more*
*than ever before to demonstrate our mastery,*
*not over nature but of ourselves.*
— RACHEL CARSON

# Contents

# Part 3: Education of Heart

# Part 4: Education of Hands

# Part 5: Schumacher Worldwide

## Part 6: Schumacher Alumni Experiences

## Part 7: The Future

# Introduction: A New Pedagogy

Satish Kumar

*Knowledge and practice (yoga) are one. When you see this, you truly see.*
— Bhagavad Gita

With this book we celebrate the first thirty years of Schumacher College. At this moment I am overwhelmed with gratitude to those who embraced the idea in the first place and saw its potential. In particular I would like to pay my tribute to the late Maurice Ash and to John Lane, the two trustees of Dartington Hall Trust who, in 1990, shared the vision of the college and gave their practical support to realize the dream. I also feel deeply indebted to the Dartington Hall Trust itself which has kept the college afloat and enabled it to flourish all these years.

No project of this nature can be established and maintained without the engagement and commitment of many staff, teachers, volunteers, funders and above all students and participants. I am holding back from the temptation of naming all those who helped the college to manifest. Suffice to say that the college is a living example of co-creation.

This book is not about the history or the practical functioning of the college. The purpose of this book is to look back and see how a new educational philosophy has evolved at the college in the past thirty years. And how this new holistic pedagogy could be applied in mainstream educational institutions.

In this book I did not choose to take the method of academic research to present this pedagogy. Rather I wanted to follow the narratives and experiences of our teachers, participants and students. So, I invited a few of our past and present teachers and some of our students and participants to write about their personal experiences and feelings about their time at the college and how that has affected their thinking and their lives. I am delighted with the outcome.

Schumacher College was founded to provide a place for the study and practice of ecological and spiritual values. It was felt that the mainstream educational system was dominated by economic and materialist values. We needed an alternative.

The study of the economy without understanding ecology, and the pursuit of materialism without spiritual values, has led to a situation where however much money we have and whatever economic growth we achieve never seems to be enough in spite of the fact that forests, wildlife, biodiversity and oceans are all being sacrificed to serve the economy. Furthermore, material success is followed by growing levels of anxiety, loss of meaning and decline in the feeling of fulfillment.

Mainstream education has played a central role in these deteriorating human conditions. Schools, colleges and universities are the pillars of the industrial and consumerist society. They are the training grounds and the upholders of this economic and materialist pedagogy. In the current educational system Nature is considered to be a resource for the economy. But in the new pedagogy Nature is more than a resource, Nature is the source of life itself. In mainstream universities students learn *about* Nature, in the new pedagogy we learn *from* Nature. Nature is the ultimate teacher and mentor. We go even further; we realize that humans are an integral part of Nature.

Those of us who wish to see the transformation from the old pedagogy to the new pedagogy, where the economy is in harmony with ecology and material well-being is complemented by spiritual well-being, need to start transforming the current pedagogy and changing mainstream educational institutions. But before we can do that we have to experiment and see if the ideas of the new pedagogy work.

Reading this book, readers will see that the answer is positive. Yes, it works. Yes, it is possible to create and live a good life without damaging the ecosphere. And yes, we can embrace outer material comfort without losing inner spiritual harmony.

It is with pleasure that we present this book to all those who are interested in a successful and radical educational experiment, an experiment where the education of head, heart and hands is integrated and fundamental.

In this book we have used head, heart and hands as separate headings for the sake of convenience. But as head, heart and hands are parts of one body, so the education of head, heart and hands is also part of one system. There is neither division nor separation.

# PART 1

# Education of Head:
# Science

# Greening of Education

### Satish Kumar

*In the modern times people do not experience themselves*
*to be part of nature, but as an outside force destined*
*to dominate and conquer nature. People even talk of a battle*
*with nature, forgetting that if they won the battle,*
*they would find themselves on the*
*losing side.*

— E. F. Schumacher

## Meeting with E. F. Schumacher

My story of Schumacher College begins with my meeting E. F. Schumacher himself. It was in 1968 when Fritz invited me to have lunch with him in an Italian restaurant in London, following an introduction by a common friend. In that very first meeting we clicked.

On a subsequent visit to London in 1972 I met him again. At that time, Fritz was an associate editor of *Resurgence* magazine. The founding editor, John Papworth, had gone to Africa, and the editorial team was looking for a new editor. Fritz said to me, "You have had plenty of editorial experience in India, how about taking on the editorship of *Resurgence*?"

I replied, "That is a very kind thought, but I am in England only for a short time. I am returning to India."

Fritz said, "But you don't have to go back to India! Why do you want to go back? Is the job of the editor of *Resurgence* not good enough?"

I said, "I am a Gandhian, I want to work with the Gandhian movement in India."

Fritz countered me energetically by saying, "But Satish, there are many Gandhians in India. We need one in England, so I urge you to take up the editorship of *Resurgence*."

That was a very persuasive argument. Spontaneously I said, "Ok! If I become the editor, will you contribute to each issue of the magazine?"

Fritz replied, "Yes, that's a deal. If you become the editor, I will certainly contribute in every issue."

Then it became an impossible deal to get out of. Thus, I stayed in England and became the editor of *Resurgence* and worked with Fritz until he died in 1977.

After his death, to honor his memory and build on his legacy, *Resurgence* launched the Schumacher Society and a series of annual Schumacher lectures, held in Bristol. These lectures where delivered by prominent ecologists and new paradigm thinkers and activists. They were attended by five hundred to a thousand people and were a great success.

## The Dartington Connection

In 1988, I was having lunch with John Lane, an artist, a regular attendee of Schumacher lectures and an avid reader of *Resurgence*. Moreover, he was also a trustee of Dartington Hall Trust, an estate of more than a thousand acres and a center for rural reconstruction, education, arts and culture. Dartington Hall was established through the inspiration of the Indian poet Rabindranath Tagore.

Over lunch John informed me that due to financial pressures and lack of numbers, Dartington Hall School had to be closed and one of the buildings, the Old Postern, with forty bedrooms was empty and they were looking for a suitable tenant. I knew the Old Postern, a beautiful fourteenth-century building which had been used to accommodate students of Dartington Hall School, and where Rabindranath Tagore had stayed. So, I said to John, "Who is going to want this building! Too big for a family, too small for a hotel, and after all it was a school. So, it should be used for a good educational purpose."

John said, "But we could not continue to run the school. What kind of educational activities can we organize there?"

I said to him, "We know these great thinkers and activists who have given Schumacher lectures, but these lectures are one-day events, there is no in-depth exploration possible in such a short time. Wouldn't it be good if we had a place where these green thinkers could spend a reasonable amount of time and go deeper into the exploration of new kinds of science, new kinds of economics and a new way of life? Most universities are wedded to the old paradigm thinking. They are committed to reductionist science, continuous economic growth, unlimited industrialization and rampant materialism leading to waste, pollution and the destruction of biodiversity and loss of natural habitats. In terms of ecological worldview, the planet is in peril. I would love to invite these thinkers and activists to teach in such a new learning center."

John said, "That sounds very interesting! Write a proposal, which I can present to the trustees of Dartington Hall!"

That was the seed of Schumacher College. After many meetings and prolonged discussions among trustees, my proposal was accepted by them, but with a certain reluctance by some. One of the trustees, Michael Young, was particularly skeptical. He said to me, "Satish, you are a dreamer! Who is going to come and learn about ecology and green perspectives and pay for it? The college may not last more than five years! But since my fellow trustees want to do something and the building is standing empty, we will give you five years to prove yourself, but I don't think you will last that long!"

I said, "Michael, it is better to try something and fail, than not try at all!"

Michael said, "I like your enthusiasm and your passion. The trustees will give you five years rent free, and we will underwrite any deficit during that time. I wish you good luck."

## Launching the College

James Lovelock, who had given a Schumacher lecture, lived near me in North Devon. I often walked with him on Dartmoor, talking about his Gaia theory. So, as I was planning to invite teachers of an earth-centered worldview to teach at Schumacher College, I said to James, "I would like to start our courses on a scientific subject. Science is good, but the old science of mechanistic thinking, which only looks at nature as an inanimate object and exploits her for the benefit of humans, is becoming a dangerous science. We need a new and holistic science. Your Gaia theory is the science of the future; will you be our first teacher at Schumacher College?"

James said, "Your invitation is tempting. Most universities at the moment reject my science of Gaia. They think that my science is not scientific enough. But Gaia, the earth, is a living organism. How can life be sustained by a dead rock! But that is how most of the scientists think of the earth—a dead rock. Therefore, I would love to explore and explain to a group of people how scientifically we can prove that earth is a living organism and not a dead rock."

I was delighted that James accepted to be our first teacher. Then I contacted Fritjof Capra, Vandana Shiva, David Orr, Jonathon Porritt, Joanna Macy, Janine Benyus, Wendell Berry and many others who had given Schumacher lectures and asked them to teach at the college. To my utter delight every single one of them accepted my invitation, and we published our year-long program in *Resurgence*.

The very first course, in January 1991, on Gaia, was a sellout with a waiting list.

## The Vision

The vision of Schumacher College was not simply to create an intellectual learning center based on an ecological and spiritual worldview. Our vision was to create a center where learning and living came together, where knowledge and experience integrated and where learning was not simply a personal pursuit but a collective journey within the context of a community. We envisioned that Schumacher College should not be solely an institution, it would be a community, a home.

Most education in universities is an intellectual pursuit. Students are perceived as if they have no body. They have no hands, no legs, no hearts, no feelings, only a head, and education is simply education of the head and only the left hemisphere of the head at that. How could education be defined and then promoted in such a staggeringly narrow way? So, we decided from the very beginning that at Schumacher College we would endeavor to practice education of head, education of hearts and education of hands. Thus cooking, crafts, cleaning and gardening became an integral part of learning. And, of course, singing, storytelling, poetry, meditation and spirituality were incorporated in the daily timetable to cultivate the heart qualities. The pursuit of beauty and elegant simplicity became an integral part of the Schumacher experience.

Michael Young had given us five years. But I am delighted that we have been here for much longer than that. Now we are celebrating the 30th anniversary. During this time students and participants have come to Schumacher College from around the world. We have about 20,000 alumni in eighty different countries. They have gone through a transformative experience at the college and gone out into the world to serve people and the planet earth. When Schumacher students leave the college, I say to them, "Go out in the world, but don't look for a job. Create your own job, a job which is regenerative, fulfilling and enhances the life of Gaia, people and yourself. Your work is not just a job, it should be a livelihood."

## Pedagogy of Freedom

The word "education" is derived from Latin *educare* which means "to bring up" or "to bring forth" or "to draw out." Thus, education doesn't mean teaching, or schooling or giving knowledge or even acquiring knowledge. Education simply means developing the qualities which are already in the student. Socrates compared a teacher to a midwife who just helps to bring forth the child.

I compare a teacher to a gardener. No one puts a tree in the seed, the tree is already in the seed. The seed knows what kind of tree it is. The gardener only helps the seed to become a tree. The gardener may find a place with some good soil to plant the seed, dig in good organic compost to nourish the seed, build a fence to protect the plant, give water to nurture it, but a gardener never tries to change an apple into a pear tree.

Teachers need to be like gardeners. They need to observe their students, understand them, help them to become who they are, support them on their way to self-realization. But never try to impose on them their idea of an "educated person."

In our modern Industrial Age, education has become confused with training, schooling or acquiring facts, information and knowledge in order to get a job. Rather than teachers helping a student become who he or she is and realize his or her true potential, teachers have become technicians or trainers or even agents to meet the needs of the market. The teacher is paid to mould the student so that he or she is fit to contribute to the economy. In this kind of educational system, the market and the economy become the masters and human beings become the servants.

This is corruption of education. At Schumacher College we want to recover the original actual meaning of the noble word "education."

We want schools and teachers to return to the true meaning of the word and dedicate themselves to the cause of helping young people discover their vocation.

The famous philosopher J. Krishnamurti once said to me, "There is nothing wrong with the market or with the economy. As long as they serve the needs of humans, they have a place in the world. But when humans are required to serve the needs of the market and the economy then we are in real trouble. Unfortunately, that is the problem at this moment in the world. This is why we need a total revolution in our idea of education. We need to liberate ourselves from the idea that education takes place only within the four walls of a school. It is not that you read a book, go to a classroom for your lessons or pass an examination and then you have finished with your education. Education is a lifelong process. From the moment you are born to the moment you die, you are on the journey of learning.

"We are learning to be free! Learning is all about liberation. We need to learn to be free from fear, free from anxiety, free from dogmas and doctrines. We need to discover and rediscover that we are born free and freedom is our birthright! Fear is a conditioning of the mind. From family, from religious belief, from the media and even from our educational systems, we are conditioned to fear. The purpose of true education is to free us from all kinds of fear."

I was deeply touched by his words.

For me this was a new Pedagogy of Freedom!

But our educational system at present is totally unaware of the fact that it is based on the Pedagogy of Fear.

I have observed that schools, colleges and universities around the world are focused on the education of heads only. No wonder that many of our young people feel inadequate, incompetent and fearful. They have never developed their heart qualities. They don't know how to relate to other people and to the natural world. This lack of emotional and spiritual intelligence is a major cause of fear. The conventional educational curriculum includes almost nothing about compassion, about a sense of service, about courage or about love! At Schumacher College our vision continues to be that these qualities should be an integral part of learning.

Most colleges and universities ignore all practical or physical skills. Most undergraduates or postgraduates coming out of universities know nothing about growing food, nothing about building a house, nothing about mending or repairing and almost nothing about cooking. They have highly trained heads superbly capable of complaining, comparing and criticizing. They are taught to control and consume. They have little or no capacity for making, producing, building or creating. There is very little in our educational philosophy or practice which promotes self-reliance and self-confidence. That is why from the very beginning of Schumacher College we incorporated these practices.

On top of this deficit in emotional intelligence and body intelligence, the current educational system is more or less indifferent to the development of the imagination. Music, art, dance, plays, poetry and philosophy are relegated to some distant and specialist corners. Instead of the arts being an integral part of everyday life, they have been exiled to museums and art galleries to be pursued by a small minority of celebrity artists whose work is marketed as commercial commodities. On the other hand, there are a small number of genuine artists, who can hardly make a living.

The educational system produces millions upon millions of young people to serve the needs of machines, markets and money. And all these young people are struggling to compete and succeed and are often afraid of not succeeding.

This fear of failure is one of the most detrimental aspects of the current pedagogy of fear.

In order to compensate for this fear of failure, young people are encouraged to focus on success for themselves and to seek big salaries, big cars, big houses and high positions. Some succeed, but many fail. This egocentric rat race results in family breakdown, mental breakdown, discontent, depression and disappointment. Therefore, at Schumacher College students are encouraged to seek fulfillment in their work and in their community rather than individual success. Moreover, they are encouraged to glow like stars glow.

SATISH KUMAR is Editor Emeritus of *Resurgence* and *Ecologist* magazines and author of *Elegant Simplicity*, published by New Society Publishers.

AN OVERVIEW

# A Unique Learning Experience

F RITJOF  C APRA

*Study nature, love nature, stay close to nature.*
*She will never fail you.*
— F RANK  L LOYD  W RIGHT

Since the early 1990s, I have taught over a dozen courses at Schumacher College. In fact, Satish Kumar invited me to teach one of the very first courses there. I still remember meeting Satish for tea in a hotel near Paddington Station in London some time in 1990, one year before the college was founded. During that meeting Satish shared with me his vision of a new kind of place-based, community-oriented, transformative learning. I found this vision so compelling that I immediately accepted his kind invitation, and I have been a strong supporter of the college ever since.

During the last thirty years, Schumacher College has been, indeed, an absolutely unique institution, providing an unparalleled learning experience. It is not a traditional college with a well-defined faculty and student body, and unlike most colleges and universities, it was not founded by any government agency, nor any individual or foundation associated with business.

Schumacher College grew out of a global environmental movement that had its roots in the counterculture of the 1960s, flourished during the 1970s and 1980s and became a central part of the global civil society that emerged during the 1990s. Thus, from the beginning its faculty has been part of an international network of scholars and activists, a network of friends and colleagues that had already existed for several decades.

Satish Kumar, the founder of Schumacher College, is an Indian spiritual teacher and Gandhian activist, who lives in the UK where he served for forty years as editor of *Resurgence*, one of the most important and beautiful ecological magazines. Satish (as he is known to his friends and disciples around the world) was a close associate of E. F. Schumacher, the environmental pioneer and author of the classic book *Small Is Beautiful*, after whom the college was named.

Before its foundation in 1991, there was no center of learning where ecology could be studied in a rigorous, in-depth way and from many different perspectives. As far as the faculty was concerned, they were outstanding scholars, many of whom had written brilliant books, but they did not have a place where they could explore their ideas and have them critically examined in the relaxed environment of a community that shared their basic values.

During the subsequent years, the situation changed significantly when a global coalition of NGOs, now known as the global civil society, formed around the core values of human dignity and ecological sustainability. To place their political discourse within a systemic and ecological perspective, this global civil society developed a network of scholars, research institutes, think tanks and centers of learning that largely operate outside our leading academic institutions, business organizations and government agencies.

Today, there are dozens of these institutions of research and learning in all parts of the world. Schumacher College was one of the first and continues to play a leading role. These research institutes are communities of scholars and activists who are engaged in a wide variety of projects and campaigns. As their scope grew and diversified over the years, so did the faculty and curriculum of Schumacher College.

From the very beginning, Satish had the vision that the college should not represent a Eurocentric view but should give voice to a broad range of opinions—that it should be international. When Americans and Europeans discuss science, technology and philosophy here, they are joined by voices from Africa, India, Japan and other parts of the world.

The same ethnic, cultural and intellectual diversity exists among the students. It has not been unusual for me to have twenty-four course participants (the limit that was established) from ten or more different countries. Participants are usually highly educated. Some are professionals in various fields; some are young students, but there are also older people; and they contribute to the discussions from a multitude of perspectives.

The level of education and experience of the course participants, who come from all over the world and engage one another in intensive discussions, is truly amazing. I have often thought that the core faculty are merely catalysts for the participants to engage in these dialogues. In a way, these diverse perspectives mirror the richness of the field of ecology, which is the central focus of the college. There is ecology as science, as politics, as technology and as a philosophy grounded in spirituality. This great diversity of ecology is embodied in the very structure and in the curriculum of the college.

## A Sense of Community

Another key characteristic of Schumacher College is the strong sense of community it engenders. Participants come here for several weeks to live together, learn together and also to work together to sustain the learning community. They are divided into working groups that cook, clean, garden—doing all the work that is needed to maintain the college, in a practice of Gandhian spirituality.

In these groups, conversations go on virtually round the clock. While they are cutting vegetables in the kitchen, they talk; while they are mopping the floor, or rearranging chairs for a special event, they talk. Everybody here is immersed in a continual experience of community and exciting intellectual dialogues and discussions.

The teaching in the morning stimulates those dialogues that go on throughout the day and evening, and the courses themselves are also largely structured around dialogues. These are not just dialogues involving two people, one student and one teacher. They are collective dialogues in which common ideas are explored and contradictory ideas are examined together. In this kind of dialogue, we collectively look at the subjects from various perspectives. We don't debate but examine and explore things from different points of view.

All this stimulates tremendous creativity. At Schumacher College, much is created collectively, from meals in the kitchen to ideas in the classroom. Creativity flourishes because there is total trust in the community. By nurturing community, a climate of trust is created that becomes a fertile ground for creativity.

At Schumacher College, Satish has created a unique learning environment where discussions take place in an atmosphere that is intellectually intense and challenging but is emotionally very safe. To the faculty who teach at the college, it feels almost like being among family, and this strong feeling of community emerges after being together for not more than a week or two.

## Systemic View of Life

To most scholars such a situation is extremely attractive, as it offers us a unique opportunity to examine our work in depth, and to try out new ideas in a safe environment. This has certainly been the case for me. During the 1990s I discussed and explored, in course after course, my synthesis of the systemic understanding of life that has emerged at the forefront of science. Over the years I presented successive versions of that synthesis as my thinking evolved, highlighting the integration of the biological and cognitive dimensions of life, the critical role of complexity theory, the extension of the systems view of life to the social dimension and the ethics and spirituality of deep ecology. My students in those courses, as well as the core faculty members Brian Goodwin and Stephan Harding, helped me enormously in clarifying my ideas with critical questions and countless helpful suggestions.

Schumacher College, then, is a unique place not only for course participants to learn but also for the teaching faculty to deeply engage over a relatively long period with a group of highly educated and highly motivated students, and to pursue a process of sustained self-exploration.

FRITJOF CAPRA, PhD, physicist and systems theorist, is a founding director of the Center for Ecoliteracy in Berkeley, California. He is a Fellow of Schumacher College and serves on the Council of Earth Charter International. Capra is the author of several international bestsellers, including *The Tao of Physics*, *The Web of Life* and *The Science of Leonardo*. He is co-author, with Pier Luigi Luisi, of the multidisciplinary textbook *The Systems View of Life*. Capra's online course (capracourse.net) is based on his textbook.

# Salt in the Stew

DAVID W. ORR

*The highest education is that which does not merely give us
information but makes our life in harmony with all existence.*
— RABINDRANATH TAGORE

Thirty years ago, when Schumacher College was founded, carbon dioxide in the atmosphere was 354 parts per million—twenty-six percent above its background level. Other heat-trapping gasses measured in $CO_2$ equivalent units would have added another 20-30 ppm. The health of soils, forests, waters and wildlife was declining almost everywhere. We were skating on thinner and thinner ice. The Cold War was over, however, and we had arrived at the "end of history" where supposedly all of the big questions about politics and economy had been answered once and for all. We skated on, confident in our science, technological domination of nature, military prowess and growing economy. We, the US in particular and the West in general, were the winners in the lottery of history. Or so we thought.

## Predicament of Present Pedagogy

Thirty years on, however, we know better. It took a teenaged Greta Thunberg, however, to call the barons of the global economy to account and a global pandemic a year later to highlight the extent of our vulnerability. Someday, historians will sort through the many reasons for our blindness, but I'll focus on one they're likely to overlook: education.

The growing gyre of climatic, ecological, public health, social and economic chaos is a consequence of how we think and what we think about. Pandemics, global warming, mass extinctions and rising ecological disorder are consequences of a pathological derangement and misapprehension of the proper and durable human place in the world. In sum, they reflect a prior disorder of mind and so constitute a crisis for those institutions that purport to improve minds. But, what does it mean to improve our capacity to think ecologically or, as Donella Meadows put it, "think in systems"?

## Civilizational Crisis

To that question, there is neither a simple nor a final answer. We can describe, however, the symptoms of the disease. For one, our predicament crosses almost every academic discipline, yet we continue to educate within narrowly defined categories and tend to deal with small questions shrink-wrapped to fit therein. For another, our vaunted research piles disconnected facts onto other disconnected facts in a cacophonic mountain of bits and pieces, the result of what historian Page Smith once described as "busy-work on a vast almost incomprehensible scale." Ours is an ecological-civilizational crisis, but we have no educational departments adequate to inform or enlighten at that scale. The crisis is one of heart, but we educate for the brain only, and mostly that part primed to calculate, not the part from which we learn to feel, empathize and love. We deal in what E. F. Schumacher called "convergent problems," not "divergent problems." The former is linear and so amenable to scientific or technological solutions. The latter are more like dilemmas that are, by definition, unsolvable but avoidable with wisdom, foresight and compassion. Increasingly our basic problems are of the latter sort; they are divergent moral and political questions "refractory to mere logic and discursive reason." In short, the cascading crisis of crises, is the result of the disconnection of knowledge from the totality of ourselves, of humankind from nature, each from the other, and from the wisdom accumulated through the ages.

While the bonds that hold us together fray, we live in splendid isolation as "economic men" maximizing our narrowly defined self-interest calculated by utility (the most useless of useless notions) while sinking under a rising tide of junk, plastic debris, ugliness, pollution, bad ideas, violence and anomie. But we were warned long ago. John Ruskin, for one, wrote:

The rule and root of all economy—that what one person has, another cannot have; and that every atom of substance, of whatever kind, used or consumed, is so much human life spent...the world is not to be cheated of a grain; not so much as a breath of its air can be drawn surreptitiously. For every piece of wise work done, so much life is granted; for every piece of foolish work, nothing; for every piece of wicked work, so much death.

A century later, E. F. Schumacher wrote similarly:

If human vices such as greed and envy are systematically cultivated, the inevitable result is nothing less than a collapse of intelligence. A man driven by greed or envy loses the power of seeing things as they really are, of seeing things in their roundness and wholeness, and his very successes become failures. If whole societies become infected by these vices, they may indeed achieve astonishing things, but they become increasingly incapable of solving the most elementary problems of everyday existence.

At the periphery of the learned world, they and others proposed a different future for humankind—a human-scaled, ecologically designed world powered by sunlight, energized by ancient wisdom and disciplined by compassion, practical know-how and neighborliness. What they proposed was not so much research but, rather, a rediscovery of the best features of what historian Peter Laslett once called "the world we've lost." That world was by no means perfect, and at some times and in some places, it could be awful. At its best, however, it was a "creative, patient, and increasingly skilful love-making that had persuaded the land to flourish." The scale of habitation and enterprise was fitted to particular places, the skills to practical needs and the culture to our need for conviviality and connection. The world of villages, small farms, practical competence, local economies and moderately sized cities was the essence of "the age-long effort of Englishmen to fit themselves close and ever closer into England."

## Schumacher College Offers a New Pedagogy

Schumacher College is four hours by train from London and two miles northwest of Totnes on highway A384. The College is situated in the Old Postern (gatehouse) to the 1,235-acre Dartington Estate in the rolling hills of Devon. The Dartington Estate buildings, music center, hotel and White Hart pub are a lovely fifteen-minute uphill walk through farm fields divided by ancient hedgerows. At the crest, the rolling Devon landscape unfolds to the horizon. It is one of the most beautiful landscapes in all of Britain. To the north and east, the estate is bounded by the River Dart on its way to the port of Dartmouth from which Puritans once sailed to the Massachusetts Bay Colony.

The history of the estate goes back to 1388 when the half-brother of Richard II built Dartington Hall. It flourished as long as wealth was measured in land but declined in the new industrial age that measured wealth as capital. Dorothy and Leonard Elmhirst purchased the estate in 1925 and made it a center for holistic education and rural renewal that included farming, forestry, music, crafts and the arts. The Elmhirsts' vision was inspired in part by Rabindranath Tagore's philosophy of education and his experience in creating the Institute for Rural Reconstruction at Sriniketan.

Tagore intended to:

Develop in the children...the freshness of their feeling for Nature, a sensitiveness of soul in their relationship with their human surroundings, with the help of literature, festive ceremonials and also the religious teaching which enjoins us to come to the nearer presence of the world through the soul, and thus to gain it more than can be measured—like gaining an instrument, not merely by having it, but by producing music upon it. I prepared for my children a real homecoming into this world.

Tagore's influence is still very much alive in Schumacher College but with a broader mission that includes meditation, philosophy, the science of ecology, systems dynamics and ecologically based design, health, restoration ecology, ecological economics as well as regenerative farming and forestry. Its essence, as its founder Satish Kumar explains in *Elegant Simplicity*, is in the practical connections between soil, soul and society. Chopping vegetables, cooking, cleaning floors, conversation, laughter, walking, meditation and music blend in a tapestry of a convivial learning community.

The college exists on the far periphery of the global educational system that deals in millions of students each year, rapid throughput, billions of dollars of research funding, trillions in capital assets and has the bulletproof assurance that goes with its assumed monopoly of solutions to what ails modern societies. It exists unmolested as long as it does not threaten the prerogatives of the dominant culture or its underlying assumptions such as the imperative of economic growth and human domination of nature.

Schumacher College, on the other hand, is one of many alternative small educational centers scattered around the world. It concerns itself more with questions than with answers. Typically, the questions posed in seminars and conversations at Schumacher are the divergent kind that challenge paradigms and pomposity of any kind. The atmosphere is seldom as certain as in the higher reaches of the academic world. The scale is minuscule—several hundred students per year. Its clock speed—the rate at which things happen—is slow. Its primary stock-in-trade is the kind of dependable old knowledge that has accumulated over many centuries. Daily routines at the college allow for serendipity and spontaneity. The focus is a kind of disciplined diversity and boundary-crossing thought. The program includes meditation, music, serious lectures, gardening, walks along the Channel coastline that mimic geologic history. In other words, it is diverse but unified around the fundamental realities of body, mind and soul. College clientele is similarly diverse. The classes in which I participated over the years included students of all ages from all kinds of backgrounds from all over the world. Still, they typically bonded quickly into a supportive community in part because they work together to keep the place going. More importantly, removed from the mad bustle and busyness of their ordinary lives, participants have the time to sort the trivial from the important and observe the world and themselves from a calmer and saner vantage point.

For students and facilitators alike, the experience of Schumacher College is rather like the effect of salt in stew: small by volume but large by effect. For most, Schumacher changed the flavor of the mysterious thing called education. And, if we are to be truly drawn forth— the root meaning of the word "education"—we need such places and times to reconnect with our soul, the soil under our feet and the Life all around us.

DAVID W. ORR is Paul Sears Distinguished Professor of environmental studies and politics emeritus, Oberlin College. He is the author of nine books including *Ecological Literacy: Educating Our Children for a Sustainable World*, published by Sierra Club Books.

# Teaching for Gaia

STEPHAN HARDING

*The debt we owe to the play of imagination is incalculable.*
— CARL JUNG

I first came to Dartington almost thirty years ago thinking that I might stay two years at most. By then I had completed my doctorate in behavioral ecology at Oxford and had spent nearly three years teaching conservation biology at the National University in Costa Rica. Once back in the UK, I came to Devon with Ponlop Rimpoche, a young Tibetan lama who wanted to visit the Buddhist community at Sharpham House. There I discovered that the nearby Dartington Hall Trust was about to establish a college to explore the causes of the ecological crisis and its cures with small groups of teachers and participants from all over the world living and learning together in semi-ashram style in the Old Postern, a spacious old vicarage nestled in the woods and fields of the 1,235-acre Dartington Estate. Satish Kumar was a lead person in this endeavor, so I met him and others at Dartington and was soon appointed as the college's resident ecologist and also as estate ecologist charged with promoting biodiversity on the Trust's lands.

## The Science of Gaia

How fitting then that Gaia as science and myth was the theme of the very first course at Schumacher College in January 1991, taught by James Lovelock himself.

Gaia was the divinity of the Earth in ancient Greece. Hesiod (700 BCE) tells us that she was the firstborn of primordial Chaos (the vast intelligence which existed before matter, time and space); also that Gaia gave birth to the starry heavens and eventually to all her living creatures including human beings. For thousands of years Gaia, our Earth, was seen as a great soul, as a sacred living presence, kind to those who loved her and ruthless towards those who did not. Sadly, this deep appreciation of our Earth's sacredness ended when mainstream Christianity and later science ruthlessly banished these heartfelt perceptions of our Earth's lustrous spherical animacy into perpetual oblivion. Or so it seemed.

Our loss of connection with Gaia is part of a much wider split between humans and nature which has led our culture to so tragically and dangerously rend the world asunder with ever-increasing frenzy and destructive power since the scientific revolution gave us the means to do so in the sixteenth and seventeenth centuries.

And so it was that Gaia languished in the outer fringes of our culture's awareness for twenty centuries during which we despoiled the Earth with exponential rapidity in furtherance of our insane imperative to dominate, rule and conquer the whole of nature. By the mid-1960s we had pushed Gaia very close the brink of global climate and ecological catastrophe—and things were getting rapidly worse.

It was around that time that James Lovelock, a brilliant independent scientist-inventor, found himself working for NASA in Pasadena, California, as part of their quest to find life on Mars. One day in autumn 1965, he was in a NASA office conversing with his colleague, the philosopher Diane Hitchcock. The pair had had spent many days puzzling deeply over some intriguingly complex questions they had discovered through Lovelock's work at NASA: why are the atmospheres of Mars and Venus virtually entirely full of chemically inactive carbon dioxide while Earth's atmosphere swims in highly reactive oxygen? And why has the amount of this oxygen in our atmosphere remained virtually unchanged at around twenty percent throughout all the many convulsive geological and evolutionary events of the last three hundred million years or so?

Lovelock writes that the answer occurred to him like a "flash of enlightenment" in the depths of his conversation with Diane Hitchcock over these questions. In that key moment Gaia returned to our culture after her long absence—not as myth but as science. Lovelock's insight comes in two parts. First, he proposes that our Earth automatically and unconsciously regulates key aspects of her surface within the narrow limits tolerable by life without the need for any external agency or any planetary divinity. Second, this "self-regulation" is an emergent property arising spontaneously out of all the myriad interactions and feedbacks amongst our planet's living beings, her rocks, atmosphere and water.

"That flash of enlightenment, Jim," I once asked him during one of our long country walks, "was it an earth-shaking moment? Was there some kind of spiritual revelation full of powerful emotion and feeling?"

"No," he said. "Not at all. It was a great intellectual idea—that's all."

Lovelock first heard the word "Gaia" from his friend and neighbor, the novelist William Golding. Back in England after his epiphany at NASA, Lovelock was walking with Golding in the meadows and fields near their village explaining his idea of a self-regulating Earth—of Earth as a superorganism.

Golding knew the myth of Gaia well and understood the science. Listening to Lovelock he felt the utter grandeur and magnificence of the myth again, more so now that he could blend it with science. Feeling that this was a major new scientific hypothesis in need of a really big name, he said to Jim, "Call it Gaia," and told him the ancient myth of Gaia born from primordial Chaos. To his credit Lovelock didn't reject Gaia because of the myth—indeed, quite the opposite. He realized that the myth and his science belonged together and thus was born his Gaia hypothesis.

Later, with the help of several other scientists, particularly Professor Lynn Margulis, a highly innovative American evolutionary biologist specializing in symbiosis, Lovelock began to gather scientific evidence showing how various intricate feedbacks between Gaia's living beings, her rocks, her atmosphere and her waters have regulated temperature, acidity and the distribution of key chemical elements on her surface over vast spans of geological time.

## Holistic Science

Many teachers and students from around the world have come to Schumacher College over the last thirty years to pioneer and cultivate more Gaian ways of being in their lives. To begin with, the college offered these pioneers short courses without academic credits, but after a few years, it became apparent that some students wanted academic recognition for their studies at the college. A generous and timely donation from Rosalie Baston allowed us to offer master's level credits on short courses in partnership with nearby Plymouth University. I was the college's academic tutor and worked with Dr. Paddy O'Sullivan from the university in supervising many superb credits projects ranging from green economics to Earth-based spirituality.

It was around 1996, after our credits option had been running for many years, that Brian Goodwin, a mathematical biologist with a powerful shamanic bent, first came to the college soon after retiring as professor of biology at the Open University. I remember a brilliant talk Brian gave then on how Darwin's ideas on natural selection were heavily influenced by his Victorian capitalist background. Schumacher College and Dartington as a whole offered Brian what he had long been searching for: a place where he could establish a master's degree that would allow students to heal the split between ourselves and Gaia by practicing the unique approach to nature which we call holistic science, matured and seasoned at the college for over twenty years now.

Brian and I and Anne Phillips, Schumacher College's director at the time, worked together to realize his dream by creating the MSc in Holistic Science accredited by Plymouth University, our crucially supportive and much appreciated academic partners for all these years. This was the college's first year-long intensive residential course. We started the MSc with two students (from Japan and South Africa) in 1998 and have been accepting up to seventeen students from all over the world ever since.

Holistic science cultivates a healthy and earthy interaction between our four ways of knowing—sensing, feeling, intuition and thinking—in relation to nature, each other and Gaia. Sensing and thinking are obviously required for any kind of scientific activity. To do science we need to sense the world in certain ways, and we need to think about what our senses reveal to us. We need to respect our intuitive insights, and we need to feel the meaning and value of what we are studying, an ability which mainstream science develops hardly at all.

The kind of learning so badly needed now in this time of planetary crisis is seldom found in classroom settings which cultivate only our rational cognitive functions. As Satish Kumar is fond of saying, we need to educate not just our heads, but also our hearts and hands in service of Gaia. Schumacher College's contribution to this kind of holistic learning over the last thirty years has been to rigorously integrate scientifically accepted understandings of Gaia and of our impacts upon her with experiential learning in class, in the college's kitchen and its vegetable gardens and deep in the nearby woods and fields.

## A Science of Qualities

For over a decade we would spend the first week of the first module of the MSc in Holistic Science by exploring a science of qualities with physicist and philosopher Henri Bortoft.

Henri helped us enter into lived experiences of nature's qualities moment by moment by redirecting our attention away from the abstract categories of the verbal-intellectual mind and instead paying close attention to our sensory experiences and intuitions when contemplating nature, in the manner pioneered by the great poet/scientist Johann Wolfgang von Goethe (1748-1832). Henri passed away in 2012, but his approach remains central to our teaching on the MSc.

In the following two weeks of this first module, we plunge ever more deeply into the qualities of nature using Goethian science, for many years with Dr. Margaret Colquhoun or Dr. Craig Holdrege, two of the world's most eminent Goethian scientists, who showed us how to perceive the emergence of a plant's qualities in its unfolding from seed to leaf to flower. Sometimes Professor Francoise Wemelsfelder would come down from Scotland to tutor us in her rigorous scientific method for quantifying people's qualitative impressions of the health of farm animals—a method our students have used with local people for assessing the health of coral reefs and even of entire landscapes.

## Chaos and Complexity

The second module, on Chaos and Complexity, was taught initially by Brian and then, for eight years or so after Brian passed away, by our MSc graduate Philip Franses. In this module we examine the contention that life at all levels of organization, from cells to organisms to ecosystems to planet, tunes itself close to the edge of chaos where just enough order prevents collapse and where just enough chaos brings

novelty and innovation. As Brian was fond of saying, "maximum coherence to the whole, maximum freedom to the individual."

We ponder the correspondences between patterns in nature and
mathematical equations from chaos and complexity theories iterated
on computers that generate exquisite nature-like patterns such as
strange attractors and the Mandelbrot set. We explore mathematical
models which track how individual bees, ants, termites and flocks
of birds organize themselves into coherent wholes and compare the
qualities of these simulations with the actual natural phenomena.
For many years, with the expert guidance of Professor Patricia Shaw,
we ended the module by applying what we'd learnt about chaos and
complexity to the dynamic life of human organizations, sometimes
even dancing tango to explore this domain.

## The Living Earth

The third module, on the Living Earth, has been taught by me since
the beginning of the MSc. Our aim is to experience the living qualities of our planet using what we've learnt in the first two modules.
We start by physically walking a stretch of land representing deep
time, a process I first experienced with Joanna Macy in the 1990s at
the college and elsewhere. Much later, in 2008, the experienced ge-
ologist Sergio Maraschin (one of our MSc students at the time) and I
expanded the process into the Deep Time Walk. Our simple innovation was to hugely expand the walk into a two-mile ramble along the
South Devon coast near the college, representing 4,600 million years
of Earth and her history. The walk (now available as an app thanks to
Geoff Ainscow and Rob Woodford) brings us a sense of the immense
age of our planet (every millimeter walked equals one thousand
years) and connects us with the astonishing evolutionary journey of
our Gaian system—of life and planet closely coupled together.

We study the science of James Lovelock and Lynn Margulis, both
of whom taught on the module, Jim for eleven years running, and we
connect with the work of other Gaian scientists. We explore aspects
of Gaia's physiology, including her temperature regulation through
geological time using science as story, mathematical modeling, a winter pilgrimage to the granite on high Dartmoor, a light sprinkling of
alchemy and some creative projects along the way. I write more about
some of this content in my book *Animate Earth* and in my forthcoming book *Gaia Alchemy*.

The MSc in Holistic Science has spawned two other master's degrees, one on Economics for Transition and the other on Ecological Design Thinking, and the college's original offering of short courses has integrated well over the years with these three postgraduate programs.

## Deep Ecology

One short course teacher who greatly influenced our work at the college was the Norwegian philosopher and mountaineer Professor Arne Naess, who taught here several times in the 1990s and whose concept of deep ecology is deeply embedded into my Living Earth module on the MSc. Deep ecology is of such immense importance at the college that our founding statute enshrines it as being at the core of our activities.

To my mind, there are three senses of "deep" in Arne's deep ecology, a phrase he coined in the early 1970s as a spur for the growing ecology movement. The first sense refers to our deepest experiences of the living qualities, magnificence and intrinsic value of nature, sometimes using scientific ecology as an aid. When we perceive the intrinsic value of another being, we know in our hearts that they matter in themselves simply because they exist, irrespective of any use they might have for us, the humans.

These deep experiences lead us to deeply question how we live, which in turn helps us develop and strengthen our deep commitment to be of benefit to all life, including all humans, who are also perceived as having intrinsic value. Over the years I've had the immense privilege of exploring deep ecology with Arne and our college teachers Per Ingvar Haukeland, Per Espen Stoknes and David Abram in the wild open spaces of Norway's mountains, lakes and forests.

Other people who have greatly influenced my own development at Schumacher include Rabindranath Tagore, the great Indian sage, poet and educator, and a major inspiration behind Dartington; and also C. G. Jung whose psychology reunifies psyche and science. Both, among many others, have shown me how to blend my love of science with a heart open to the miraculous qualities of nature.

The smallness of Schumacher College is our greatest strength, for our carefully crafted alchemical vessel for deep ecological transformation only works with a few people at a time. Our smallness, to use E. F. Schumacher's phrase, allows the education we offer to be of "human scale," ensuring that the learning is personal, supportive, convivial and transformative.

The evidence in favor of our "small is beautiful" approach in education is the pro-Gaian work of our alumni all over the world. Several young men and women from South America are working in new ways to save the Amazon rainforest based on what they learnt here. Others helped Christiana Figueres set up the Paris climate agreement in 2015, and yet others have gone on to help the localization and transition movements and to start green businesses. Some are working to protect Indigenous cultures; others have set up sister colleges in various parts of the world. Some are introducing Schumacher ideas into academia, and others have set up ecological food growing systems in their local area. One such alumnus is our MSc graduate Justin West who established a forest garden at the college well over a decade ago. More recently the gardens have been further developed into a superbly effective food-producing educational resource by Jane Gleason and her teams of growers.

I hope that I've managed to convey something of how we have been practicing whole body education for head, heart and hands here at Schumacher College for the last thirty years. Much of mainstream education trains us to be efficient cogs in the globalized industrial machine that is ripping our planet to shreds, but Schumacher College educates us for right relationship with each other and with Gaia. Now is the time for this educational model to spread far and wide, and fast, for our chances of avoiding the direst consequences of the global crisis are quickly slipping through our fingers. Time is running out.

STEPHAN HARDING, born in Venezuela, received his doctorate from Oxford University. He is the author of *Animate Earth*, published by Green Books.

# Transforming Lives

RUPERT SHELDRAKE

*Science without religion is lame,*
*religion without science is blind.*
— ALBERT EINSTEIN

I first taught at Schumacher College in 1991, soon after it first opened, when I led a five-week-long course. I've taught there almost every year since then both in short courses and in the MSc in Holistic Science program. I am currently a Fellow of the college.

I think of it as my academic home base and feel far more closely aligned with its aims, objectives and ethos than with any other academic institution. It combines an emphasis on holistic perspectives, ecological awareness and practical activity in a way that is in harmony with my own aims and objectives. I love teaching there because the classes are small and intimate, and there is an ashram-like sense of community, enhanced by the way in which participants take turns cooking and cleaning, as well as studying and playing together. Teachers are not separate from this community but part of it, which makes teaching there so rewarding.

The first time I taught there, my older son, Merlin, was three years old and my younger son, Cosmo, one and a half. My wife, Jill Purce, led the group in chanting and in a May Day ceremony. Cosmo is now an internationally known musician, and Merlin is a biologist with a strongly ecological perspective who is now himself teaching at Schumacher College, so I feel I have a family connection with the college, as well as a personal one. What I have been teaching at Schumacher College can be summarized in the following way.

## Nature as Machine

Conventional science since the seventeenth century has been based on the machine theory of nature: nature is mechanical and inanimate. There's no consciousness anywhere in the universe, everything is machine-like. Animals and plants are just automatic machines, and so are we. In Richard Dawkins' vivid phrase, we are genetically programmed "lumbering robots." Our brains are nothing but complex computers.

Coupled with that machine approach is the reductionist approach to nature. Matter is made up of atoms, which are now believed to be made up of sub-atomic particles, and the most solid foundation for scientific explanation is to reduce everything to the smallest bits, the most fundamental subatomic particles, such as quarks. Following this line of reasoning, the most prestigious and important kind of biology is molecular biology which reduces life to the smallest possible bits, molecules, genes and proteins.

In this approach to nature, there is no such thing as God, or spirit. Consciousness is confined to human heads and is nothing but the mechanical activities of brains. "Minds are what brains do," in the words of the standard materialist summary. This is the kind of science that is taught in practically every school and college all over the world, in India and China and Africa and South America, as well as in Europe and North America.

## Nature as Living Organism

Holistic science has a different approach. It starts from the idea that nature is made up of different levels of organization. Cells exist in tissues, tissues in organs, organs in organisms, societies of organisms in ecosystems, ecosystems in Gaia, Mother Earth. There are many levels of organization in nature, and there is no reason that we should think that one level, the smallest, is the most important and the others should be reduced to the smallest possible particles. All the levels are important, and nature is made up of many levels. At each level, the whole is made up of parts, and the whole is more than the sum of the parts. This is the basic premise of holistic science, and of course, the Gaia Hypothesis, as proposed by James Lovelock, fits into that holistic model because the earth is seen as a living organism in its own right. In turn Gaia is part of the solar system, which in turn is part of the galaxy, which is itself a gigantic organism.

In the 1920s, the great philosopher Alfred North Whitehead put forward what he called the Organismic Philosophy of Nature. This is another way of expressing the holistic approach. Basically, it involves changing the fundamental metaphor. Instead of saying that nature is made of machinery, we can say that nature is made of organisms. The whole universe is like a gigantic organism. The Big Bang was like the hatching of the cosmic egg, and the universe has been growing ever since and cooling down and creating new structures, much more like a growing embryo than like a machine.

In many ways, this view that nature is made up of organisms is what everyone believed before the scientific revolution of the seventeenth century. In the Middle Ages, all the universities in Europe would have been a bit like Schumacher College, teaching science holistically. They followed Aristotle and St. Thomas Aquinas, the great philosopher and theologian, who lived in the thirteenth century. The standard doctrine was that nature is alive, the earth is alive, the stars are alive, the sky is full of the presence of God and the heavenly bodies have spirits and souls. All plants and animals have souls. The fact animals are called animals is because the Latin word for soul is *anima*—they're beings with souls. The whole of nature was animate. The theology was one of Christian animism: God is the God of a living world. God's presence and being shine through all of nature. Nature is within God, and God is within nature. That was the standard medieval view. This is how nature is seen in shamanic cultures, in Hinduism and other Indian religions.

This is precisely what the scientific revolution overthrew, replacing it with the machine theory of nature. Mechanistic science involves a tremendous rupture with this traditional understanding. Through the missionaries of science, we have now exported this mechanistic model to the whole world.

What's happening now is that we are rediscovering a more ancient view of nature, an animistic view, which is found in all ancient cultures, but of course we are not turning back the clock to pre-mechanistic animism, we are developing a post-mechanistic animism.

## The Age of Reason

In Europe, there were two main reasons why mechanistic science was so successful. First, in the seventeenth century, when this kind of science got going, there was a period of tremendous religious warfare in Europe, especially in the Thirty Years War that began in 1619 on the continent, with Protestants killing Catholics and vice versa. This meant that a lot of people were very upset that religion was causing wars and conflicts. The supporters of science in the seventeenth century cleverly argued that science is not about quarrelling over biblical texts or ecclesiastical power structures, it's about looking at God's work in nature, providing a third way to God that was neither Protestant nor Catholic, but transcended both, leading directly to the heart of the Divine Being. God, they said, is a mathematician and an engineer. The machinery of nature was made by an engineering God who thinks mathematically. Through science and reason, we can discover the mathematical laws of nature, which are ideas in the mind of a mathematical God.

Kepler, Galileo, Descartes and Newton all had this idea that they were finding out the mind of God through science. Their supporters managed to present science as being more divine and religious than religion, which gave it a lot of intellectual prestige. Science wasn't atheistic to start with. All the great founders of science were deeply religious men.

By the eighteenth century, this prestige became the basis for the Enlightenment, the idea that science and reason could lead humans forward progressively in a way that would take us beyond all the quarrels of the past. Progress was possible through science, reason and technology. This became the standard intellectual point of view by the end of the eighteenth century, and it was often associated with anti-religious propaganda. Secondly, science began to enable engineers to produce useful things, such as steam engines and electrical technologies, like telegrams and electric motors, and now the internet and smartphoneTechnology has taken over our lives. Moreover, modern medicine has conferred immense benefits, and many of us would not be here without it. So, the prestige of science is now so immense that every government in the world wants to have academies of science and engineering and science colleges. In medieval Europe, there was a separation of church and state. Now there is no separation of science and state. Science is a state-sponsored enterprise everywhere in the world through academies of science, government grants, national curricula and research agencies.

## Science and Spirituality

Mechanistic science creates an inevitable tension between science and spirituality. Its worldview says that nature is inanimate, purposeless and non-conscious. There is no such thing as God or spirit in this mechanical world. Everything proceeds automatically. Obviously, this belief system strikes at the root of all religions, which see God working in nature, interacting with human beings and interacting with events in the world. That's why people pray; they are asking for divine help in practical matters. So if there is a completely mechanical universe that works non-consciously, and minds are nothing but the physical activity of brains, then religion must be rubbish, which is why militant atheists put their faith in mechanistic science and dismiss all religions as childish superstitions. So there is an inevitable conflict there, and for many years people dealt with this by having two separate worlds—a public world and a private world.

At work, you go along with the mechanistic worldview, on which our educational, political and commercial activities are based, but when you go home, you can be a practicing Christian or Jew or Hindu or Muslim, but it's in a separate compartment. There are different realms of authority, and they are separate.

This is true in Europe, but we have exported this split to all other countries too. I used to work in India at an international agricultural research institute in Hyderabad, and this is how all my Indian colleagues behaved. Nearly everyone in the institute was religious. I hardly ever met any atheists, and when my colleagues went home in the evenings after doing mechanistic science at work, which none of them publicly questioned or challenged, they became conventionally religious. I had dinner with some of my Hindu colleagues at their homes, which had domestic shrines with pujas being held, and they didn't see any conflict at all. My Muslim colleagues would fast during Ramadan, and many would pray five times a day. They managed to inhabit completely separate realms. The same thing happens in other countries, like Japan where many scientists take part in the cherry blossom festival and visit Buddhist temples, Shinto shrines and holy mountains. Mechanistic science caused splits in European and all other cultures.

Things are now changing with the rise of holistic science and consciousness studies. For example, scientists are looking at altered states of consciousness through meditation. Some scientists have now started studying other spiritual practices as well. This convergence of science and spirituality is the theme of my two most recent books, *Science and Spiritual Practices* and *Ways to Go Beyond and Why They Work*. In these areas, we are not talking about an ideological conflict, we are talking about complementary activities. If I meditate and find that I feel better and sleep better and scientists study me meditating and find that my blood pressure drops, levels of stress hormones decline and so on, these are scientifically measurable effects, and indeed the effects on well-being are measurable too.

Now that scientists have started looking at spiritual practices in these ways, they have found that, in general, spiritual and religious practices make people happier, healthier and live longer. This must also mean that people who don't have these practices are unhappier, unhealthier and live shorter lives. These traditional practices turn out to be very relevant to health and therefore relevant to medicine. Indeed, you can now get a prescription for meditation from a psychiatrist if you're depressed because they have found that people who meditate are less prone to depression than people who don't. Moreover, meditation has no side effects, unlike antidepressant drugs— and it's cheaper!

Religious fundamentalism is a response to scientific fundamentalism. Dogmatic atheists like Richard Dawkins claim that science shows there's no such thing as God, evolution is just a matter of chance mutations and natural selection, and almost everything in the Bible is wrong. In response, biblical literalists adopt a biblical fundamentalism that enrages Dawkins and his friends, who then attack them, and they attack back. So, these wars are between fundamentalists on both sides. What's much more interesting is an attempt to explore the ground in between.

It would be difficult to have scientists sign up to some kind of agreed religious principles because some are Christian, some are Jewish, some are Muslim, some are Hindu, Sikh, Jain, Daoist or Buddhist, and some are anti-religious atheists, non-religious agnostics and secular humanists. It might be possible to persuade scientists of all these kinds to agree to something that was fairly general, like a

Hippocratic Oath. But I doubt if it would work very well. Many scientists work on destructive technologies like weapons, toxic chemicals for use in agriculture and new ways of extracting fossil fuels. They are not evil people, but just doing their jobs, which they find plausible ways of justifying.

Rather than have some kind of verbal statements, I think that spiritual practices could have a more transformative effect. Practices are about *experiences*. Most people who are religious are not religious because they've studied a whole lot of beliefs and memorized dogmas. They are religious because they've been brought up that way and value the practices. For example, going to church together means going to a holy place, being part of a community, celebrating festivals together, praying together and singing together. I think that if scientists were to add a spiritual dimension to their work, it would be best done through some shared activity. For example, once a year each laboratory could have a festival, maybe a celebration of the day on which it was founded, like a birthday, then people could celebrate together and offer prayers or intentions that would bring the community together. Or they could go on a pilgrimage together, a scientific pilgrimage.

Science is both part of the problem and part of the solution. If we have new technologies, like better solar panels and wind power and possibly free energy technologies, they are going to come about through scientific research, so science is definitely a part of the solution. Science funding is part of the problem and possibly part of the solution. Right now, science funding is very conservative. It would be good to have think tanks explore what scientists could do to help make the world a better place.

## Roles for Schumacher College

Schumacher College is a pioneering example of holistic education. But what we need is holistic education in schools and colleges everywhere, not just in one college in one country for a small number of people. Ideally, Schumacher College could help holistic education spread into colleges throughout the world.

One obvious way would be to have online courses that could be used in colleges and schools. Right now, if you are teaching in a school and you want to have holistic material for your courses, where do you get it from? There aren't textbooks yet, and where do you find someone who could do the teaching? If you wanted to roll out holistic education all over Britain, you'd need thousands of teachers to do this and they don't exist. So, online courses would be one way that Schumacher College could help do this. For example, people who have graduated from Schumacher College who are doing holistic science in Brazil could produce online courses in Portuguese.

Another way in which Schumacher College could help transform other educational institutions is through running teacher training courses, or training people who could teach holistic modules in existing colleges of education.

Schumacher College could also team up with forest schools and other outdoor education projects, helping to develop course materials, textbooks and children's books that convey a holistic perspective.

There is no question that Schumacher College is of greater relevance than ever. The only questions are about how to make it more effective in transforming the lives of more people, who can in turn become leaders as we move towards more ecologically sustainable and spiritually rewarding ways of life.

*This essay is based on dialogue with Satish Kumar.*

 RUPERT SHELDRAKE has a PhD in biochemistry from the University of Cambridge. He became well-known for his proposition of Morphic Resonance which states that "nature systems have a collective memory." His latest book is *Science and Spiritual Practices*, published by Coronet. sheldrake.org

# A New Biology

BRUCE H. LIPTON

*The most beautiful and profound emotion*
*we can experience is the sensation of the mystical.*
*It is the power of all true science.*
— ALBERT EINSTEIN

## Epigenetics

I now recognize that I was at the right place at the right time when I entered graduate school at the University of Virginia's department of biology in 1967. Learning experiences there launched me on the path of an amazing life adventure. Virginia's biology department was the right place, and the timing was perfect; in recognition of it being designated as a Center of Excellence, the department had just received a massive federal grant—funds to hire distinguished faculty and acquire state-of-the-art technology, including a new electron microscope suite in which I spent most of my graduate career.

The upgrade brought Irwin R. Konigsberg, a world-famous pioneer in stem cell cloning techniques, to the department. I was subsequently honored to be selected as a graduate student under his mentorship. My studies combining stem cell cultures and electron microscopy became pioneering research that presaged the new revolutionary field of *epigenetics*.

In the late 60s and early 70s, my research results and conclusions were shunned by my colleagues, all of whom were committed to *genetic determinism*, the belief that genes controlled biology. In contrast, my research revealed that genes were not self-actualizing, meaning that they do not control their own activity, but were controlled by their environment. In the face of collegial alienation, I left the scientific community, yet I continued my research on the mechanisms by which environmental signals shape genetic expression. Incorporating the principles of quantum physics in my cell studies revealed the mechanics of a new life-enhancing theory, the science of *Conscious Evolution*, which, in total surprise to me, introduced me to the realm of spirituality.

Ostracized by my medical science peers, I left formal academia and found support for my insights of a new biology from a community of other "reformed" scientists, whose personal insights also caused them to leave conventional academia. My lectures on epigenetics, quantum biophysics, fractal geometry and spirituality began to draw a vastly different audience primarily comprised of ecologists, environmentalists and groups that encourage self-empowerment through consciousness raising and spirituality.

## The Magical Moments

A friend and colleague, Rupert Sheldrake, suggested that I would find a very supportive community of researchers and students at Schumacher College. As fate would have it, months later in 2011, I received a letter from Schumacher College inviting me to present a course on the new biology. Without hesitation, I accepted the invitation and returned an abstract for a program entitled, "The Biology of Belief: The Science of Personal and Global Transformation."

Months later, after an eighteen-hour trek from California using planes, trains and automobiles, I stood facing the historic Dartington Hall, the centerpiece of Schumacher College's campus. A bit frazzled from the two-day trip to Devon, England, I stood transfixed in front of this magnificent six-hundred-year-old medieval edifice, trying to conceptualize the history that had surrounded this building since its foundation was laid in the late 1300s.

At that moment, I had a premonition that I was again at the right place at the right time. I think I anticipated that by being present on this campus and immersed in an historic energy field I would acquire a better sense of civilization's evolution. Little did I anticipate the surprise that greeted me when I entered the historic home of Schumacher College. Though the building presented a stark ancient facade, inside the buzz of an interactive community of faculty, students and researchers provided a vibrancy of life not concerned with history but focused on creating a new version of life, a better future founded on consciousness, health and harmony with each other and with our provider, Mother Earth. The food served at that first meal, freshly picked from the biodynamic gardens maintained on the campus, was as vital as the energy of the student volunteers that prepared it.

I attended a class on holistic biology after the meal on my first day at Schumacher. I admit, I believe I am a pretty good lecturer, but I felt like an enchanted child, sitting cross-legged on the floor, watching Dr. Stephan Harding weave science, anecdotes and personal stories into a profoundly informative presentation on ecology and evolution. I was personally overjoyed to befriend Stephan and share amazing insights about environment and evolution, and especially stories of his personal history with James Lovelock, founder of the Gaia Hypothesis.

On that first evening on campus, the Schumacher magic grew even greater, for I found myself now sitting at the feet of Satish Kumar, a great humanitarian and co-founder of Schumacher College. It was a special honor to attend his presentation and later directly engage with Satish. In our private conversations, he offered his heart and wisdom, providing support that buoyed me up and encouraged me to pursue my theories on consciousness and spirituality as a foundation for advancing planetary evolution.

Psyched about the nature of the community I just entered, I looked forward to presenting my course. It was a wonderful "welcome home" experience when I met the students in my program. The class represented a vast cross-section of humanity: young, old, professionals, students desiring to become professionals, others seeking self-empowerment, all of them energized and anxious to participate in experiencing a new vision of biology and evolution.

It became clear that the vision and intentions of Schumacher College students was far beyond that of the conventional students I had taught at bigger colleges and universities. The joy of their participation, which they describe as "deep immersion," expanded the meaning and context of the messages contained in my lectures. The students in the program held a great positive view of the planet's future and were imbued with the desire to change the world, in spite of the challenges they faced in a world beset by an evolving global chaos.

## The Biology of Belief

My program on the Biology of Belief introduced leading-edge science that was shattering old myths and rewriting the fundamental beliefs of human civilization. The presentation introduced the idea that we were in the midst of an incredible evolutionary event, a new biology that would take us beyond environmental collapse, economic upheaval and racial and religious extremes, to reveal that such chaos was a natural step in an unfolding process, rather than the tragic end to a broken planet.

With the support of Stephan Harding, I offered a synthesis of modern science and ancient spiritual wisdom in assessing the past and future of Gaia's evolution. Our collective story provided hopeful insight into the unfolding destiny of our species—and how we each play an active role in nurturing our civilization's evolution.

The presentations reviewed a series of recent, remarkable discoveries in science that unlocked the mystery of the body-mind-spirit-world connection. The ancient belief that *all life truly is interconnected* took on a new empowering significance in light of advances in fractal geometry, quantum physics and epigenetics.

Fractal geometry, the principle upon which Nature is designed, is the mathematics that represents a practical realization of the Hermetic maxim "As above, so below." Nature's fractal structure expresses a hierarchy of repetitive and self-similar patterns, which collectively are useful in visioning the past and future of life on this planet.

Quantum physics principles, applied to biological mechanisms, reveal the powerful force that invisible energy fields, which include "spirit," have on shaping the origin and character of the biosphere.

Our discussions focused on the failure of neo-Darwinism, with its emphasis on random mutations and a struggle for survival, as being a major factor in disconnecting us from Nature. In contrast, the new science of epigenetics provides the mechanism by which the environment and the web of life control organismal genetics and evolution. Frontier sciences also emphasized the fact that the Jean Baptiste de Lamarck's theory of evolution, published fifty years before Darwin's theory, offered a more accurate assessment of evolution and emphasized the important role of environment in shaping evolution's unfoldment.

The course concluded with the story of civilization poised to take an incredible step forward in the growth of our species. Collectively, these new scientific insights show that we are on the threshold of a major evolutionary event—the emergence of a new giant super-organism called *Humanity*. Each human is the equivalent of a "cell" in the body of Humanity. As we learn, live and reinforce Humanity's new communal story as a thriving organism, we are provided with evidence that we are here on the planet to "re-grow the Garden" and to thrive into the future.

Schumacher College provided me with a wonderful opportunity to return to the school in 2015 and 2016, so that I could update and expand upon the story of conscious evolution. Since those years, evolutionary chaos has human civilization precariously balanced on the knife-edge between extinction and evolution. Our uncertain future is dependent on the actions we engage in today.

This is the fundamental significance of celebrating the existence of Schumacher College. The school was designed to unveil a revolutionary vision of life science that illuminates the hidden connections among biology, psychology, environment, spirituality and our imminent evolutionary upheaval. Schumacher College represents a global resource that offers new sustainable awareness that can enhance our evolution, while training responsible co-creators that can facilitate the opportunity to heal ourselves and the planet.

Happy 30th Anniversary Schumacher College, civilization salutes you!

BRUCE H. LIPTON, PhD, cell biologist and award-winning lecturer, is an internationally recognized leader in the new biology. Bruce, recipient of Japan's prestigious Goi Peace Award, is the author of the bestselling *The Biology of Belief*, *The Honeymoon Effect* and co-author with Steve Bhaerman of *Spontaneous Evolution*.

# From the Quanta to the Seed

DR. VANDANA SHIVA

*Look deep into nature*
*and then you will understand everything better.*
— ALBERT EINSTEIN

I have had the privilege and honor to be associated with Schumacher College since its very beginning when Satish Kumar invited me to be a faculty member.

Over the years, as I returned to teach courses at the college, the faculty apartment in the Old Postern started to feel like home.

## From the Mechanistic to the Quantum Paradigm

I remember the first course I was invited to offer was a course on quantum thinking with David Bohm. Unfortunately, Professor Bohm was hospitalized, and I had to teach the entire five-week course. Prof. Bohm passed away on October 27, 1992. As I reflect on my first course at Schumacher, I realize how indebted I am to the college and to Prof. Bohm in my intellectual evolution.

Physics had been my passion from childhood. Quantum theory became my passion in university. I had studied David Bohm's books during my MSc in Physics. I wanted to do a PhD with him, but he suggested I go to Canada and study with his student and co-author Jeff Bub, because Canada had scholarships and Birkbeck College at the University of London where Bohm worked did not.

So, I did my PhD on "Hidden Variables and Non-Locality in Quantum Theory" at the University of Western Ontario in Canada with Jeff Bub as my guide.

The four quantum principles which I learnt during my doctoral studies, and which have guided my thinking for a transition from the mechanical worldview of the industrial age to the ecological world view of the age of Gaia, are:

1. Non-locality, non-separability and interconnectedness, non-separation:
   Mechanistic thought is based on our separation from nature, and on nature as being constituted of discrete particles separate from each other. In the quantum world there is no separability, everything is interconnected.

2. Potential not fixed determinate qualities:
   Mechanistic thought is based on fixed immutable entities that cannot change. Quantum theory is based on potential which is always unfolding.

3. Uncertainty and indeterminateness, not certainty:
   The mechanical world is based on determinateness and certainty. Quantum theory is based on irreducible uncertainty and indeterminateness, on probability and possibility.

4. No excluded middle, not duality and not exclusion, always "And" not "Either-Or":
   In the mechanical world there are particles and there are waves. Quanta can express themselves as both waves and particles.

Over the years I have offered many courses and participated in many conferences at Schumacher College where I have been able to expand on these four principles.

In his book *Wholeness and the Implicate Order*, Bohm had synthesized these principles as the "implicate order" and "enfoldment"—the structure and process which is the ground from which the reality of particular objects emerges. Bohm considered that the world of appearances and what we take for reality are "surface phenomena, explicate forms that have temporarily unfolded out of an underlying implicate order."

As he wrote:

In the enfolded [or implicate] order, space and time are no longer the dominant factors determining the relationships of dependence or independence of different elements. Rather, an entirely different sort of basic connection of elements is possible, from which our ordinary notions of space and time, along with those of separately existent material particles, are abstracted as forms derived from the deeper order. These ordinary notions in fact appear in what is called the "explicate" or "unfolded" order, which is a special and distinguished form contained within the general totality of all the implicate orders.

A particular conference at Schumacher College that I remember was a conference on technology with Doug Tompkins, Jerry Mander and Edward Goldsmith.

Technology means tools. Humanity has evolved tools to transform what nature gives to meet our needs. We can evolve tools that work in harmony with nature or tools for war with nature. We can evolve tools for improving human well-being or tools for profits and control. We can evolve tools through democratic participation, or tools can be imposed.

When particular technologies that serve the powerful are forced blindly on society without social and ecological assessment and without democratic participation, they can have a destructive impact on nature and society.

Tools and technologies used to extract and burn fossil fuels are disrupting the earth's climate systems leading to climate change. Fossil fuels used to make chemicals such as pesticides and herbicides are pushing species to extinction. Biotechnologies have accelerated the disappearance of biodiversity. The emergence of information technologies, digital technologies and artificial intelligence are creating new challenges which have not been fully assessed.

Blind imposition of technologies without assessment has been referred to as Techno Utopianism by the thinkers and activists who met at the technology conference in Schumacher College. These will be important issues for our times and for the future.

## Nature as Teacher: The Inspiration of Tagore

During my first visit to Schumacher College, I went to the archives of Dartington Hall to understand how the institution had started. In the archives I discovered the links between India and Dartington, between Rabindranath Tagore and Schumacher College.

Tagore had created Shantiniketan, the University of the East, based on learning from nature.

I had spent a few months in Shantiniketan before going to Canada because Dr. Samar Biswas, who was supervisor of my studies, had been invited to start the physics department in what was otherwise a university of culture. Tagore was also concerned about the peasants around Shantiniketan, and he wanted to introduce a rural development program. So, while in New York, he wrote to Cornell University to introduce him to their best student. Thus in 1920, Tagore met Leonard Elmhirst, a Cornell student. In 1921, Elmhirst came to India as Tagore's secretary. In 1922, in the village of Surul, he set up an Institute of Rural Reconstruction.

Elmhirst's *The Poet and the Plowman* and Tagore and Elmhirst's *Pioneer in Education* tell the story of Elmhirst's period in Shantiniketan.

After a few years, Tagore sent Elmhirst to start a Shantiniketan of the West in Dartington. In 1925, Dorothy and Leonard Elmhirst purchased the neglected fourteenth-century Dartington estate and started Dartington Hall Trust.

Tagore's idea of education was based on learning from nature because, for Tagore, nature is a teacher, not an object of exploitation. As he wrote: "Nature stands as an image of mother and teacher to the human beings which provides everything we need, and it teaches us the secrets of better life. Its each and every activity has certain hidden secrets that human mind and eyes need to read and observe."

Learning from nature teaches us diversity, it teaches us life and living, it teaches us mutuality and giving ,it teaches us creativity and living within limits, it teaches us how to not take more than we need, and leave enough ecological space to share with other species, other humans and future generations of all beings.

The illusion of nature as dead matter and mere raw material to be exploited, combined with the illusion of limitless growth on a planet with ecological limits, has in a few short centuries brought humanity to the brink of ecological collapse. Avoiding collapse needs a new consciousness of nature and the earth as living organism and of humans as earth citizens along with all other species. As Tagore wrote: "The highest education is that which does not merely give us information but makes our life in harmony with all existence."

This is the idea of education for harmony with all existence based on nature as teacher that gave birth to Shantiniketan in India and

Schumacher College in the UK, and to the Bija Vidyapeeth/Earth University in Doon Valley in India.

## The Seed and Soil as Teachers

I had done my MSc in particle physics in Punjab. In 1984, Punjab erupted in violence. The same year, a pesticide plant owned by Union Carbide leaked in the city of Bhopal, killing thousands. Because of violence in Punjab and Bhopal, I felt compelled to look at why agriculture had become so violent and to seek nonviolent ways of farming. I wrote a book, *The Violence of the Green Revolution*. In 1987 I realized how the corporations, whom I call the Poison Cartel, that had introduced war chemicals in agriculture, now wanted to introduce GMOs and patent and own seeds. That is when I started to save seeds and later started Navdanya, the movement for conserving biodiversity and agroecology.

Satish Kumar was visiting me at Navdanya's biodiversity conservation farm in Doon Valley, and while walking around the farm started to imagine and plan a learning center, an Indian Schumacher College. Today this has grown to be the Bija Vidyapeeth/Earth University where the seed, the soil and the farmers are our teachers. Schumacher College has inspired and influenced Bija Vidyapeeth. Here we are working with our hands and with the soil, which is an important part of education.

Education and expertise that have grown from the distorted worldview that nature is dead matter, that we are separate from nature and her masters and owners, facilitate exploitation and have brought us to the precipice. Climate catastrophe and the sixth mass extinction threaten the very future of humanity and all species.

We need an education for healing the earth, for working with the seed and the soil to regenerate the earth.

As the examples of learning centers like Schumacher College and Bija Vidyapeeth show, saving and sowing seeds of hope and growing gardens of diversity has become a vital part of education in our times.

VANDANA SHIVA is an eco-feminist and promoter of seed freedom and food sovereignty. She is the author of more than twenty books, including *Earth Democracy* and *Soil not Oil*. navdanya.org

# Science in the Service of Soil

WES JACKSON

*To be interested in food but not in food production
is clearly absurd.*

— WENDELL BERRY

## The Schumacher Visit

My first experience with Schumacher College, beautifully situated on the Dartington Estate surrounded by an impressive forest, overrode the usually restrictive reality of small rooms and shared bathrooms. If I remember right, we dined exclusively on good vegetables.

Beyond the setting were the people engaged in the necessary radical thinking of what we must do. It was the thinking not only of E. F. Schumacher but his founding disciple, Satish Kumar. Since then I have been fortunate to have the memory of that time come back as I read the writings of others who have come and gone over the years.

My experience at Schumacher College was consistent with the spirit of E. F. Schumacher, the man I met when he visited the Land Institute in March 1977, scarcely five months before his death the following September. Had I met him one more time, maybe I would have called him Fritz as many of his friends did.

A little about that visit deserves mention. The Land sponsored an evening lecture in our town of Salina, Kansas, where Schumacher told two memorable stories to a regional audience. The first had to do with lorries carrying biscuits from Edinburgh to London meeting lorries carrying biscuits from London to Edinburgh. "I wondered," he said, "that they don't exchange recipes." Then he added, "But then,

I am just an economist, and there must be something about the added value of the transport."

His second story was about how he and some friends from Europe went across the United States, right through our part of the country. It was at the height of the Great Depression and the period of the Dust Bowl. The story featured the young visitors' stop at a small town somewhere in Kansas, maybe just for fuel, food, whatever, and while there Schumacher engaged a local man by asking, "Well, how is it going?"

"Alright," the local said.

"Well, what do you do?"

"I work on that farm over there," he said, pointing across the road.

"So, you are a farmer."

"Yes, I used to own that farm, but I had no money to pay the hired hand, so I paid him in land. Now he owns the farm."

"Well, that is a sad story."

"Oh, no, he has no money either, and now he is paying me back in land."

Our Salina Community Theater had few empty seats that night, and the locals received a bit of a taste of what was to come out of the Land Institute. It was a perfect launch of what we already were and to a large degree did become. I mean to say that his writings and that visit plus the intellectual traffic through Schumacher College helped establish an evolving standard for "what is up" here on the Great Plains of Kansas. Once Schumacher College came into existence, we could learn a bit of what's going on from the array of visitors to that place.

## In Search of Perennial Grain

Scarcely three months after what we still call the Schumacher Visit, I had an epiphany, of sorts, that led to our efforts to solve the ten-thousand-year-old Problem of Agriculture. Here's how that happened. As mentioned, it was in 1977. I had just read the General Accounting Office (GAO) report of soil erosion in the United States. (The GAO's job is to see how effectively US taxpayers' money is being spent.) From the report it looked to me like erosion was about as serious as when the US Soil Conservation Service was born back in the mid-1930s. I thought, how can this be, given the thousands of miles of terraces, grass waterways, shelter belts and high motivation of practicing farmers? Within a few days, I took our student interns to the never-plowed Konza Prairie, and what did we see? No detectable soil erosion, no fossil fuel dependency, no chemical contamination of the land. The only visible industrial product was the barbed wire fence. Coming and going to that native prairie sixty miles away, we passed corn with soil erosion; soybeans with soil erosion; sorghum with soil erosion. We all knew that fossil fuels had been spent for fertilizer, traction and pest control. Back home with the GAO study and the field trip to the Konza in mind, I began to think about that prairie ecosystem and most natural land ecosystems: rainforest, alpine meadow, desert scrub and more. They all feature perennials growing in mixtures. And so, the question: Why do humans not have perennial grains growing in mixtures? We have had 10,000–12,000 years of agriculture, and the problem of soil erosion and its disastrous consequences has been noted and written about back to the Greeks. Why no perennial grain polycultures? It would save our soils and reduce our labor in the fields.

I thought of how humans have used plants for various purposes and considered four contrasting categories: Some plants are herbaceous, some woody, some perennial, some annual. We eat the seed from some, and we eat or use the vegetative part of others. We have mixed crops, or polycultures, and we have monocultures. When one considers the four pairs in all combinations, we come up with sixteen. In the figure on the following page, you see that four are irrational since there's no such thing as a woody annual. Of the twelve possible combinations remaining, eleven of those are in the human inventory. But what of that blank?

Why have there been no herbaceous, perennial seed-producing polycultures organized and used by humans? If there had been, it would be a perennial grain polyculture—a domestic prairie. If we had such an ecosystem, might not there be some of the same efficiencies inherent within the natural integrities of the prairie? Could they also be present on the farm?

I talked to my geneticist and ecologist colleagues about the possibility of perennial grain polyculture. Their response was something like, "Well, Wes, everybody knows that's not possible. Not even a perennial monoculture seems possible. A plant will either allocate its resources to the root or to the seed, but it can't do both." Many, but

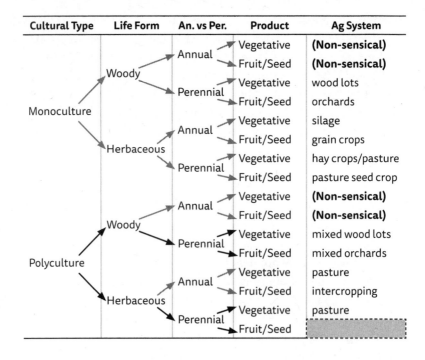

| Cultural Type | Life Form | An. vs Per. | Product | Ag System |
|---|---|---|---|---|
| Monoculture | Woody | Annual | Vegetative | **(Non-sensical)** |
| | | | Fruit/Seed | **(Non-sensical)** |
| | | Perennial | Vegetative | wood lots |
| | | | Fruit/Seed | orchards |
| | Herbaceous | Annual | Vegetative | silage |
| | | | Fruit/Seed | grain crops |
| | | Perennial | Vegetative | hay crops/pasture |
| | | | Fruit/Seed | pasture seed crop |
| Polyculture | Woody | Annual | Vegetative | **(Non-sensical)** |
| | | | Fruit/Seed | **(Non-sensical)** |
| | | Perennial | Vegetative | mixed wood lots |
| | | | Fruit/Seed | mixed orchards |
| | Herbaceous | Annual | Vegetative | pasture |
| | | | Fruit/Seed | intercropping |
| | | Perennial | Vegetative | pasture |
| | | | Fruit/Seed | |

not all, of my scientist friends whom I treasure may have doubted me, but my environmentalist friends, such as those who have ventured to Schumacher College, were encouraging.

So, we continued to plunge ahead, all the while reckoning that if we stopped with a perennial grain monoculture, we would miss half the point. So, we set our sights on perennial grain polyculture: a domestic grain-producing prairie. Some considered that still too pure.

My friendship with Wendell Berry, who taught at Schumacher College, began in 1980, following the publication of *New Roots for Agriculture*. I called on him to give a lecture at the Land at the dedication of our first greenhouse. In that talk he introduced us to both the literary folk and scientists, members of the formal culture who looked to nature as a standard. As he talked, I was especially taken with Alexander Pope's *Epistle to Burlington*, where he admonishes us to "consult the genius of the place in all." Wendell gave several examples, citing passages from Shakespeare, Spencer, Milton, as well as Virgil.

With the GAO report and the Konza field trip on my mind in 1977, I wrote a piece for the Land's *Land Report* and for a Friends of the

Earth publication called *Not Man Apart*. I laid it all out, admitting it would take fifty to a hundred years to develop perennial grain polycultures.

So much for that time some four decades ago. Where are we now? David Van Tassel is working on a wild perennial which shows promise to be an oilseed crop called silphium. It is in the sunflower family. Pheonah Nabukalu, from Uganda, came to us as a postdoc to work with Stan Cox on sorghum, and later became a full-time staff member. Their perennial sorghum breeding is going on at the Land and in Africa, along with a winter nursery in Puerto Rico. Lee DeHaan is working on intermediate wheatgrass.

We call the grain from this perennial plant Kernza.® It is being grown on at least five continents and is now somewhat commercialized. Shuwen Wang is working on perennial wheat, with good results but no releases yet. Brandon Schlautman is doing evaluations on promising legumes.

We were instrumental in appropriating the wild perennial rice species from the Philippines and went on to help fund that research. Our concern was for the Chinese uplands, where erosion is serious. Our friends in China, under the direction of Fengyi Hu, have made it possible for farmers to grow thousands of acres of perennial rice in China. Three-year-old plants are still experiencing high yield two times a year. Nearly all of those acres are in paddy rice to date, but that is changing.

From China perennial rice has spread to the uplands in Viet Nam, Laos and Cambodia. As Soil Association president, Schumacher would have loved that story.

Other species are also being considered. We're helping support scientists at Saint Louis University and Missouri Botanical Garden develop a global inventory of herbaceous perennials as possible new "hardware" for agriculture. (I don't like that word for organisms, although it is useful for now.) Perennials on the land introduce a whole new dimension to farming in the future, because annual grain "hardware" is so limited.

So, here is the story on that. Farmers and agronomists have the *burden* to be *prescriptive*. Hunger is on the line. Ecologists have had the luxury to be descriptive. They have been trying to understand primarily how the world is or works. With perennial polycultures, the *descriptive* and *prescriptive* can become one, bringing two scientific cultures together. Ecological agriculture may be—just may be—our last best hope to keep alive all that we have discovered during our prodigal journey. By that I mean what we have learned about the journey of the universe, and the framework of the journey from minerals to cells, both now scientifically verifiable.

If we are successful, we will protect our potential for producing food by reducing soil erosion and getting rid of fossil fuels and chemicals. A whole different kind of flowering is needed and seems possible for meeting our bona fide human needs. Leading this orchestra is our ecologist and research director, Tim Crews. He and his colleagues are studying mixtures of various perennials, with ecological intensification as a major goal. The Land Institute researchers, along with an increasing number of colleagues around the world, are out to fill that blank on the figure.

One last but necessary consideration: The last poem, "For the Children," from Gary Snyder's book, *Turtle Island*, captures much of the challenge ahead of us.

> The rising hills, the slopes
> of statistics
> lie before us.
> The steep climb
> of everything, going up,
> up, as we all
> go down.

Snyder's poem continues on with a note of hope.

> In the next century
> or the one beyond that,
> they say,
> are valleys, pastures,
> we can meet there in peace.

The Land Institute research effort has contributed and still contributes to those "rising hills," the "slopes of statistics." Our researchers make things happen with fossil-powered tractors, combines, lots of lab equipment and three greenhouses. All of that industrial equipment contributes to those "rising hills, the slopes of statistics." How can we justify this? Here is what I believe: Once established, the new perennial grain mixtures, in a pinch, will not require the industrial world that brought them into existence. Their creatureliness remains. Should one of our ancestors, Rip Van Winkle-like, appear from the first millennium of agriculture, he or she would know what to do with these creatures, with less time spent managing weeds. If in a polyculture, whole-field crashes due to insects and pathogens should be less. And here is the point: The industrial or material world can't say that. A creaturely worldview now seems possible and necessary.

Once we assess our technologies against a background of ecosystem concepts that feature creatureliness, information-intensive becomes a way of being, and energy intensity declines. This will be essential as we put a cap on carbon emissions and keep ratcheting that cap down. So, let us imagine an "information imperative" gradually replacing much of our "energy-intensive culture," perhaps led by our oldest and most necessary work—growing food. After all, the first work task given our forebearers in the Judeo-Christian world was to care for the garden. Buddhist economics would also embrace that admonition.

And so, Schumacher College, keep on keeping on.

WES JACKSON is the President Emeritus of the Land Institute. His latest book is *Nature as Measure*. He received a Right Livelihood Award in 2000. landinstitute.org

# Healing the Divided Brain

IAIN McGILCHRIST

*Whether life is worth living*
*depends on whether there is love in life.*
— R. D. LAING

Congratulations to Schumacher College and all those teachers and students who have participated in the life of the college for reaching this landmark year of 30th anniversary. Schumacher College has been a pioneer college in elucidating the ecological and spiritual paradigm for our time.

We are now facing crises that will test not just each one of us individually but the whole of humanity, and indeed the living world as a whole: Gaia. We face, above all, the possibility of devastating climate change, the pollution of the earth and sea, the destruction and desecration of the natural world and the driving to extinction of the ancient cultures of Indigenous people, along with possible mass migrations leading to the breakdown of civil order.

But we also face a crisis less tangible, but no less serious for humanity: we are experiencing a crisis of meaning. Not coincidentally, far more of us than ever before in the history of the world live divorced from Nature, alienated from the structures of a stable society and indifferent to the divine. These three elements have always been what have provided us with an overarching sense of belonging: our relations with the living world, with one another and with God. Alas, they are barely still open to us; we have seen to that. We exist in the world, of course, but we no longer *belong* in this world.

Each of these divorces has come about very swiftly, in a mere

200–250 years—the twinkling of an eye in relation to the age of humanity. And they have each come about because we think we know best. In the eighth-century Chinese classic, *The Secret of the Golden Flower*, it is written that "the conscious mind is like a violent general of a strong fiefdom controlling things from a distance, until the sword is turned around." The sinologist Thomas Cleary comments:

> Zen Buddhism traditionally describes the mechanism of delusion as mistaking the servant for the master. In the metaphor of this passage, the general is supposed to be a servant but instead usurps authority. According to Zen/Taoist psychology, the conscious mind (which does the thinking) is supposed to be a servant of the original mind, but the activity of the conscious mind tends to become so self-involved that it seems to have become an independent entity. When "the sword is turned around" in the metaphor of our text, the original mind retrieves command over the delinquent conscious mind.

This text was unknown to me when I wrote *The Master and His Emissary*, in which I describe the overthrow of the Master, the right hemisphere of the brain, by his own emissary, the left hemisphere. In that book I argued that we have succumbed twice in the West, and are now succumbing for the third time, to the temptation to see the world only through the eyes of the left hemisphere emissary. In the past this has invariably coincided with the overreaching of an empire, as today, and the collapse of a civilization, as I fear awaits us tomorrow. But never has the hold of the left hemisphere on us been more complete than it is today. Its form of attention to the world and way of being in it confront us wherever we look.

A member of the Swiss Parliament, Lukas Fierz, recalls as a boy meeting his celebrated neighbour, Carl Gustav Jung. In the course of conversation,

> Jung told us about his encounter with a Pueblo chief whose name was Mountain Lake. This chief told him that the white man was doomed. When asked why, the chief took both hands before his eyes and—Jung imitating the gesture—moved the outstretched index fingers convergingly towards one point before him, saying "because the white man looks at only one point, excluding all other aspects."

Many years later, Dr. Fierz, who is a physician and a founding member of the Green Party in Switzerland, recalls that a significant adversary of that movement was a successful industrialist and self-made billionaire:

> I asked him what in his view was the reason for his incredible entrepreneurial and political success. He took both hands before his eyes and moved the outstretched index fingers convergingly towards one point before him, saying, "because I am able to concentrate on only one point, excluding all other aspects." I remember that I had to swallow hard two or three times, so as not to say anything...

The secret of success—of a kind—and the formula for ruin. Such narrow, hyperfocused attention is the characteristic mode of the left hemisphere: temporarily useful, but effectively blind to the bigger picture, indeed to everything except its perceived goal at a moment in time.

One consequence of not seeing the longer-term consequences of our actions, or the broader consequences at a moment in time, is that we are constantly surprised by the way things do not turn out as we expected. As a society, we pursue happiness and become measurably less happy over time; we privilege autonomy and end up bound by rules to which we never assented, and more spied on than any people since the beginning of time; we pursue leisure through technology and discover that the average working day is longer than ever, and that we have less time than we had before. The means to our ends are ever more available, while we have less sense of what our ends should be, or whether there is purpose in anything at all. We carefully predict and monitor the stock market in order to avoid a crash: it promptly crashes. We are so eager that all scientific research result in "positive findings" that it has become progressively less adventurous and more predictable, and therefore discovers less and less that is significantly new. We grossly misconceive the nature of teaching and research in the humanities as utilitarian, in order to get value for money, and thus render it pointless and, in this form, certainly a waste of resource. We "improve" education by dictating curricula and focusing on exam results to the point where freethinking, arguably an overarching goal of true education, is discouraged; in our universities many students are, in any case, so frightened that the truth might turn out not to conform to their theoretical model that they demand to be protected from discussions that threaten to examine the model critically; and their teachers, who should know better, in a serious dereliction of duty, collude. We over-sanitize and cause vulnerability to infection; we overuse antibiotics, leading to super-bacteria that no antibiotic can kill; we make drugs illegal to protect society, and, while failing comprehensively to control the use of drugs, create a fertile field for crime; we protect children in such a way that they cannot cope with— let alone relish—uncertainty or risk, and are rendered vulnerable. The left hemisphere's motivation is control, and its means of achieving it alarmingly linear, as though it could see only one of the arrows in a vastly complex network of interactions at any one time. Which is indeed all it can.

But in broader terms, the consequences are even more numerous. Because of the narrow, piecemeal nature of left hemisphere attention, we have lost the sense of wholeness; our thinking has become narrow and dogmatic; we see categories as more real than the unique living beings that compose them; we have become curiously disembodied in our way of being—detached, abstract, driven by theories, rather than valuing our intuitive understandings, mechanical and even in a sense devitalized.

The evidence is plentiful that spending time close to Nature, having a habit of regular, especially communal spiritual practices and belonging to a community with shared aspirations, where one can trust and be trusted, all have a truly staggering effect on health, both physical and mental, happiness, resilience and the sense of fulfillment. Similarly, being deprived of these can lead to anxiety, anger and frustration, problems with attention and cognition and the psychological and physical concomitants of stress. Of course, the irony is that each of those elements of a good life is rightly valued not for its utility but for itself; yet even those whose values never rise above the utilitarian should, on purely rational grounds, embrace them.

In the world as it is today, we need more than ever what Schumacher College stands for: the values of a close and nurturing relationship with Nature, the values of a shared life with common purposes and the cultivation of a sense of the sacred. In a saner world, Schumacher College would be hardly the exception: it would be the rule. For what it has to teach is now more urgently needed than ever, both for our own thriving as individuals and for the saving of whatever we can from coming disaster.

In 1983, the American philosopher and novelist Walker Percy wrote: "You live in a deranged age—more deranged than usual—because despite great scientific and technological advances, man has not the faintest idea of who he is or what he is doing." In Schumacher College, we have a shining example of how to redress this predicament. It is a small beacon of sanity in a very strange world. I am deeply moved by having been welcomed into the world of Schumacher College on several visits when I have given talks and seminars there. It is something I will always treasure.

I cannot finish without a word of thanks specifically to Satish Kumar, for his wisdom and guidance, and for the example he sets of what a human being can become and the difference that one person can make. Let us take our lead from him. Once again, many congratulations to Schumacher College on its 30th anniversary, and may there be many more.

 IAIN McGILCHRIST read English at New College, Oxford. He is a Fellow of the Royal College of Psychiatrists and the author of *The Master and His Emissary*, published by Yale University Press.

# PART 2

# Education of Head:

# Economics

SMALL IS BEAUTIFUL

# Buddhist Economics

E. F. Schumacher

*Today we have a temporary aberration called "Industrial
Capitalism" which is inadvertently liquidating its two most
important sources of capital, the natural world and properly
functioning societies. No sensible capitalist can do that...If we
treat nature as model and mentor and not as a nuisance to be
evaded or manipulated, we will certainly acquire much more
reverence for life that we seem to be showing right now.*
— Amory Lovins

*We named the College to honour E. F. Schumacher because
he was one of the rare economists who was brave enough to
link spirituality with economics. His classic essay, "Buddhist
Economics," written in 1966, is an outstanding statement of that
intention. Once I asked him, "Why did you connect economics
with Buddhist principles?" He said, "Economics without ethics
is like a flower without fragrance, a well without water,
words without meaning or marriage without love."*

*Here we reprint the essay in order to pay our tribute to a
visionary economist of the twentieth century.*
— Satish Kumar

"Right Livelihood" is one of the requirements of the Buddha's Noble Eightfold Path. It is clear, therefore, that there must be such a thing as Buddhist economics.

Buddhist countries have often stated that they wish to remain faithful to their heritage. So Burma: "The New Burma sees no conflict between religious values and economic progress. Spiritual health and material well-being are not enemies; they are natural allies." Or: "We can blend successfully the religious and spiritual values of our heritage with the benefits of modern technology." Or: "We Burmans have a sacred duty to conform both our dreams and our acts to our faith. This we shall ever do."

All the same, such countries invariably assume that they can model their economic development plans in accordance with modern economics, and they call upon modern economists from so-called advanced countries to advise them, to formulate the policies to be pursued and to construct the grand design for development, the Five-Year Plan or whatever it may be called. No one seems to think that a Buddhist way of life would call for Buddhist economics, just as the modern materialist way of life has brought forth modern economics.

Economists themselves, like most specialists, normally suffer from a kind of metaphysical blindness, assuming that theirs is a science of absolute and invariable truths, without any presuppositions. Some go so far as to claim that economic laws are as free from "metaphysics" or "values" as the law of gravitation. We need not, however, get involved in arguments of methodology. Instead, let us take some fundamentals and see what they look like when viewed by a modern economist and a Buddhist economist.

There is universal agreement that a fundamental source of wealth is human labour. Now, the modern economist has been brought up to consider "labour" or work as little more than a necessary evil. From the point of view of the employer, it is in any case simply an item of cost, to be reduced to a minimum if it cannot be eliminated altogether, say, by automation. From the point of view of the workman, it is a "disutility"; to work is to make a sacrifice of one's leisure and comfort, and wages are a kind of compensation for the sacrifice. Hence the ideal from the point of view of the employer is to have output without employees, and the ideal from the point of view of the employee is to have income without employment.

The consequences of these attitudes both in theory and in practice are, of course, extremely far-reaching. If the ideal with regard to work is to get rid of it, every method that "reduces the workload" is a good thing. The most potent method, short of automation, is the so-called "division of labour," and the classical example is the pin factory eulogised in Adam Smith's *Wealth of Nations*. Here it is not a matter of ordinary specialisation, which mankind has practised from time immemorial, but of dividing up every complete process of production into minute parts, so that the final product can be produced at great speed without anyone having had to contribute more than a totally insignificant and, in most cases, unskilled movement of his limbs.

The Buddhist point of view takes the function of work to be at least threefold: to give a man a chance to utilise and develop his faculties; to enable him to overcome his ego-centredness by joining with other people in a common task; and to bring forth the goods and services needed for a becoming existence. Again, the consequences that flow from this view are endless. To organise work in such a manner that it becomes meaningless, boring, stultifying or nerve-racking for the worker would be little short of criminal; it would indicate a greater concern with goods than with people, an evil lack of compassion and a soul-destroying degree of attachment to the most primitive side of this worldly existence. Equally, to strive for leisure as an alternative to work would be considered a complete misunderstanding of one of the basic truths of human existence, namely that work and leisure are complementary parts of the same living process and cannot be separated without destroying the joy of work and the bliss of leisure.

From the Buddhist's point of view, there are therefore two types of mechanisation which must be clearly distinguished: one that enhances a man's skill and power and one that turns the work of man over to a mechanical slave, leaving man in a position of having to serve the slave. How to tell the one from the other? "The craftsman himself," says Ananda Coomaraswamy, a man equally competent to talk about the modern West as the ancient East, "can always, if allowed to, draw the delicate distinction between the machine and the tool. The carpet loom is a tool, a contrivance for holding warp threads at a stretch for the pile to be woven round them by the craftsmen's fingers; but the power loom is a machine, and its significance as a destroyer of culture lies in the fact that it does the essentially human part of the work." It is clear, therefore, that Buddhist economics must be very different from the economics of modern materialism, since the Buddhist sees the essence of civilisation not in a multiplication of wants but in the purification of human character. Character, at the same time, is formed primarily by a man's work. And work, properly conducted in conditions of human dignity and freedom, blesses those who do it and equally their products. The Indian philosopher and economist J. C. Kumarappa sums the matter up as follows:

> If the nature of the work is properly appreciated and applied, it will stand in the same relation to the higher faculties as food is to the physical body. It nourishes and enlivens the higher man and urges him to produce the best he is capable of. It directs his free will along the proper course and disciplines the animal in him into progressive channels. It furnishes an excellent background for man to display his scale of values and develop his personality.

If a man has no chance of obtaining work, he is in a desperate position, not simply because he lacks an income but because he lacks this nourishing and enlivening factor of disciplined work which nothing can replace. A modern economist may engage in highly sophisticated calculations on whether full employment "pays" or whether it might be more "economic" to run an economy at less than full employment so as to ensure a greater mobility of labour, a better stability of wages and so forth. His fundamental criterion of success is simply the total quantity of goods produced during a given period of time. "If the marginal urgency of goods is low," says Professor Galbraith in *The Affluent Society*, "then so is the urgency of employing the last man or the last million men in the labour force." And again: "If...we can afford some unemployment in the interest of society—a proposition, incidentally, of impeccably conservative antecedents—then we can afford to give those who are unemployed the goods that enable them to sustain their accustomed standard of living."

From a Buddhist point of view, this is standing the truth on its head by considering goods as more important than people and consumption as more important than creative activity. It means shifting the emphasis from the worker to the product of work, that is, from the human to the sub-human, a surrender to the forces of evil. The very start of Buddhist economic planning would be a planning for full employment, and the primary purpose of this would in fact be employment for everyone who needs an "outside" job; it would not be the maximisation of employment nor the maximisation of production. Women, on the whole, do not need an "outside" job, and the large-scale employment of women in offices or factories would be considered a sign of serious economic failure. In particular, to let mothers of young children work in factories while the children run wild would be as uneconomic in the eyes of a Buddhist economist as the employment of a skilled worker as a soldier in the eyes of a modern economist.

While the materialist is mainly interested in goods, the Buddhist is mainly interested in liberation. But Buddhism is "the Middle Way" and therefore in no way antagonistic to physical well-being. It is not wealth that stands in the way of liberation but the attachment to wealth; not the enjoyment of pleasurable things but the craving for them. The keynote of Buddhist economics, therefore, is simplicity and non-violence. From an economist's point of view, the marvel of the Buddhist way of life is the utter rationality of its pattern—amazingly small means leading to extraordinarily satisfactory results.

For the modern economist, this is very difficult to understand. He is used to measuring the "standard of living" by the amount of annual consumption, assuming all the time that a man who consumes more is "better-off" than a man who consumes less. A Buddhist economist would consider this approach excessively irrational: since consumption is merely a means to human well-being, the aim should be to obtain the maximum of well-being with the minimum of consumption. Thus, if the purpose of clothing is a certain amount of temperature comfort and an attractive appearance, the task is to attain this purpose with the smallest possible effort, that is, with the smallest annual destruction of cloth and with the help of designs that involve the smallest possible input of toil. The less toil there is, the more time and strength is left for artistic creativity. It would be highly uneconomic, for instance, to go in for complicated tailoring, like the modern West, when a much more beautiful effect can be achieved by the skilful draping of uncut material. It would be the height of folly to make material so that it should wear out quickly and the height of barbarity to make anything ugly, shabby or mean. What has just been said about clothing applies equally to all other human requirements. The owner-ship and the consumption of goods is a means to an end, and Bud-dhist economics is the systematic study of how to attain given ends with the minimum means.

Modern economics, on the other hand, considers consumption to be the sole end and purpose of all economic activity, taking the factors of production—land, labour and capital—as the means. The former, in short, tries to maximise human satisfaction by the optimal pattern of consumption, while the latter tries to maximise consumption by the optimal pattern of productive effort. It is easy to see that the ef-fort needed to sustain a way of life which seeks to attain the optimal pattern of consumption is likely to be much smaller than the effort needed to sustain a drive for maximum consumption. We need not be surprised, therefore, that the pressure and strain of living is very much less in, say, Burma than it is in the United States, in spite of the fact that the amount of labour-saving machinery used in the former country is only a minute fraction of the amount used in the latter.

Simplicity and non-violence are obviously closely related. The optimal pattern of consumption, producing a high degree of human satisfaction by means of a relatively low rate of consumption, allows people to live without great pressure and strain and to fulfil the pri-mary injunction of Buddhist teaching: "Cease to do evil; try to do good." As physical resources are everywhere limited, people satisfy-ing their needs by means of a modest use of resources are obviously less likely to be at each other's throats than people depending upon a high rate of use. Equally, people who live in highly self-sufficient local communities are less likely to get involved in large-scale vio-lence than people whose existence depends on worldwide systems of trade.

From the point of view of Buddhist economics, therefore, produc-tion from local resources for local needs is the most rational way of economic life, while dependence on imports from afar and the con-sequent need to produce for export to unknown and distant peoples is highly uneconomic and justifiable only in exceptional cases and on a small scale. Just as the modern economist would admit that a high rate of consumption of transport services between a man's home and his place of work signifies a misfortune and not a high standard of life, so the Buddhist economist would hold that to satisfy human wants from faraway sources rather than from sources nearby signifies failure rather than success. The former tends to take statistics showing an increase in the number of ton/miles per head of the population carried by a country's transport system as proof of economic progress, while to the latter—the Buddhist economist—the same statistics would indicate a highly undesirable deterioration in the *pattern* of consumption.

Another striking difference between modern economics and Buddhist economics arises over the use of natural resources. Bertrand de Jouvenel, the eminent French political philosopher, has characterised "Western man" in words which may be taken as a fair description of the modern economist:

> He tends to count nothing as an expenditure, other than human effort; he does not seem to mind how much mineral matter he wastes and, far worse, how much living matter he destroys. He does not seem to realise at all that human life is a dependent part of an ecosystem of many different forms of life; As the world is ruled from towns where men are cut off from any form of life other than human, the feeling of belonging to an ecosystem is not revived. This results in a harsh and improvident treatment of things upon which we ultimately depend, such as water and trees.

The teaching of the Buddha, on the other hand, enjoins a reverent and non-violent attitude not only to all sentient beings but also, with great emphasis, to trees. Every follower of the Buddha ought to plant a tree every few years and look after it until it is safely established, and the Buddhist economist can demonstrate without difficulty that the universal observation of this rule would result in a high rate of genuine economic development independent of any foreign aid. Much of the economic decay of southeast Asia (as of many other parts of the world) is undoubtedly due to a heedless and shameful neglect of trees.

Modern economics does not distinguish between renewable and non-renewable materials, as its very method is to equalise and quantify everything by means of a money price. Thus, taking various alternative fuels, like coal, oil, wood or water-power: the only difference between them recognised by modern economics is relative cost per equivalent unit. The cheapest is automatically the one to be preferred, as to do otherwise would be irrational and "uneconomic." From a Buddhist point of view, of course, this will not do; the essential difference between non-renewable fuels like coal and oil on the one hand and renewable fuels like wood and water-power on the other cannot be simply overlooked. Non-renewable goods must be used only if they are indispensable, and then only with the greatest care and the most meticulous concern for conservation. To use them heedlessly or extravagantly is an act of violence, and while complete non-violence may not be attainable on this earth, there is nonetheless an ineluctable duty on man to aim at the ideal of non-violence in all he does.

Just as a modern European economist would not consider it a great economic achievement if all European art treasures were sold to America at attractive prices, so the Buddhist economist would insist that a population basing its economic life on non-renewable fuels is living parasitically, on capital instead of income. Such a way of life could have no permanence and could therefore be justified only as a purely temporary expedient. As the world's resources of non-renewable fuels—coal, oil and natural gas—are exceedingly unevenly distributed over the globe and undoubtedly limited in quantity, it is clear that their exploitation at an ever-increasing rate is an act of violence against nature which must almost inevitably lead to violence between men.

This fact alone might give food for thought even to those people in Buddhist countries who care nothing for the religious and spiritual values of their heritage and ardently desire to embrace the materialism of modern economics at the fastest possible speed. Before they dismiss Buddhist economics as nothing better than a nostalgic dream, they might wish to consider whether the path of economic development outlined by modern economics is likely to lead them to places where they really want to be. Towards the end of his courageous book, *The Challenge of Man's Future*, Professor Harrison Brown of the California Institute of Technology gives the following appraisal:

> Thus we see that, just as industrial society is fundamentally unstable and subject to reversion to agrarian existence, so within it the conditions which offer individual freedom are

unstable in their ability to avoid the conditions which impose rigid organisation and totalitarian control. Indeed, when we examine all of the foreseeable difficulties which threaten the survival of industrial civilisation, it is difficult to see how the achievement of stability and the maintenance of individual liberty can be made compatible.

Even if this were dismissed as a long-term view, there is the immediate question of whether "modernisation," as currently practised without regard to religious and spiritual values, is actually producing agreeable results. As far as the masses are concerned, the results appear to be disastrous—a collapse of the rural economy, a rising tide of unemployment in town and country and the growth of a city proletariat without nourishment for either body or soul.

It is in the light of both immediate experience and long-term prospects that the study of Buddhist economics could be recommended even to those who believe that economic growth is a question of choosing between "modem growth" and "traditional stagnation." It is a question of finding the right path of development, the Middle Way between materialist heedlessness and traditionalist immobility, in short, of finding "Right Livelihood."

REGENERATIVE ECONOMICS

# New Story

JONATHAN DAWSON

*Infinite growth of material consumption*
*in a finite world is an impossibility.*
— E. F. SCHUMACHER

I was listening to a radio program on Black History Month in which a Black woman was reliving her excitement at her introduction to Black history and culture in her classroom. A teacher had introduced a module on the music, history and politics of Africa and the Black diaspora, and suddenly a whole world opened up for the schoolgirl that this woman had been, radically changing her life's path. A great swathe of experience and knowledge that had previously been invisible to her suddenly was given a language, in the process radically reframing how she understood the world and her place within it.

I felt and shared her excitement, recognizing that is precisely what has drawn me to the profession of educator and specifically what has taken me to Schumacher College.

We live in an era which, in the words of Thomas Berry, lies between stories—where the narratives and norms we have inherited from our parents' generation no longer make sense, but in which the new narratives we need to guide us through the next stage of our planetary journey are struggling to be born. I see Schumacher College as having an important role to play as midwife to the new story.

Such a transition of narratives is required perhaps nowhere as urgently as in the two fields that I specialize in here at the college— economics and education. My own first rush of excitement at the existence of a whole other world beyond that which my habitual stories prescribed was on the subject of money. Here, diving into a wealth of anthropological research, I found that the dominant narratives around money—its origins and functions, how and why it is created and the influence this all has on the workings of our economy—are spectacularly wrong. This opened up the door for radical, out-of-the box thinking... and activism.

Since then, I have found myself as a researcher and educator seeking out other foundational creation myths underpinning the dominant paradigm that are ripe for challenging and demolition. Schumacher College is the perfect place to do this, as the core instinct is to always "go upstream" to explore the root of the societal challenges we face rather than, as is all too common, to tweak at the level of symptoms.

Looking specifically at our nine-year-old Economics for Transition postgraduate program (that is to be superseded by a new offering, Regenerative Economics, from 2020/21), for example, this is, to the best of my knowledge, the only accredited economics course in the world that begins with a deep dive into holistic science and earth systems design.

There are two reasons for doing this. First, to make explicit our understanding that the economy is a subsystem of the planetary ecology rather than vice versa, as is generally, if largely unconsciously, assumed. Second, because a guiding hypothesis at the college is that, at least to some degree, the multiple crises in our social and economic systems have their common root in the gulf between human and other-than-human system design. In short, if you want to learn how to create a money system that is efficient, generative and equitable, you are likely to pick up a good number of clues by taking a walk in the forest and studying how it thrives.

## Economics of the Commons

Perhaps the cornerstone concept, connecting many of the other threads we weave into the new economy tapestry, is that of "the commons." Once again, there exist here foundational myths of the dominant market-based orthodoxy that are ripe for overturning. The "tragedy of the commons" is an idea that has entered our societal subconscious—the core hypothesis being that community-managed resources and spaces will tend to overuse and deterioration because it is in the interests of the individuals who form the community to maximize their own personal usage beyond what is sustainable. This theory has entered our collective belief systems and has indeed been used to justify the transfer of land and resources from communities to corporations across the global South for the last fifty years.

But this does not stand up to any kind of empirical examination. The tragedy of the commons hypothesis was generated by Professor of Human Ecology Garret Hardin in 1968 on the basis of zero empirical evidence. It has since been contradicted by a mass of fieldwork, much of it done by the esteemed economics Nobel Prize winner Eleanor Ostrom. What Hardin missed was that we are not isolated individuals making decisions solely on the basis of our self-interest but rather are embedded in communities that engage our loyalty and that make and enforce rules governing collective behaviour.

And so, the commons have been rediscovered as if by magic, a whole mode of social organization and governance that has never gone away but has been rendered invisible by our division of the world into two opposing camps (socialism/more state versus capitalism/more market), and a whole world of human experience has come vibrantly alive. Alliances are being built between traditional commoners occupying ancestral lands (mostly in the global South) and digital commoners creating distributed governance models and open-source platforms (mostly in the global North).

## Beyond Development

Another module on the program, Beyond Development, goes way upstream in questioning many of the core assumptions underlying the development paradigm, enquiring not into "How can we do development better?" but rather "What are the root causes of power and wealth imbalances in the global family and how can we all, North and South, free ourselves from the oppressive legacy of colonialism in all its forms?"

My excitement at the uncovering and languaging of paradigm-busting ideas is not limited to the curriculum. I am, if anything, even more excited by the pedagogical experiments and innovations at the college—what we refer to as an education of head, heart and hands. My interest in this dates back to my work as an educator in Findhorn, from where I moved to the college. An early memory from that period was in teaching about ecological footprints. I noticed that as long as we remained at the cognitive level, the students' response bypassed emotional engagement as they went straight into problem-solving mode, with any initial distress in response to the data seemingly soon forgotten.

So, I experimented in dividing the group up into four circles representing the span of humanity from richest to poorest, each circle representing the ecological space their culture takes up, from a huge finger-tip to finger-tip circle for the North Americans to a dense huddle for the Africans. The response was immediate and electric. Catharsis, passion, deep engagement and, over time, behavioral change. The lesson was clear: While cognitive engagement is essential, we have many other learning faculties begging to be engaged.

Schumacher College is a perfect place for experimentation of this kind. There is a deep, lived understanding of the need for total engagement—intellectual, embodied, emotional and spiritual—in the learning process. As Fritz Schumacher himself put it, *education* can help us only if it produces the "*whole* person." The aim here is much more than mental stimulation alone but is rather about creating the conditions in which the whole person can flourish.

The Beyond Development course, for example, includes a Theatre of the Oppressed workshop, drawn from the experience of radical educators and dramatists working together with the urban poor in Brazil. Here, the students have an opportunity to play out their own experiences of oppression.

Students not only discuss abstract ideas relating to economic structures but experiment with representing these structures with their bodies, drawing on constellation practices. It is one thing to absorb the data describing how market-based activity is dwarfed by the unaccounted-for value of ecosystem services and unpaid work in the core economy, such as childcare and housework. It is quite another—and far more impactful—to map out these proportional relationships with the students' bodies on the floor in the form of an iceberg, with the monetized economy as the visible tip above the waterline.

## It Is All About Love

A module that ran as part of the economics course in the early years of the program, Drawing on Indigenous Wisdom, included an overnight, fasting vigil in the woods. This is not frivolous. If we are to develop a qualitatively different relation with the other-than-human world, there is only so far one can go while sitting in the library. UK journalist George Monbiot has a lovely way of expressing this: "Acknowledging our love for the living world does something that a library full of papers on sustainable development and ecosystem services cannot: it engages the imagination as well as the intellect."

And fundamentally that is what it is all about—love. Something I deeply appreciate about Schumacher College is the ease and lack of embarrassment with which love—in words and in actions—is included as a necessary part of the learning journey. This is economics education fit for the needs of the twenty-first century.

I cannot help but think that Fritz Schumacher would have deeply approved of what we are up to in the college and would feel flattered and delighted that we see ourselves as following in his lineage. Fritz was a champion paradigm buster, using a delightful mix of irreverence, intelligence and lucidity to undermine the cult of gigantism that dominated the narrative landscape of the period in which he lived. The distributed systems, social enterprise and human-scale local economies that lie at the heart of our curriculum find their roots squarely in the world of his imagining.

"Wisdom," Schumacher wrote, "demands a new orientation of science and technology towards the organic, the gentle, the nonviolent, the elegant and beautiful." This is what we are seeking to create, in our teachings and our actions.

JONATHAN DAWSON is Senior Lecturer in Economics at Schumacher College where he leads the Regenerative Economics postgraduate program: schumachercollege.org.uk/courses/postgraduate-courses/ma-regenerative-economics. A former president of the Global Ecovillage Network, he is also one of the principal authors of the Gaia Education sustainability curriculum: gaiaeducation.org/about

# People and Planet Connection

ANN PETTIFOR

*I never feel discouraged.*
*I can't raise the winds which might take us into a better world,*
*but I can put up the sail so that when the winds come,*
*I can catch it.*
— E. F. SCHUMACHER

There is a sustained and luminous arc that stretches from the corridors of Schumacher College to the city of Burlington, Vermont. It is not just a meteorological arc. It is an economic and political arc too. It is the Green New Deal, whose seeds were sown at a gathering convened by Satish Kumar at Schumacher College in November 2007. The ever-branching tree that emerged from that event is now firmly rooted in the campaign of Senator Bernie Sanders of Vermont. He was a candidate for the presidency of the United States of America, and the Green New Deal is at the heart of his offering to the American people.

## Economics, Ecology and Equity

The November 2007 Schumacher College gathering was defined as a "Think Tank on Economics, Ecology and Equity." Present at that meeting were many distinguished ecologists, economists and monetary theorists, identified in the photo below. They included Vandana Shiva, world-renowned environmentalist and thinker; Manfred Max Neef, a brilliant Chilean economist; Arturo Escobar, the radical anthropologist; Bernard Lietaer, engineer and economist, who taught me a great deal about the monetary system; and Paul Ekins, prominent advocate of sustainable economics and founder of the platform TOES (The Other Economic Summit) which shadowed G7 summits and promoted a new economics grounded in social and spiritual values. (The TOES platform was later to be transformed into the New Economics Foundation.) Richard Douthwaite, the radical Irish monetary reformer, sadly no longer with us, was there too as was the now-departed Brian Goodwin, radical ecologist. Wolfgang Sachs of the Wuppertal Institute for Climate, Environment and Energy and Colin Tudge, distinguished British science writer and broadcaster, brought formidable intellectual heft to the discussions. Another distinguished and now much-missed participant was Margrit Kennedy, a woman who had done so much important work on the nature of credit and its ability to multiply exponentially thanks to the magic of compound interest.

Present also were three people who were to become architects of the Green New Deal: Colin Hines, former coordinator of Greenpeace International's economics unit; Andrew Simms, political economist and environmentalist; and myself, a humble activist and political economist.

After the gathering at Schumacher College, Colin returned to London and began to corral prominent environmentalists and radical economists into a group whose purpose would be to draft a Plan B for

**Think Tank on Economics, Ecology and Equity**
November 14–18, 2007—Schumacher College

the planet. That plan became the Green New Deal, published in July 2008 by the New Economics Foundation.

Fundamental to the Green New Deal then and now is the integration of economy, ecology and equity. Before the Schumacher meeting, we all tended to stick to our own silos, whether economy, ecology or equity. Satish, by insisting on the integration of these themes, helped bring together ideas and people often believed to be in conflict. Sparks then flew, of course. Those of us focused on economics and the monetary system were often impatient with the green movement's lack of interest in, and understanding of, the international financial system. Similarly, while there was agreement on the need for systemic *ecological* change, there was frustration that the emphasis on individual behavior change and community change neglected systemic *economic* change. Environmentalists were equally frustrated by mainstream economists—perceived as overwhelmingly preoccupied with limitless growth. As a result, there was little engagement between environmentalists and economists.

That was to change with the Green New Deal.

After twelve formative years working on the sovereign debts of the world's poorest countries, I was concerned with two issues. First, the deregulated international financial architecture and the way in which the finance sector recklessly inflated credits, aimed these at speculation, consumption and production and then deflated these debts, often catastrophically. The finance sector recklessly aimed a hose of the propellant we know as credit at speculation, consumption and production, which in turn fuelled greenhouse gas emissions.

My second concern was with the origins and nature of money, banking and debt—often ignored in mainstream texts and misunderstood by many in the green movement. It was my interest in these two complex subjects that landed me an invitation to the November 2007 meeting, and that caused Satish to invite me over the next ten years to lead a number of workshops and courses at the college.

## A Sense of Belonging

I was quite unprepared for what was expected of me when I first stepped off the train after the long journey from London, having arrived at Totnes to run a workshop at Schumacher. On arrival at reception, I was quietly escorted to a beautiful self-contained tutor's flat overlooking the garden. Such a gift it was. I can picture it now. A quiet and simply furnished space, profoundly welcome after the stress of office screens, emails and social media and the hurly-burly of London life.

A little later I joined students gathered around a fire in the living room downstairs. Satish perched on a low stool and introduced us to the rules and routines of the college. Then he began to tell stories of his family back in India, of travels as a Jain monk around his country, and of his historic journey for peace, walking across the Indian subcontinent and Europe to London and Washington and of his very changed life as an adult in Britain. More of the guests offered their own stories, until, after a communal session of herbal tea drinking, we retired to bed.

That night I slept like a lamb.

The next morning, we gathered first for a period of meditation. Then breakfast at long shared tables bustling with fresh, wholesome bread, cereals and fruit. I remember the simple delight at being allocated my own napkin and ring for use throughout my stay. It made me feel I belonged. After that there was assembly in the hall where we were encouraged to stretch and move our stiffened limbs. An inspiring poem or piece of prose was read, and tasks and roles allocated. Some had to sweep the breakfast room and main reception rooms, others had to clear up after breakfast. Some were allocated to the kitchen to share in the preparation of the main midday meal or in the clearing up after it. In the afternoon some joined Satish in the sacred and therapeutic process of making, kneading and preparing the staff of life—a loaf of bread.

With our household tasks allocated and done, we moved into classes, where I began to lead discussions on the nature of money and of the international financial system—and the impact of both on the ecosystem. The sessions were free-flowing, stimulating and demanding. Some lasted fully two hours, and I remember feeling mentally drained after each session, so demanding were the questions and so intense the scrutiny by our varied group of international students. After lunch came the afternoon ramble in the nearby woods and across the surrounding fields, before returning for tea, more sessions on money, banking and debt, another delicious communal meal and, finally, tales by the evening fire.

## The Green New Deal

All the while the Green New Deal was buried in a report at the New Economics Foundation, with only the occasional endorsement by UN staff, the European Greens, the US Green presidential candidate, Jill Stein and, to our surprise, President Obama during his re-election campaign in 2012.

The original group led by Colin Hines continued to gather periodically in my flat where, on each occasion, I would cook a simple bowl of risotto or pasta, accompanied by salad, while Colin and others would bring bottles of fine wine. While Colin always ensured our gatherings were convivial, we were not averse to fierce arguments and differences, political and economic. We were to mourn one member of our group, Susie Parsons, who died suddenly in 2018, but who had brought good food, laughter and wise counsel to some of our more tempestuous meetings. Regular attendees included Caroline Lucas, then a Member of the European Parliament, but later to become a Member of Parliament; Richard Murphy, accountant and tax expert; Geoff Tily, Keynesian macroeconomist; Andrew Simms and Ruth Potts of the New Economics Foundation; two ex-CEOs of Friends of the Earth, Charles Secrett and Tony Juniper; Jeremy Leggett, the Solar Century entrepreneur; and Larry Elliott, senior economist at the *Guardian*.

And then in February 2018, two American activists, members of a group known as the Justice Democrats, knocked on my door in search of advice for a forthcoming campaign they were organizing. The campaign was part of the US mid-term Congressional elections, and the Justice Democrats were supporting a candidate, a Ms. Alexandria Ocasio Cortez, who was challenging a powerful sitting Democrat. In passing we discussed the Green New Deal, and on their return, in July 2018, they shared a Google doc headed: "A Green New Deal, with Justice for All. Practical. Possible. Inevitable." These were the words that were to help AOC, as she is now known, to win an extraordinary victory.

The rest is history. Senator Bernie Sanders, in his campaign to become the Democratic presidential candidate for the 2020 election, embraced it. On his website, Sanders explains the Green New Deal thus:

The climate crisis is not only the single greatest challenge facing our country; it is also our single greatest opportunity to build a more just and equitable future, but we must act immediately.

The key points are:

- Transform our energy system to 100 percent renewable energy and create 20 million jobs needed to solve the climate crisis.
- Ensure a just transition for communities and workers, including fossil fuel workers.
- Ensure justice for frontline communities, especially under-resourced groups, communities of colour, Native Americans, people with disabilities, children and the elderly.
- Save American families money with investments in weatherization, public transportation, modern infrastructure and high-speed broadband.
- Commit to reducing emissions throughout the world, including providing $200 billion to the Green Climate Fund, rejoining the Paris Agreement and reasserting the United States' leadership in the global fight against climate change.
- Invest in conservation and public lands to heal our soils, forests and prairie lands.
- End the greed of the fossil fuel industry and hold them accountable.

Those that took part in the Think Tank on Economics, Ecology and Equity at Schumacher College in November 2007 would not have dreamed of the distance their ideas and debates would travel, and of the influence and power of their contributions. Only Satish Kumar, I suspect, would have had an inkling of how the clash of ideas and of disciplines could sow fresh seeds from which great transformations grow.

ANN PETTIFOR is a Fellow of New Economics Foundation, and her latest book, *The Case for the Green New Deal*, is published by Verso.

NEW ECONOMICS

# Local Is Beautiful

HELENA NORBERG-HODGE

*The global economy is built on the principle that one place can
be exploited, even destroyed for the sake of another place.*
— WENDELL BERRY

My association with Schumacher College goes back to the very beginning. In fact, I was lucky enough to teach the second-ever course
there (James Lovelock's course was the first). Over the past thirty
years, under the visionary influence of Satish Kumar, the college has
established itself as the world's pre-eminent place of deep ecological
learning.

As it happens, my life had already been profoundly affected by the
writings of E. F. Schumacher even before my association with the college. In his seminal book, *Small Is Beautiful*, Schumacher articulated
a fundamental rethinking of conventional economic assumptions,
based upon his experience of an Indigenous land-based culture in
Burma. His perspective was invaluable to me when I found myself
working as a linguist in the remote Himalayan region of Ladakh, or
"Little Tibet," in the mid-1970s—a region that had never been colo-
nized, and had been sealed off from the outside world until 1974.

## Life in Ladakh

Like the people Schumacher encountered in Burma in the 1950s,
the Ladakhis lived beyond the reach of the consumer culture and its
growth-based economic worldview. Speaking the language fluently,
I became aware that the Ladakhi people were not afflicted by the
psychological insecurity, competitiveness and social divisiveness so

common in industrial societies. Instead they exhibited a profound spiritual grounding, as well as an irrepressible *joie de vivre*. They had very little money, and yet there was no poverty, no unemployment or homelessness. I became aware, as had Schumacher in Burma, that these were not a people who needed to be "developed" according to Western standards and priorities. In *Small Is Beautiful*, Schumacher made the case for decentralized, locally sensitive and culturally relevant development. I quickly became interested in exploring such a path in Ladakh, especially as the fossil fuel-based global economy was starting to make significant inroads into the region.

*Small is Beautiful* gave me the audacity to write to the Indian government seeking permission to demonstrate alternative technology in Ladakh. Together with a group of local community leaders, we introduced a range of decentralized, renewable technologies that were adapted to the cultural and ecological realities of the region. With more than three hundred days of sunshine annually, solar was an obvious choice, so we demonstrated passive solar architecture, greenhouses, solar water heating systems and photovoltaics. We were also able to develop locally made ram pumps and small-scale hydropower systems.

Since I was the only outsider to speak the language, I regularly found myself engaged in a kind of "counter-development," which consisted of providing information about the impact in the West of the industrial products and modern lifestyles that were being promoted with such gusto by government leaders and mass media alike. It became necessary to explain to my Ladakhi friends (who had never before encountered the concept of toxicity) why they shouldn't bake their bread on asbestos, store their butter in old petrol tins or use DDT on their crops. It also became important to expose the reality behind the one-sided glamorized media images of modern life, explaining that many people in the West struggle with loneliness, stress and depression, and that increasing numbers of people are actively searching for more sustainable and equitable alternatives to the consumer culture.

## The Western Globalized Economy

My experiences in Ladakh impelled me to see my own culture through different eyes. The waste and injustice of our capital- and energy-intensive economy became more obvious, and for the first time

I understood the high psychological and social price of a type of development that isolates people from one another and cuts us off from the natural world.

I saw that the speed, mobility and competition demanded by the modern economy erode the complex web of community relationships that, in places like Ladakh, support the formation of secure identities. From the school to the supermarket, from the workplace to the online world, the contact we have with others tends to be brief and transactional, with superficial facades emphasized over deep, interpersonal knowing. Only through seeing my own society through the lens of Ladakh was I able to recognize the dramatic cost of this kind of emotional and spiritual impoverishment.

I similarly saw how the globalizing economy undermines local economies, thereby destroying decentralized land-based livelihoods and continuously drawing ever more people into large, explosively growing urban centers. I also recognized that this kind of "progress," although global in its reach, is by no means an inexorable, evolutionary path: in the UK just as much as in Ladakh, it is the consequence of a particular set of economic policies, underpinned by a myopic worldview.

## Economic Localization

The lessons from Ladakh are more pertinent now than ever. Along with my organization, Local Futures, I continue to work around the world to promote a shift away from corporate globalization—towards a balance between city and country and a strengthening of smaller, more human-scale economies that meet the needs of people and the planet. We call this shift economic localization. As pioneers of this shift, we have been working for forty years to help build a worldwide movement for localization.

Localization is a structural path towards the "Small Is Beautiful" reality that Schumacher envisioned. Essentially, it is about revitalizing local economies by shortening the distances between production and consumption wherever possible. Decentralizing the production and distribution of our basic needs is the most effective way to reduce fossil fuel use and greenhouse gas emissions, but the benefits don't stop there. In the case of local food, for example, it also stimulates agricultural diversification, reduces the pressure to use chemical pesticides and fertilizers, helps restore agricultural and wild biodiversity, improves food security and increases the number of meaningful, productive livelihoods. Smaller-scale economic structures like those found in local food systems encourage a healthier relationship not only with the earth but also within the local community. They provide visible bonds of interdependence, and are a prerequisite for active and participatory democracy.

## Economics of Happiness

A sense of connection to community and the living earth is a fundamental human need. Studies are revealing that the mounting epidemics of depression, anxiety and suicide are linked to disconnection. We evolved in multigenerational communities, deeply connected to the plants, animals and landscapes on which we depended. In our work around the world, we see increasing evidence that human-scale localized economies are the best way to provide an "economics of happiness."

And yet, over the past thirty years, economic policy has continued to favor large-scale production, long-distance trade and ever more technology. It has increasingly exempted multinational firms from taxes and regulation, giving them an enormous unfair advantage over smaller businesses. Today, in fact, sixty-nine of the hundred largest economies in the world are not countries, but private corporations, giving them an inordinate amount of control over not just the economy but government policy as well: the amassed wealth of multinational corporations has enabled them to consolidate ownership of the media and to buy the favors of political parties.

Why have our supposedly democratic governments chosen to pursue this path? After many decades of studying the mechanisms and impacts of globalization around the world, I'm convinced that it is not because of innate human greed or evil intention. Rather, it is because the system has become so big, and the perspectives of those working within it have become so narrow and specialized, that people can remain unaware of the systemic impacts of this globalizing model.

We are all swimming in this system. Just as a supermarket shopper cannot know the effects of their purchases on people and ecosystems on the other side of the world, most policymakers and CEOs are so far removed from the real-world impacts of their decisions that they can easily believe the convenient rhetoric of "trickle-down economics" and "comparative advantage." It's as if our arms have become so long we cannot see what our hands are doing.

When we learn about the enormous power of global business—and see that almost every government is committed to its growth—we can easily believe that there's no possibility of changing things. However, when we become aware of what is happening at the grassroots around the world, a very different image emerges. We see that the "Small Is Beautiful" reality is being created in small pockets in virtually every country, with greater dedication than ever before.

## Grassroots Movements

Unseen by the global media and unsupported by governments or mainstream academia, this diverse grassroots movement has been quietly growing as more and more people act upon their yearning for greater connection to one another and to the natural world. From the flourishing of local food initiatives like farmers markets and community gardens, to the widespread revival of and appreciation for Indigenous knowledge, traditional skills and artisanal crafts, people are reaching beyond the confines of the consumer capitalist imagination and recreating human-scale economies that would, no doubt, please E. F. Schumacher.

Young people are walking out of so-called successful jobs in big cities to seek a life closer to the land and community. New farmers' movements are emerging in places as diverse as the UK, Palestine and Japan, partly driven by the realization that local food systems can reverse climate change and ecocide while strengthening community and local economies. And studies are emerging that underline the effectiveness of therapies—like Alcoholics Anonymous and "therapeutic horticulture"—that reconnect people to each other and to the natural world. Place-based educational institutions like Schumacher College, as well as the burgeoning "ecoversities" network, are becoming bastions of the interdisciplinary and nature-based wisdom that is key to responding to our global crises with systemic solutions.

Humanity is at a crossroads, and we must choose between the two paths that lie before us. One of those paths leads to further globalization, urbanization, centralization and technological dependence. Do we really want 5G wireless technology if it is going to hook us all more deeply to our smartphones and to insidious agents of social disconnection like social media? Do we want to fund further research into artificial intelligence, if it means destroying more livelihoods and surrendering more of our civil rights to centralized profit-oriented technocracies? Do we want our governments to persist in their commitment to global trade via "free-trade" treaties and infrastructure spending, if it means the continued growth of global monopolies and a further expansion of unsustainable resource-intensive production? Or do we want to choose the other path, the one that leads towards a diversity of smaller, more human-scale and place-based societies?

We need to recognize, just as Schumacher did, that the direction of our economy is not determined by some inevitable force of "progress" but is the result of policies that can be changed and assumptions that must be questioned. Let's come together to articulate our own visions of progress and join hands to strengthen the worldwide localization movement—the best way to help us realize our dream of a more peaceful, just and prosperous world.

 HELENA NORBERG-HODGE is the director of Local Futures and winner of a Right Livelihood Award. She is the author of *Local Is Our Future*. localfutures.org

# Less Is More

### Juliet B. Schor

*I want to say, in all seriousness, that a great deal*
*of harm is being done in the modern world*
*by belief in the virtuousness of work,*
*and that the road to happiness and prosperity*
*lies in an organized diminution of work.*

— Bertrand Russell, "In Praise of Idleness"

What a delight to relive my experiences at Schumacher College, thirty years after its founding! I had the good fortune to teach at the college a number of times in the early years. It was a formative experience for me, my family and, I believe, for many of the participants as well. The combination of engaging with pathbreaking ideas and the intentional daily routine was transformative.

I have a vivid memory of my first encounter with Satish, who approached me after a talk I'd given at Oxford to ask if I'd be interested in teaching at Schumacher College. While my summers are ordinarily reserved for research, the opportunity to live communally again was irresistible. I especially wanted my children—who were quite young at the time—to have that experience. During both my college and graduate school years, I'd been involved in political and intellectual efforts at communal living. But it had been twenty years since I'd had that experience. We had three teaching visits to Dartington as a family, and I also came for a memorable and highly productive meeting devoted to developing an alternative economic vision. For the children, the time was pure joy, with days filled with cooking, costuming and community. For my co-teacher and husband, Prasannan Parthasarathi, and I, the opportunity to have the Schumacher experience and teach people from around the world who were doing vital work was enriching. We had the extraordinary privilege of being paired with two intellectual giants—Vandana Shiva and Martin Khor—although the structure of the courses meant that we were not there together. We will always be grateful to Satish Kumar, Stephan Harding, Julia Ponsonby and other members of the community.

At the time of my first visit to Schumacher, I was close on the heels of a book on work-time and its relationship to economic growth and well-being. Its title was *The Overworked American: The Unexpected Decline of Leisure*, but the analysis was relevant not just to the United States but many countries around the world. The core of the argument was that unchecked capitalist economies have a tendency to transform productivity growth into more production, rather than using it to reduce hours of work. This was a theme that many in the United Kingdom were aware of, as it was in the tradition of John Maynard Keynes' famous essay "Economic Possibilities for Our Grandchildren," published in 1930. Keynes argued in favor of progressive diminution in the work week, to perhaps fifteen hours, as technological advances solved the problem of economic necessity and allowed humans to turn to the things that make life worth living. However, in the post-WWII era, this powerful vision had been pushed off the agenda, as governments turned to maximizing growth and consumption. In my work I'd argued that, in many countries, employers preferred that jobs be structured with long hours. As a result, much of the rapid productivity growth of the postwar era went to expanding production. I identified what I called the "cycle of work and spend," in which the long hours spent on jobs yielded growing incomes which in turn were spent. Households became acclimated to the higher spending, and so the cycle repeated itself. It was a model in which the structure of labor markets (long hours) determined the level of consumption. This was in contrast to the standard economic model in which the causal factor is workers' preferences or popular views that excessive materialism and consumers are the motor force of growth.

I believe that my preoccupation—shorter working hours in paid employment—is foundational for achieving the holistic, regenerative and life-affirming economy and society that is the core of the Schumacher vision. One reason is obvious. As is now well understood by nearly all but economists, infinite growth is not possible on a finite planet. Economists have great faith in the ability to decouple growth in marketed output from growth in resource use, but there will always be significant limits to that decoupling. And in any case, the global economy is far from achieving even moderate decoupling of total resource use from GDP. While rich countries have begun that process, much of the progress is illusory—caused by relocating resource-intensive growth to the global South, where GDP is becoming more, rather than less, resource intensive. For the ecologically minded, it's clear that the human footprint on the planet has become grossly unsustainable. This is true with respect to fossil fuels and other greenhouse gas-emitting materials. It's true for water use, soil practices, biodiversity and toxics. The modern economy, on both the production and consumption sides, is not viable at current scale, much less if it aims for continuous expansion. At the same time, progress in innovation, technology and productivity per hour worked is highly desirable. The shorter hours vision is not one of technological stasis. But if we keep getting more productive, and we cannot expand the economy for ecological reasons, then shorter hours of work become imperative. There's no other viable way to downsize (or "rightsize") an economy. The principle of holism, which is also foundational at Schumacher, is also represented in this approach. The labor market is tied to the consumer market which in turn is tied to the production side of the economy. Changes in working hours ripple through all the sectors of the economy and, by extension, ecosystems.

The alternative of a shorter hours market economy is also intimately connected to the nature of daily life, another fundamental principle of life at Schumacher. Unlike many centers of alternative intellectual activity, Schumacher is constructed on the principle that how we spend our time and organize our daily lives matters. There should be no separation between what we think and believe and how we act. So, the days are structured with enough time outside of the "classwork" to meditate, cook, clean, explore our surroundings, make friends, exercise, sing, perform and, yes, be idle. This is the type of life (and economy) that shorter paid work makes possible. We may have fewer possessions, or less money to buy services than in a maximal growth environment, but we will be richer in social connection and time for introspection and creativity. We can share work and income more equitably, instead of continuing on the current path in which a growing minority lacks access to paid employment and a shrinking majority is overworked. Life at Schumacher was a learning experience from the point of view of living differently.

I am writing these words as the coronavirus pandemic has put many countries on lockdown. Aside from the public health lessons that this experience should be teaching us, it's also an object lesson in economics. In the United States—a highly market-oriented economy—something like twenty million people lost their jobs after just a few weeks of shutdown. Millions more are in poverty and desperate about losing their homes. The failure to mount a solidaristic response is evidence of the pathology of the system. But the virus may also be teaching those practicing social isolation the lesson that my research and teaching has been directed to. We are consuming what we need—food, medicine and a few other basic items. We are learning to make do with what we already have. We have stopped wasting. Paid work, for many, has slowed down, or come to a standstill. We are focusing on remaining safe and healthy. Many of us are trying to give what we can to support those with less. And we are practicing gratitude to the many among us who are on the front lines of keeping the majority safe—whether they are health care workers, agricultural laborers or the people who are delivering food and medicine.

And people are walking. Walking and walking. It is a sight to behold, as I look out my window to see neighbors taking up this neglected practice. Satish, whose adult life began with a historic walk from India to Europe and North America, has taught us about the profound changes that can come from walking.

While the deprivation of the current moment may feel extreme to many in wealthy countries, it has turned us in the direction that Schumacher College has been advocating for thirty years. We are living more simply, more intentionally and more lightly on the earth. My deepest hope is that the lessons of this difficult time remain with us as the virus ebbs. Rather than return to "business-as-usual," a way of living that has been destroying people and planet, perhaps the values and daily life practices of the lockdown will become the new normal, paving the way for a life-affirming, non-violent culture and economy.

JULIET SCHOR is an economist and sociologist at Boston College. She is the author of *The Overworked American*, *The Overspent American* and *Plenitude: The Economics of True Wealth*. Her forthcoming book is *After the Gig: How the Sharing Economy Got Hijacked and How To Win It Back*.

# Nature Has No Waste

## Gunter Pauli

*Never doubt that a small group of thoughtful,*
*commited citizens can change the world.*
*Indeed, it is the only thing that ever has.*
— Margaret Mead

When Fritjof Capra and I laid a last hand on our book, *Steering Business Toward Sustainability* (UNU Press, 1995), he suggested I join him in the summer in Devon at his course hosted by the Schumacher College. He did not hide the fact that, even though I lived in Japan, travel would not be reimbursed and the pay would be small. However, we would have a unique opportunity to share and spread the findings of our book. Fritjof told me the story about the monk who walked the world and who inspires people to teach in this uniquely British setting. I never received a formal invitation. Fritjof asked me to accompany him, and so I showed up.

Fritjof built the course on his mastery of understanding of the *Web of Life* (Random Books, 1996). He valued the chance to present the concept of his book to a small but very committed audience. I joined as the head of a think tank at the United Nations University charged with imagining a scientific backbone for innovative business models that would start from the hypothesis that whatever we do had to be at least zero emission and zero waste. Fritjof planned to include a few early examples of our approach in his forthcoming book and was keen to expose his audience to the logic of how to design business models that would bring society and the earth back on a dynamic evolutionary path inspired by Nature.

At the time I was toying with the design of a new economic model. We wanted to learn from Nature. Nature has no waste; Nature has no unemployed. We would not only turn production and consumption into systems capable of responding to the basic needs for all, we would put Nature back on its evolutionary path. This one week in Schumacher was an early platform that permitted me to share and dialogue, while learning from deep ecology and embracing novel visions which others put forward.

The economic model that emerged was labeled later the Blue Economy, the title of my book which has been translated into nearly fifty languages. We propose that we use what we have. We generate value and refuse to compete on the basis of being the cheapest. We respond to basic needs and succeed, thanks to achieving multiple benefits. The Blue Economy model replaces the efficiency so heralded by the globalized economy with resiliency, so desperately needed by communities.

As a single father then with two young boys, I decided to expose my young teenagers to this environment. So, we shared a family room. Carl-Olaf and Laurenz-Frederik played soccer with Fritjof during the breaks. Then my sons took the initiative to build a forest hideout and to invite all participants to a drink and a cake inside the woods just a two-minute walk from the classroom of the Old Postern. Their logic was simple yet compelling: how can you learn from Nature and not be inside Nature. While I discovered Schumacher College, my children could not imagine that there was any other way that adults could learn innovative ideas to care for themselves and the earth without having the children take care of their parents. Schumacher College brought a framework, and many got the opportunity to cherish their freedom to think, propose and act.

So, it was my first visit to Schumacher, now twenty-five years ago. I discovered this remarkable setting with a simple pedagogy, a clear framework to a welcoming family setting. I was quickly aware that this learning platform was and remains unique. The spiritual leadership that guides this world to the discovery of the latest trends in inner and outer sustainability emanated from Satish Kumar. While I was keen on pioneering broadband internet and moving the world towards digital connectivity, it was not clear how my blend of high-tech media and discovery through networking scientists and entrepreneurs would be compatible with the Schumacher approach. Schumacher College gave me the benefit of the doubt. I reverted to the oral presentation, the dialogues in circles, and dropped the internet altogether while at Schumacher. I used this space to disconnect from the electromagnetic fields and could connect with the participants through dialogues on the clustering business as if it were an ecosystem.

During my multiple stays, I was able to do as Fritjof did, present my book. When I was finally ready to publish *The Blue Economy* (Paradigm, 2010), Satish Kumar created space in the calendar to present the concept that focuses on responding to the basic needs of everyone for water, food, health, housing, renewable energy and a platform for learning.

This approach to embrace the new, the pioneering and the cutting edge, while maintaining a strong link to the systemic approach, brought a new energy together. This ensured that I could expose my mind to diverse audiences. The invisible and yet clear force behind all this was always Satish Kumar. Sparing with his words, modest with his presence, unnoticed when around but determined with his vision, and capable of mobilizing those who have no time, to give time. Thanks to his invisible aura, Satish has an impact not just on the participants but certainly on his lecturers.

Over the years I returned to Schumacher, sharing the platform with Amory Lovins and Anders Wijkman, cherishing this opportunity to push the content of Blue Economy forward and to create the action platform. We networked and conspired at a school that was not a school for teaching but rather a platform for personal and societal transformation through learning, exchanging and dialoguing.

It is heartening that we can now celebrate not only the past thirty years but also the present and the future of Schumacher College. An amazing wealth has emanated from this unambitious effort where everyone was and is happy to converge. I have no doubt that Satish surpassed his dreams and co-created this legacy from where we grew the seeds, which spread around the world and continue to disperse. It is not important to know how the seeds got from here to there, as we know that the environment in which all seeds from Schumacher College sprout have clearly the touch of Satish Kumar for which we are so grateful.

GUNTER PAULI is an innovator. Under his leadership a small detergent company constructed the first ecological factory out of wood with a grass roof. He relied on palm oil, realizing too late that he tried to clean up the rivers in Europe, while unknowingly destroying the rainforests in Indonesia. This motivated him to pursue a radical new approach, embracing the concept of zero emissions and zero waste. He is the author of twenty-three books. His latest, *The Economy of Happiness*, is published in combination with twenty-five fables that translate the core content into stories for children to be inspired by.

# Turning Economics into Art

KATE RAWORTH

*The economy is a wholly owned subsidiary*
*of the environment.*
— HERMAN DALY

*The best way to learn is to teach.*
— LATIN PROVERB

Teaching at Schumacher has taught me how to teach.

This is in good part thanks to the holistic philosophy and way of life of the college, which deeply invites a holistic approach to teaching and learning in response.

It is also thanks to Jonathan Dawson, program coordinator of the MA in Economics for Transition, who is one of the most inventive and outstanding pedagogues I have ever had the chance to teach alongside. Through working with students in spaces that he creates and hosts, I have learned how to bring ideas into a room, roll them around a while, invite others to pick them up and then watch as they bring those ideas back quite wonderfully transformed.

As a teenager I wanted to be an artist—a set designer or a sculptor. That love of art has never left me, and so I have always been visually playful with economics, drawing and redrawing its key diagrams, exposing the metaphors that underlie them, then making those metaphors visible and tangible. When teaching about regenerative design, I often pull out a piece of garden hosepipe to illustrate the difference between a linear and circular economy. In sessions on the absurdity of endless GDP growth, I bring along a toy airplane to symbolize the notion of economies that must "take off" but are never allowed to land.

When I first brought my bag of toys into the classroom at Schumacher, rather than seeing them merely as a playful illustration of the point I was making, Jonathan invited me to make them the focus of the learning journey. How can we use metaphor, play and subversive creativity to challenge and change the dominant frame of economics? And so, it has been through Schumacher that I find myself realizing what it means to be an artist-economist, every year diving deeper into exploring the power of language, art and performance with the students.

The holistic setting and lifestyle of the college is also a profound way to experience and embody new economic thinking. I believe that a key starting point for twenty-first century economics—as I set out in my book *Doughnut Economics*—is to recognize, from the outset, the contribution of four distinct ways that we humans tend to provision for our wants and needs: through caring work in the household, through collaborative work in the commons, through exchange-based transactions in the market and through public provision by the state. Of course, mainstream economics focuses its attention on growing national income, or GDP, and so fixates on the market and the state, while profoundly neglecting the vast contribution to well-being arising from unpaid and unpriced value generated by the household and the commons.

In most university settings, it is hard for students to appreciate the foundational role of the household: ironically, they are trying to grasp its importance at the very moment in their lives when they have been plucked out of a household setting, and are typically living in halls of residence and eating in canteens, without their parents, siblings or even family pets to care for day to day.

At Schumacher, in contrast, the value and importance of the household's caring labor—and the contribution of the commons—is understood not through theory but through lived experience. Every day before and between classes, students take part in community service: preparing the shared meals, gardening, cleaning the common rooms, serving the meals and clearing away. I profoundly believe that twenty-first century economics will be practiced first and theorized later, and at Schumacher that practice begins daily as a way of life.

Schumacher's approach to learning radically reinvents the classroom experience. Many universities still teach with students seated in long, tight rows, facing a lecturer and screen at the front, based on a deep assumption that this is what learning looks like. But look at the faces of those students in rows and you'll know it is not. Enter a classroom at Schumacher—taking off your shoes before you do— and you'll find students seated in a circle, some on cushions, some in chairs, others stretched out on a rug on the floor. And rather than hear a long lecture, with one voice speaking to the many, you'll find conversation, small group huddles, team working, silent reflection in the woods and playful enactment. It is a powerful demonstration of the old adage: "Tell me and I will forget. Show me and I may remember. Involve me and I will understand."

Teaching in this setting, I always have the experience of learning as much as I share and leaving with ideas that had never occurred to me before. Working with Jonathan—as we have moved from teaching economics to exploring how to change the frame of economic thinking through metaphor, art and play—I have been blown away time and again by the students' inventiveness. It's a beautiful thing to bring an idea into the room and invite others to take it and run with it, and then to see it get renamed, redesigned, reinvented and recharged before your very eyes. And so, thanks to years of teaching at Schumacher, I feel compelled to add to the adage:

> Tell me and I will forget.
> Show me and I may remember.
> Involve me and I'll understand.
> Hand it over to me and I will astound you.

KATE RAWORTH studied economics at the University of Oxford. Her book, *Doughnut Economics*, is published by Random House. doughnut economics.org

# Only Connect

### ROBERTO FRAQUELLI *and* MONA NASSERI

*Imagination is more important than knowledge.*
*Knowledge is limited. Imagination encircles the world.*
— ALBERT EINSTEIN

Q: *How many Ecological Design Thinkers does it take to change*
*a light bulb?*
A: *Several...they love teamwork, and they're likely to take their*
*time redefining the problem, and of course answer the question*
*with a question—what do we need the light for, what powers it*
*and what is the ecological impact of the activity the light enables?*

The Ecological Design Thinking program was created at Schumacher College in 2014 to explore creative and practical ways of moving us all away from self-interest towards a restorative and regenerative culture. We invite and encourage students from all walks of life—architects, musicians, human rights lawyers, environmental scientists and others—to spend time together working on projects developing a personal and professional praxis that makes such a paradigm shift possible.

Spending time together working through problems and exploring ideas gives us all a chance to learn something—together. This is one of the foundational principles that differentiates Schumacher College from many other Design Thinking programs that focus largely on individual talent and performance, often in order to maintain the thermo-industrial model of society.

Problems, especially ecological ones, are by nature complex and interconnected, which means that there is very rarely a straightforward answer. Such challenges require a gentle interdisciplinary approach that combines creative design processes, deep listening and an ecological awareness. We encourage our students to develop an open mind and a passion to (re)learn in order to seed a lifetime's inquiry and commitment. We equip them with a bespoke set of tools and processes that align their true nature to their dreams. We provide them with an ecological compass to help navigate through the opportunities and challenges of making a significant contribution to the well-being of our planet.

> Ecological Design Thinking changes the state of the "inner designer" before the "designer" attempts to change the "outer world," so deeper and better questions are asked before solutions are enacted. The "new designer" operates from within the natural world as part of a true and loving partnership.
> — Professor Seaton Baxter

Our master's program is a work in progress, forever evolving and adapting. Each cohort brings a new energy to our studio practice, and each project we work on brings new discoveries and a deeper understanding of who we are and how we want to be. While living and learning alongside our sister programs, growers, volunteers and the wider Schumacher college community, our students begin to develop a critical understanding of the relationships between our environment, society and economy and positive opportunities for restorative and regenerative intervention.

## A Mandala of Learning

Theory and critical understanding are complemented with lots of hands-on activity. During our first module, Design and Ecology, students explore Gaia theory, deep ecology, planetary boundaries, but are also tasked with creating a mandala—a symbolic manifestation of their ecological inquiry. Each of us is encouraged to locate something of beauty within ourselves and then to let it out and share it with the world. One of our students, Victor, a professional concert pianist, composed a beautiful piece of music (influenced by Debussy) that he presented in collaboration with his fellow student, Astrid, who sequentially set drops of coloured inks into a shallow pool of water. It was a beautiful symbiotic live performance where we were all transfixed and transported into their world.

Celebration, fun and unpredictability are some of the more relaxed attributes and events we embrace in our program that weave daily into our slightly more structured design methodologies. Together these opposites help inform and develop personal insights that help us explore higher levels of consciousness.

> The alternative learning of Ecological Design Thinking, which challenges and disrupts all conditions of our traditional education system, has been an invaluable learning curve and has really enabled and encouraged me to "think outside the box" providing me with leverage to truly reflect on modern-day systems and their impact on me.
>
> — Lauren Fields, graduate

## A Prison Project

Working with Dartmoor Prison to improve the visitor's experience was a project none of us had had previous direct experience with, but the challenge seemed a great opportunity. Our brief was to see if it was possible to improve the visitor experience to try to make it less stressful, as security requirements can be frustrating and time-consuming, especially for children. Dartmoor Prison has the reputation of being the most remote prison in the UK and a significant challenge for many families visiting. It can take up to two hours for visitors to be processed and checked before they can see their loved ones in prison.

Being ecological designers, students undertook the project with open hearts, eager to learn and explore opportunities, and to engage meaningfully in an area which none of the group had previous experience of. Working from principles developed during the course—to work *with* rather than *for* people; adopting a systems perspective; enhancing connections with nature and working ecologically for social transformation—students began to work with the prisoners towards an idea. Equipped with a plan, a design scheme based on the surrounding Dartmoor landscape, some eco-friendly paint and a few brushes, students spent two incredible days working with the prisoners to create an interactive mural for visitors to Dartmoor prison.

> Changing the order of things, co-investigating and co-creating with the prisoners into a creative and transformative practice that is humanizing and can eventually lead to a cultural change. We didn't change the penitentiary system, but within

this old dominant system, we created humanized structures and experiences for everyone—them and us.

— Regina Ganem, graduate.

There are many personal stories, most of which celebrate a wonderful sense of humanity felt by the exercise of working alongside each other. Moira Brooke-Williams, from the charity Choices, which supports families and friends of prisoners and helped coordinate the project, said: "As for me I think it was one my best days in the job—something I wasn't expecting." But a memory that we all cherished, and perhaps one unexpected outcome to the project, was a comment shared by a prisoner during our closing circle. He had taught himself to paint watercolors while serving his time. He kindly spent one afternoon teaching a few of our students how to paint.

His comments and reflection related to the fact that in prison he had not experienced a sense of self-worth and dignity; but he had a talent and skill that he now felt he could gift to others. When he shared his story with us, we all felt a sense of humility and an air of humanity filled the room.

## A Beginner's Mind

Listening with a loving ear and learning to learn with a beginner's mind are perhaps our only way of journeying into unknown territories, treading carefully, respectfully and with humility. *How* you do it—more than *what* you do—seems to evidence change, and sometimes having too much knowledge and expertise does more to obscure the heart than it does to reveal it.

In recent years the world has been witnessing the rise of a young generation of activists who dare to demand a future different from the one their parents desired a generation ago. These inspiring young people who question world leaders and policymakers nourish their courage with their power of imagination.

## Power of Imagination

Being a teacher for sixteen years, former Ecological Design Thinking student Amy Seefeldt is acutely aware of the crucial role of imagination in children's and adults' well-being. She is also conscious of the threat that the education system poses to imaginative minds. Amy was an academic dean in Woodstock, a 160-year-old international boarding school situated in the foothills of the Himalayas, in north India, when she decided to take a year's sabbatical to study at Schumacher College in the Ecological Design Thinking program. After completing her master's degree in 2016, on her return to Woodstock, Amy started a Center for Imagination.

The Center for Imagination is a conceptual and physical space where students are encouraged to imagine new ways of learning and new paths of action. They are inspired to discover their passion, take responsibility for shaping their future and let their imagination take them beyond the do's and don'ts of mainstream society towards a future they want for themselves. "After all, when the imagination is set free, the horizons of possibility are infinite," Amy explains.

In March 2018, two years after setting up her center, Amy was visited by a new EDT cohort. A team of eight students were invited to Woodstock to exchange knowledge and contribute to the Centre for Imagination by getting involved in a range of projects around the school. This was an exceptional opportunity for our EDT students to work alongside Woodstock students and staff on issues such as energy, student safety, well-being and the guiding principles of the school. By learning about ecology-centered design, empathic problem solving and design tools, Woodstock students found the experience equally beneficial.

> *As you grow older, you will discover that you have two hands;*
> *one to help yourself and another to help others.*
>
> — Audrey Hepburn

Roberto Fraquelli: For over thirty years, Roberto has designed products, environments and experiences for organizations all over the world. In 2007 he accidentally stumbled across Schumacher College, falling in love with its approach towards living an ecological inquiry. Since then his work explores natural ways of transitioning towards a regenerative mindset, and he was invited to become a member of our Schumacher faculty in 2017.

Mona Nasseri: Mona is a faculty member on the Ecological Thinking Program. Her work on the transformative role of embodied knowledge—where her craft and design background met her interest in psychology and spirituality—brought her to Schumacher College in 2014. Her doctoral thesis is an exploration of the role of unmediated relationship with the environment in the evolution of human consciousness. Her recent research and practice are focused on enhancing resilience in rural areas by capitalizing on local wisdom.

# Transition Design

## TERRY IRWIN AND GIDEON KOSSOFF

*Design, if it is to be ecologically responsible and*
*socially responsive, must be revolutionary and radical.*
— VICTOR PAPANEK

We are delighted to contribute to this book about Schumacher College, the place where we met many years ago and which remains an important touchstone in our lives. Terry came to Schumacher as a professional designer looking for a way to reorient her practice to be more sustainable and meaningful. She attended a three-week short course with Fritjof Capra in 2002 and returned a year later to undertake the master's degree in Holistic Science (MSc). Gideon, a social ecologist and environmental activist, had joined the college in 1998 as the administrator on the MSc, but also served as the college librarian, building a diverse collection of over 8,000 volumes. Schumacher's teachers, students and staff had a profound effect on us, and their ideas, and the place itself, continue to influence the work that we are engaged in as faculty members in the School of Design at Carnegie Mellon University, USA.

Our time at Schumacher College (Gideon from 1998–2007 and Terry from 2002–2007) was a nexus for educators, scientists, environmentalists and others who were exploring ideas connected to chaos and complexity theories, living systems, Goethean science, Gaia theory, ecopsychology and archetypal psychology, eco-design, alternative economics and anti-globalization and related fields. Chief among our teachers was scientist/embryologist Brian Goodwin, our dear friend and mentor who, along with ecologist Stephan Harding,

developed the master's degree in Holistic Science that attracted leading thinkers from around the world. The program was ahead of its
time in its awareness of the limitations of reductionist science and
in its emphasis on holism, the dynamics of complex systems and the
need for a science of qualities.

In the MSc in Holistic Science program, we were privileged to
know and study with many Schumacher teachers, including James
Lovelock who taught us Gaia theory; physicist and philosopher Henri
Bortoft who lectured on Goethe's ideas about wholeness and its tem-
poral nature; and Margaret Colquohoun and Craig Holdrege who
taught us to *practice* Goethe's way of science. We studied how chaos
and complexity theories offer a new understanding of how nonlinear
systems (social systems, ecosystems and the earth itself) change and
evolve, but we also studied Indigenous place-based ways of knowing
with teachers such as Native American scholar Gregory Cajete, anthropologist Hugh Brody, philosopher David Abram, eco-designers
John and Nancy Jack Todd, and environmental educator David Orr,
as well as many others. This combination of rigorous science combined with qualitative ways of knowing, grounded in an understanding of "place" (the limits of the ecosystem or watershed that we are
always embedded within), provided a completely unique educational
experience.

Schumacher College co-founder Satish Kumar's background in
activism and Jainism infused mindfulness into the daily life of the
college—everyone cooking, cleaning, gardening and meditating together in a place that was beautiful, functional, productive and con-
ducive to "other ways of knowing." Like the title of this book, learning
at Schumacher enabled the integration of head, heart and hand.

During our years at Schumacher, we were also fortunate to watch
the emergence of the Transition Town movement and were at the very
first meeting held by Rob Hopkins in Totnes. That experience introduced the idea of and need for entire communities and societies to
transition to different ways of living, working and inhabiting place.

In 2007, we moved to Scotland in order to continue our research in
the doctoral program at the University of Dundee in the Centre for the
Study of Natural Design with Seaton Baxter, who was a frequent visitor to Schumacher College and external examiner on the MSc. Terry's
research focused on how principles from living systems could in-

form a more sustainable and appropriate design process, and Gideon began research to integrate his ideas about non-hierarchical forms of social organization into a framework for guiding societal transitions towards more sustainable futures. Gideon's doctoral research argued for a new area of design focus—Transition Design—that was to become the focus of our combined research efforts in the coming years.

## Embedding Ideas from Schumacher College into New Curricula at Carnegie Mellon University

In 2009, Terry was offered the headship of the School of Design at Carnegie Mellon University, Pittsburgh. We were both in the midst of our PhD research but decided that the opportunity to embed some of the ideas we had been exploring for years into a traditional design program was too good to pass up. We moved to Pittsburgh in July of 2009, where Gideon finished his PhD in 2011 and Terry began leading efforts to redesign all of the school's curricula at the undergraduate, master's and doctoral levels. Terry actively applied many of the principles of chaos and complexity theories, learned at Schumacher College, to the co-design approach she facilitated with the faculty, framing for initial conditions so that a new design would emerge from the wisdom of the group. The one parameter she insisted on was to integrate design for society and the environment (sustainable design) into the heart of programs.

As Head of School, Terry felt that the pedagogical ideas she experienced at Schumacher would be essential to the faculty leadership who were charged with the delivery of new curricula. In 2013, we traveled with five faculty leaders to Schumacher on a learning exchange. For several days, faculty at Schumacher taught ecology, Gaia theory and principles from chaos and complexity theories to School of Design faculty (who were also required to participate in work groups cleaning, cooking, gardening, etc.). In return, our faculty worked with those at Schumacher to provide input on a new master's program with a design component: the Ecological Design Thinking master's degree.

The faculty who traveled to Schumacher College returned invigorated, replenished and committed to integrating sustainability into new curricula. But more importantly, they believed that new and different ways of knowing could be introduced into a mainstream university. That belief and commitment continues to the present. As an example, Mark Baskinger, one of the School of Design faculty who made the original trip to Schumacher College in 2013, has worked closely with Stephan Harding to develop a "deep time walk" that School of Design freshmen make as an introduction to the undergraduate program. Upon arrival in their studio, a lecture with Stephan is Skyped in to acquaint them with key themes including Gaia theory, deep ecology and the importance of place.

In 2011, Cameron Tonkinwise joined the faculty at the School of Design, bringing knowledge and experience in philosophy and eco-design, and we began a close collaboration that over the next two years led to the formalization of the Transition Design concept. In 2014, the school launched new programs that placed sustainability and systems thinking at the heart of all curricula and introduced three areas of focus: Service Design, Design for Social Innovation and Transition Design. We also launched a four-year doctoral program in Transition Design that today has sixteen students and five graduates from seven countries.

## The Emergence of the Transition Design Approach

Transition Design was informed by many of the ideas about living systems, holism, place, Indigenous ways of knowing and alternative economics, among others, that were taught at Schumacher College. The term "transition" was an acknowledgement of the many transition-related projects and initiatives that were springing up around the world: Commons Transitions; Just Transitions; The Next Systems Project; Socio-Technical Sustainability Transitions; Rapid Transitions. But Transition Design really began to take shape as a result of a conversation (and heated arguments) between Terry (a designer), Gideon (a social ecologist) and Cameron (a philosopher). It has now evolved into what we describe as a transdisciplinary approach to addressing complex problems such as poverty, climate change, biodiversity loss, waste, crime, the opioid epidemic, lack of access to healthy food, the growing gap between rich and poor, all manner of problems connected to globalization and many more.

Transition Design argues that we need to address these inter-related, interdependent problems with ecologies of synergistic interventions at multiple levels of scale and over short, medium and long horizons of time. Interventions may be directed at the material structure of everyday life (artifacts, technologies, infrastructure), but they are just as likely to be directed at its non-material aspects (beliefs, assumptions, worldviews, values). It argues that these interventions, when connected to each other and to long-term visions, can seed and catalyze positive systems transitions (communities, cities and entire societies) toward more sustainable, equitable and desirable long-term futures. Transition Design uses the tools and methods of designers (visualization, prototyping, user-centered/qualitative research, fore-sighting) to enable transdisciplinary teams, grassroots communities and as wide a range of stakeholders as possible to co-create visions of their desired long-term futures; build capacity within the community for productive, civic conversation; and develop ecologies of interventions aimed at shifting the system over long arcs of time.

## Collaborations between the School of Design and Schumacher College

Since 2014, Transition Design has been a focus for both of us in our teaching and research. Gideon teaches and advises on the master's and doctoral program, and Terry just stepped down after ten years as the Head of School and, along with Gideon, will launch a Transition Design Institute at Carnegie Mellon University. Most importantly, Transition Design has become a bridge to Schumacher College. In 2016, we taught a one-week short course in Transition Design at Schumacher College, along with our collaborator, Cameron Tonkinwise (who is now a professor at the University of Technology Sydney in his native Australia), followed by a two-day Transition Design Symposium. Both events were extremely successful and provided an opportunity for faculty at the School of Design to attend and gain a deeper grounding in the emerging discipline. In 2018, the course expanded to ten days and was again followed by a two-day symposium with ten speakers addressing topics related to transition and systems change (transition design and transition towns, alternative economics, alternative education, commoning, socio-technical transitions, policy, civil society, narrative, behavior change, among others).

These courses and symposia at Schumacher College have brought together people from around the world from a diverse spectrum of disciplines, who are now integrating Transition Design into their research, teaching and practices. Today Transition Design is found in programs and curricula in over twenty universities around the world, and we are delivering workshops to introduce the approach to both design practitioners and businesses alike.

Our work in Transition Design was and continues to be informed by Schumacher College and the people we met through it. Its unique brand of place-based learning has enabled it to serve as an educational partner with a mainstream research university such as Carnegie Mellon, and we are continuing to explore ways to strengthen the partnership through faculty and student exchanges and the convening of events such as Transition Design Symposia.

On a personal level, Schumacher College continues to feel like home to both of us. A place that holds great meaning for us to which we can return and replenish ourselves and reconnect with friends that are like family. In an era in which mainstream education becomes ever more mechanized and commodified, creating links to alternative educational centers like Schumacher College is crucial. It reminds us of and reinforces the idea that connections between head, heart and hand are essential to living well, sustainably and gracefully in place.

TERRY IRWIN has been a design practitioner for more than forty years and was a founding partner of the international design firm MetaDesign. From 2009 to 2019, she was the head of the School of Design at Carnegie Mellon University (CMU), Pittsburgh. She holds an MFA from the Allgemeine Kunstgewerbeschule, Basel, Switzerland (1986) and an MSc in Holistic Science from Schumacher College/Plymouth University (2004). She is currently a professor in the School of Design and is the director of the Transition Design Institute at CMU.

GIDEON KOSSOFF is a social ecologist and environmental activist with a PhD in design from the Center for the Study of Natural Design at the University of Dundee, Scotland (2011). He is currently the associate director of the Transition Design Institute at Carnegie Mellon University as well as a member of faculty in the School of Design and an advisor in its doctoral program in Transition Design.

# PART 3

# Education of Heart

# Radical Activism

## Bill McKibben

*We showed that we are united*
*and that we, young people, are unstoppable.*
— Greta Thunberg

My first memory of Schumacher College is, oddly, the Eurovision Song Contest. We'd just arrived by train and bus, "we" being myself, my wife, the writer Sue Halpern, and our then-young daughter. We pushed her on the tire swing for a while, ate some excellent bread rolls at dinner and then joined in with old friend and co-teacher David Abram to see what the students were up to. They were, it turned out, deeply absorbed in the pan-European singing contest, which apparently is loved in direct proportion to the horribleness of its songs. And they were horrible. We cheered for Malta, I think, and luxuriated in having come from America, home to rhythm, blues, jazz and soul.

And then the next morning, the actual specialness of the surroundings began to sink in. We wandered the woods and hedgerows, visited the great estate down the road—and most of all we began to appreciate the intellectual milieu we'd dropped into, different than any college on the planet. Here were people deeply engaged in the work that—twenty years ago—all academics should have been engaged in. Because back then, at the turn of the century, we still had a little bit of time.

## A Time of Optimism

My topic, as always, was global warming. Having written the first book for a general audience on the topic all the way back in 1989,

I was ready to discuss where we stood and what we were going to do. It was a period of relative optimism: the world had recently gathered at the Kyoto conference, and seemed to be taking some initial steps. We were still in the business of offering warnings of what was going to come: this was before Hurricane Katrina and Sandy, before the firestorms in California and Greece and Australia, before the great droughts that decimated Mesopotamia and Central America, sending migrants fleeing by the millions. There was still quite a bit of sea ice in the Arctic, coral reefs had not yet undergone wholesale bleaching, and we hadn't yet seen the all-time record temperature readings (129 degrees Fahrenheit!) in Asian and Middle Eastern cities. It seemed at least possible that we would take the clear and logical steps to move towards a clean energy regime in time to prevent the worst damage. And the intellectual currents around Schumacher were similarly optimistic: people were deep in the serious study of the Gaia hypothesis, for instance, looking for ways the planet might help adjust to its fever.

The years since have seen an endless cascade of bad news. In the US we rejected the Kyoto accords, and then sabotaged the Copenhagen talks. In China they turned to coal to power galloping economic growth, spiking carbon levels and poisoning big cities. The fossil fuel industry continued its unabated denial—indeed, as we now know from great investigative reporting, they were engaged in an exercise as sweeping in its cynicism as Schumacher was sweeping in its sincerity. Literally, companies like Exxon knew everything there was to know about climate change, and yet bankrolled an enormous architecture of deceit and disinformation. It was a world polluted by greed and lies as profoundly as it was polluted by carbon and methane.

## Global Campaign

In the years since, I've gone from thinking and talking about the great environmental upheavals of our time to trying to do something about them. At a certain point, it became clear to me that we had won the argument about climate change—the scientific consensus was deep and robust—but that we were losing the fight, because the fight wasn't about reason and data. As usual with fights, it was about money and power. So, the time had come to try and assemble some power—which meant that teaching and writing would take a bit of a second place in my life. Instead we started trying to build broad-based popular movements, because history indicates that they are the only thing that sometimes allows the small and many to stand up to the mighty and few. This was, I think, the great Gandhian insight, and the development of nonviolent social movements may have been the most important invention of the twentieth century (the only other possible contender is the solar panel). Not that I had any idea how to do it: our first iteration, 350.org, was literally the work of myself and seven undergraduates at the small rural college where I teach in New England. But there was an unfilled ecological niche, and our small start quickly turned into the first global grassroots climate change campaign—in 2009 our initial day of action managed to simultaneously host 5,200 rallies in 181 countries, what CNN called "the most widespread day of political action in the planet's history." Schumacher was, of course, represented!

## Grassroots Movements

In the years since, I've felt a very special kinship with that corner of Britain. We've concentrated our work on the targets that seemed to us to offer the most leverage—giant oil companies, banks and the like. I've been to jail more times than I would have expected, and we've had our share of victories, stopping various pipelines and frack wells and so forth. The movement has kept swelling—it's led, mostly, by various frontline and Indigenous campaigners, and in recent years we've seen wonderful developments like Extinction Rebellion, the Sunrise Movement with its Green New Deal and, of course, the wondrous Fridays for the Future, emerging from Greta Thunberg's school strikes. (There are, thank heaven, thousands of Gretas scattered around the world, young people of enormous talent and courage.) This work is all useful—but by necessity focused on structural change, pulling the levers of politics and finance in an effort to staunch the flow of carbon. At the same time, of course, one is conscious of the need for a similar movement that arises more locally, aimed at changing how daily life can be lived. And for that the Transition Town effort, birthed in Totnes, has been such an inspiration. I know that the spirit of Schumacher is deeply embedded in that work too, and I am always cheered to see Rob Hopkins and his colleagues at work because I can place them so easily in their geography.

We will know, I think, in the next ten years how much we've been able to salvage of the planet that we knew. The scientists make it fairly clear that our period of high leverage is limited; we have to make fundamental transitions by 2030, and if we don't, our chances of maintaining a world anything like the one we were born on will have passed. So many people are working so hard to make those changes possible, from the engineers producing ever-cheaper solar panels to the campaigners pushing to change laws. Schumacher College is a place where all those kinds of efforts are honored: where the line between science and humanities and politics and religion and art are blurred in the best possible ways. I have no ability to forecast the future, and I do not waste much time figuring out whether I am an optimist or a pessimist; energy is best used fighting for a better future. But I do have the hope that some years hence those of us still around will gather once more at Schumacher, this time to look back a little and see what we managed to get done. A surprisingly large amount of the answer will be traceable back to this small building amidst the hedgerows.

BILL MCKIBBEN teaches at Middlebury College in Vermont, USA. He is the author of a dozen books, including his classic, *The End of Nature*. He is the winner of a Right Livelihood Award.

# Narratives of Hope

JONATHON PORRITT

*You wouldn't abandon a ship in a storm*
*just because you couldn't control the winds.*
— THOMAS MORE

Organizational milestones (as in big anniversaries like Schumacher College's 30th!) materialize episodically in the lives of those involved in that organization and encourage all sorts of retrospective reflection. To paraphrase Charles Dickens for a moment, those intervening thirty years represent, for me personally, both the best of times, in terms of gathering awareness and engagement on sustainability issues, and the worst of times—wasted decades—in the entire history of humankind.

I say that for one simple reason: because we didn't do what we could have done from the late 1980s onwards, it's now by no means certain that we still have time to do what we still need to do to avoid irreversible runaway climate change—the kind of climate change which would precipitate the collapse of human civilization. These three wasted decades now imperil the future of our species on planet Earth.

All the teaching I've done at Schumacher College has always been future-focused—looking at the importance of utopian thinking (in May 1993) or the future of corporate sustainability and progressive social movements. But to make sense of our future, we must first understand our past—including the immediate, near-term past in terms of these wasted decades.

113

## Science Suppressed

I don't doubt that historians will have little difficulty in identifying those who were principally responsible for these wasted decades. From the mid-1970s onwards, a number of the biggest oil and gas companies in the world conducted their own research into the science of global warming, and the implications for humankind if we continued to emit billions of tons of greenhouse gasses every year. Their science was spot on; they accurately predicted where we would be by 2020, and explicitly surfaced the likelihood of runaway climate change at some point in the first half of this century.

However, instead of putting all that science into the public domain, they initiated a thirty-year campaign to obscure the science, to fund climate-denying think tanks and to lobby furiously against *any* measures that politicians advanced to get on top of the challenge. Bill McKibben has described this thirty-year record as "the most consequential lie in the history of humankind." More than half of the greenhouse gasses in the atmosphere today were emitted during that time—a lethal doubling of an already massively serious problem.

So much for a generation of corporate climate criminals—and they know who they are, as do a growing army of lawyers who are intent on holding them to account. At the same time, there was no shortage of politicians under the sway of Big Oil, assiduously engaged in suppressing the science of climate change throughout those three decades.

Three wasted decades—precisely the period of time that Schumacher College is now looking back on, simultaneously inviting contributors to think ahead over the next thirty years. And either we will have done what we need to do by 2050, or the role of Schumacher College will be looking very different indeed! My principal conclusion is that to get things landed within that timeframe, we're going to have to fundamentally rethink how we set about this challenge.

## Thinking Through a Future Lens

The reason why I love the discipline of thinking about things through a future lens is that it keeps the area of inquiry as open as one needs it to be. I chose to teach a course on utopianism at Schumacher to answer a number of pressing questions on my mind at that time: Why were most sustainability narratives so godforsakenly gloomy—both environmentally and socially? Why had the groundbreaking Brundtland Report (*Our Common Future*, published in 1987), with all its solutions-oriented, upbeat framing, failed to get any serious traction with politicians—and not even that much traction with social justice and environmental NGOs? How could that be turned around? And did the history of utopianism in Western civilization have anything to teach us?

One thing I quickly discovered was that many people on the left are by no means persuaded that utopian thinking is a valid way of framing ideas about a better world, seeing it as escapist, elitist or even illusionist. For such critics, utopian thinking is a dangerous distraction from the hard-edged business of winning the arguments and "maintaining the struggle." To be honest, I didn't get that then, and I still don't now. I see absolutely no incompatibility between short-term campaigning for greater social justice and conjuring up more positive visions of the future to encourage people to fight for a better world.

There is still a serious dearth of positive visions, even as the worsening impacts of climate change have given rise to a proliferation of dystopian visions of the apocalyptic world that now awaits us, following in the footsteps of Cormac McCarthy's utterly depressing *The Road*. All the psychological evidence tells us that very few people choose to get involved in climate campaigning, or even in adopting more environmentally responsible lifestyles, from having had their spirits crushed by unrelenting images of personal trauma and societal collapse.

It's interesting that Christiana Figueres, one of today's most resolute climate champions, chose to structure her new book in 2020 (*The Future We Choose*, co-authored with Tom Rivett-Carnac) around two dramatically contrasting scenarios: the first where business-as-usual politics continues to dominate the global economy for the next decade, leading to a literal hell on Earth by 2050; and the second premised on a dramatic shift to ultra-low-carbon, fair and inclusive ways of creating and distributing wealth, delivering a balanced but unapologetically utopian vision of a better world by 2050.

## A Positive Picture

Pretty much everything I've done since my deep dive into utopia at Schumacher College has been geared to promoting positive, solutions-based narratives about the future. It underpins everything we do through Forum for the Future, working with a very wide range of different partners, and it was the central proposition behind *The World We Made*, which I wrote ten years ago, conjuring up a positive but strenuously realistic picture of what our lives might look like in 2050. It's the central proposition behind my new book, *Hope in Hell*, analyzing prospects for the extraordinarily rapid transformation that we need to secure in order to avoid runaway climate change. For me, this has always been a world that is awash with "good stuff," with instantly available solutions, with life-enhancing alternatives to the crazy consumerist chaos of our lives today.

So, I'm all the more baffled by the difficulties we still face in selling these positive, visionary ideas to mainstream politicians. If they bite at all, it's usually grudgingly and very selectively (with the rest of their policies still as conventional and backward-looking as ever), and with little thought as to the level of investment required. To be fair, 2020 saw some real breakthroughs around the big idea of a Green New Deal—in the USA, the UK and the EU—and it was indeed uplifting to see all the opposition parties (Labour, Lib Dems, Greens, Scot Nats, Plaid Cymru) proposing variations of the Green New Deal in the UK's general election in December 2019.

There's one aspect of this worth calling out. We already have ample evidence that the climate emergency acts as an amplifier of social inequality, disproportionately affecting the poorest and most vulnerable in society. It's simply impossible to imagine humankind successfully navigating the decades of radical decarbonization ahead of us without addressing the deep structural inequalities that blight the lives of so many billions of people today. This reality is increasingly captured in the idea of a Just Transition.

It's highly significant that this factor features so prominently in both the Green New Deal in the USA (which has committed unequivocally to protecting the interests of those in the fossil fuel industries who lose their jobs) and in the EU's emerging Green Deal, which proposes a €100 billion Just Transition Mechanism to support those European nations most vulnerable to the impacts of rapid decarbonization.

I see this emergence of a proper climate justice movement in Europe as one of the most hopeful developments in the wider sustainability world today. It also opens the door to the next era of radical campaigning. I'm as enthusiastic about the Green New Deal as anyone, especially those aspects that address historical injustices (like the appalling state of our housing stock in the UK), but *none of this* is going to happen within the current political structures in the UK (over-centralized, Whitehall-dominated and disempowering) and the current economic orthodoxy (with a still obsessive focus on economic growth at all costs).

While continuing to promote the power of positive solutions, I have to accept that utopian visions of a better world can indeed be both self-indulgent and counterproductive unless combined with hard-edged, highly practical plans for driving delivery at the local level and breaking down political barriers. This was one of the most important insights for me at Schumacher College in 1993: positivity counts for next to nothing without an unstinting commitment to the radical transformation of society.

In that regard, we should not underestimate the strength of the climate movement, and the speed with which things are changing; embedded in the whole emergency story is the idea of *emergence*— of new ideas and perspectives in people who've never thought much about this before; of new organizations seizing the moment; of new collective energy; of new artistic expressions of concern; of new and improbable alliances. I've always loved Rebecca Solnit's mushroom analogy:

> After a rain, mushrooms appear on the surface of the Earth as if from nowhere. Many do so from a sometimes vast underground fungus that remains invisible and largely unknown. What we call mushrooms, mycologists call the fruiting body of the larger, less visible fungus. Uprisings and revolutions are often considered to be spontaneous, but less visible long-term organizing and groundwork—or underground work—often lay the foundations.

What's more, bit by bit, people are beginning to realize there's something much more profound going on here than simply solving the climate crisis. You don't have to get very deep into a conversation about climate change without opening up wider considerations of how we're living our lives, our hopes and fears, our anxieties about the future, of today's economic insecurity. It's as if the climate emergency is giving us all permission to open up whole areas of our lives that often stay hidden—precisely the kind of deep connectivity that Schumacher College is so well placed to explore over the next thirty years.

 JONATHON PORRITT is founder director of Forum for the Future. He has a degree in modern languages from the university of Oxford. He was director of Friends of the Earth and chairman of Sustainable Development Commission. jonathonporritt.com

# Love for All

## Satish Kumar

*I offer you love.*

— Mahatma Gandhi

### October 2, 2019

On Thursday evenings I hold a fireside chat at Schumacher College. Short course participants, graduate students, volunteers and guests, all are welcome to these chats. They are informal and open to all.

I start the chat with the current topic of the week. Then everyone is invited to ask and explore any questions they might like to raise.

2019 was the 150th anniversary of Mahatma Gandhi. I led a course on the life and philosophy of Mahatma Gandhi; the following is the gist of my talk.

Mahatma Gandhi was a champion of Love Revolution. For him love should permeate all and every aspect of our lives. Be it political, social or personal, all human activities should be informed by love. Love should be the organizing principle of individual lives as well as of the whole of society. For Gandhi love had no borders and no boundaries, no limits and no conditions. He said, "Where there is love there is life and where there is love there is light."

Love as a basis of personal relationships has been accepted and advocated by many. All religions and most philosophical traditions preach and promote love as a foundation for personal behavior. But for Mahatma Gandhi love should also be the motivation behind political policies, economic decisions and business behavior.

The practice of love among friends and family members is good but not sufficient. Love has to come out of the confinements of homes, temples and monasteries. Love should be practiced in the corridors of political power and in the marketplace.

All our activities of agriculture, education, medicine, arts and crafts should emerge from the foundation of love. All our work should be "love made visible." Teachers should teach not just to earn money but because they love children and they love teaching. Earning a living is only a means to an end. The true purpose is to love and to serve children. Similarly doctors need to practice medicine because they love to heal the sick, farmers need to produce food because they love to feed the hungry, politicians need to go into politics because they love to serve people, traders engage in business because they love to meet the needs of their communities. Every profession needs a vocation.

In order to bring love into every sphere of society, Mahatma Gandhi developed the concept of *Sarvodaya*. This word has many meanings, including the well-being of All, love for All and the happiness of All. Here All means *All*: all human beings and all sentient beings. Harmony at all levels.

Mahatma Gandhi rejected the utilitarian idea of "the maximum good of the maximum number." Political and economic policies should be designed for the good of All, and not just for the majority. Political and social philosophy must respect the dignity of all life and not accord higher status to any one form of life. All life means all non-human life as well as human life. We must love animal life, plant life and every other form of life. Pollution of oceans and rivers with agro-chemicals and plastic is violence. Contamination of the air with excessive carbon emissions and greenhouse gasses shows a lack of love for the living planet. Destruction of forests, cruelty to animals in factory farms and the poisoning of the soil with herbicides and insecticides are a consequence of an absence of compassion. Diminishing biodiversity is the result of diminishing kindness.

Political philosophies like utilitarianism, socialism and capitalism see human life above all other forms of life. And since, according to this view, human life is superior to the life of plants, animals and oceans, humans are accorded the right to control them, exploit them and use them as they wish. This anthropocentrism is contrary to the Gandhian philosophy of nonviolence and love, which is the foundation of Sarvodaya. The Mahatma believed that the value of non-human life should not be measured in terms of its usefulness to humans, because all life has intrinsic value. Therefore, reverence for All life is the fundamental principle of Sarvodaya.

The holistic philosophy of Sarvodaya insists on changing human attitudes, human hearts and human relationships with nature. Our attitude needs to be based in the unity of life rather than the separation and dualism between human life and the rest of life. An inner transformation is the prerequisite for changing human behavior.

According to the science of evolution all life has evolved from the same source, from the same single origin. Oceans, forests and animals are the ancestors of humankind. All living beings are made of the same basic five elements: earth, air, fire, water and consciousness. Trees, animals and humans are all made of these same five elements.

Sarvodaya moves away from the story of separation and embraces the story of relationship. We are all connected. Unity and diversity are complementary. Evolution is a journey from unity to diversity and not a descent from unity to separation and dualism. Diversity is not division. Diversity is the celebration of unity. All forms of diversity are interrelated through the intricate web of life. Through love of life, love of the earth and love of nature, we take care of all life on earth, without discrimination, without judgment and without ifs and buts.

The mindset which separates and divides humans from nature also divides one group of humans from another group of humans. We divide people in the name of caste, class, nationality, politics, gender, race and religion. We begin to put one caste, class, nationality, politics, gender, race or religion above other. We turn human diversity into human division. Such division leads to competition, conflict and war. We devise our politics in the interest of one group rather than another. The national interest of one country is seen to be in conflict with the interest of another country. Class conflict leads to class war. The welfare of the working class is perceived to be contrary to the welfare of the bosses. All this is a consequence of separational and dualistic political philosophy.

Sarvodaya perceives the clash of interest among humans to be the result of the conditioning of our minds. In the greater scheme of things, all humans have a common interest. That common ground can be found in love. All people wish to be happy, healthy and want to live in harmony with each other and in harmony with planet earth.

Therefore, with a consciousness based in love, we share our happiness and well-being with others. We care for each other, and we care for the earth. We design our policies to serve the interest of All, without exception. The principle of Sarvodaya suggests that we should give no offence to anyone and make no enemy of anyone. Love even those with whom we disagree. Love without borders and love without frontiers! Love has more power to win the hearts and minds than any amount of bombs and weapons. "Conquer with love," said Gandhi.

Talking about All seems to be too broad and vague. To love All, where do we start in our political decision making? Mahatma Gandhi answered that question. He said that when you are making a policy decision and allotting funds from the government budget, ask yourself who will benefit from this decision? If your decision is going to benefit the poorest of the poor, the weakest of the weak and the most deprived members of society first, then that decision reflects your love for All. Mahatma Gandhi rejected the trickle-down theory of economic decision making. The economics and politics of love have to be reflected in urgent and immediate action to end social injustice and the exploitation of the poor and the weak.

In terms of our love for the whole of planet earth, Mahatma Gandhi also had a simple formula. If human activities produce waste and pollution of the air, water and soil and inflict pain and suffering on animals, then those activities are contrary to our love of the earth. Moreover, humans need to practice humility. We need to take from nature to meet our genuine needs and do so with gratitude and not exploit natural resources to meet our cravings, greed, extravagance and desires to hoard, accumulate and possess unnecessary stuff. Gandhi said that "the Earth provides enough for everybody's need but not enough for anybody's greed." Nature is not merely a resource for the economy, nature is the source of life. Love for the earth in practical terms means caring for the earth.

This is not simply a lofty ideal. It is pragmatic and practical politics. It has been proven again and again that the politics of separation, division, conflict and competition is stressful, wasteful and counterproductive. The politics of serving the interest of one group against another or the interest of humans against nature has been tried, and it has failed over and over again. Mahatma Gandhi believed that "power based on love is a thousand time more effective and permanent than the one derived from fear of punishment." Therefore, Mahatma Gandhi asks us to give the politics of love a chance.

The ideal of love is considered to be a spiritual ideal. But for Gandhi there is no division between practical and spiritual. Practical has to be spiritual, and spiritual has to be practical. Therefore, the solutions to our environmental problems, personal unhappiness, social divisions, economic inequality, international conflicts, racial discrimination and umpteen other pressing issues lie in one great idea; the idea of Sarvodaya: Love for All.

SATISH KUMAR is the author of *Elegant Simplicity*, available from resurgence.org/shop

## ECOLOGY AND SPIRITUALITY

# A Polar Star

MARY EVELYN TUCKER

*Each community can take from the bounty of the earth*
*whatever it needs for subsistence, but it also has the duty to protect*
*the earth and to insure its fruitfulness for coming generations.*
— POPE FRANCIS

The first time I walked into Schumacher College, I felt at home. A rustic setting surrounded by woods where a rambling country house was populated by seekers—what more could one ask? For those of us in the United States, Schumacher College was a polestar—a place that drew remarkable thinkers and artists, educators and writers. The abundant creativity and verve was alluring—one could count on being changed by coming there. The combination of place and people is still unique in the English-speaking world. What makes it so special? Certainly E. F. Schumacher's vision and Satish Kumar's leadership along with leading-edge programs like Holistic Science directed by Stephan Harding.

But let's look first at the place and bioregion. The college is located in a setting of immense beauty—both cultivated and wild. This combination has a charm that appeals to people coming from urban and rural areas alike. There are gardens for flowers and vegetables—sustaining beauty for the eyes and bounty for the table. There are trails in the woods providing walks for young and old alike. Nearby is the heath with open vistas and a chance to join Stephan for a Deep Time Walk. Dartington Hall beckons with its stunning gardens and ancient trees. And the local city of Totnes is a model Transition Town, inspired by resident Rob Hopkins.

Behind the country house where the college is located is a stand of redwoods marking a place for some of the most primeval trees on the planet. I was amazed to see them there and spent many serene moments bathing in their presence.

Thus, the grounds and the surrounds of Schumacher bring one into a space of contemplation and reimagination. This is a place where one can reflect on our world with its myriad problems and promise. It is a space inviting the inner and outer journey to be woven together once again. It is a place of renewal and revitalization for the tasks still awaiting. With holistic pedagogies and transdisciplinary methods, Schumacher has moved beyond the boundaries of traditional academia.

Every part of Schumacher calls us to a holistic way of being in the world. Central to this is the community that is present here—the staff and teachers as well as learners and participants. The spirit of the people and place begin to mingle and marinate in the programs. The rhythm of the day provides a context in which the community can arise. From nourishing organic food at each meal to touching base at morning and evening gatherings, a togetherness emerges that is natural and grounding. This togetherness is reinforced by the programs that shape the day—lectures and discussions with provoking questions. How can one describe this unique combination of place and participants except to say it is generative of new ways of being and living in our world. The international blend of people assures an awareness of global concerns along with an awareness of bioregional commitments.

This is inspired by teachers who open up space for challenge and disagreement as well as synergy and symbiosis. E. F. Schumacher himself left a legacy of creative thinking, combining ecology and economics with Buddhist interdependence and meditation. Satish Kumar picked up this legacy with his Jain heritage of simplicity and wholeness. He moved this toward ecological spirituality, which has been a defining characteristic of the college under his leadership. His work has grounded the educational vision of the college rooted in the well-being of both people and planet. This has been complemented by the magazine he has edited for many years, now called *Resurgence & Ecologist*. Following Brian Goodwin, Stephan Harding developed a program on Holistic Science based in his understanding of the

Animate Earth. This has opened up space for exploring what James Lovelock has named Gaia and Thomas Berry called the living Earth community.

Into this setting my husband, John Grim, and I brought our projects of the Yale Forum on Religion and Ecology, as well as Journey of the Universe. These were inspired by our close work with the cultural historian Thomas Berry, our teacher and colleague for over thirty years. Berry created the history of world religions program at Fordham University where we all met and studied together. He first came to Schumacher in 1996 for a gathering on earth jurisprudence organized by the Gaia Foundation.

Berry worked for a decade with our colleague Brian Thomas Swimme, and together they wrote *The Universe Story*, published in 1992. Brian came twice to teach the Universe Story at Schumacher in 1997 and in 2003. It was with Brian that John and I created the *Journey of the Universe*, a multimedia project of an Emmy-award-winning film, a book, twenty podcast interviews and three online classes. John and I brought this work to Schumacher in June 23–27, 2014, when we showed the film at the Tagore Festival at Dartington Hall and followed up with a workshop.

## World Religions, Spirituality and Ecology

Earlier John and I taught a summer course on religion, spirituality and ecology. This arose from a ten-part conference and book series we had organized at the Harvard Center for the Study of World Religions from 1996–1998. Our question was how can religious and spiritual perspectives help solve environmental challenges? What are the environmental ethics that will motivate people within the religions for environmental protection and eco-justice? If eighty-five percent of the world's people are involved with religion and spirituality, we should bring them into discussions on ecology.

The assumption of the Harvard series was that science and policy approaches are necessary but not sufficient for solving environmental problems. Values and ethics, religion and spirituality are needed for the task of transforming human consciousness and behavior for a sustainable future. This included perspectives from all the world's religions—Western, Asian, and Indigenous. These perspectives were the focus of our Schumacher workshop.

After the Harvard conference series, the Forum on Religion and Ecology was formed at a culminating meeting at the United Nations in 1998. We brought the Forum to Yale in 2006 and with numerous others have been midwifing efforts to establish a new field of religion and ecology within academia and as a moral force for change in the larger society.

## Environmental Ethics

For many years religious communities were so absorbed in internal sectarian affairs that they were unaware of the magnitude of the environmental crisis at hand. To be sure, the natural world figures prominently in the major religions: God's creation of material reality in Judaism, Christianity and Islam; the manifestation of the divine in the karmic processes underlying the recycling of matter in Hinduism and Jainism; the interdependence of life in Buddhism; and the Dao (the Way) that courses through nature in Confucianism and Daoism. Despite those rich themes regarding nature, many religions turned from the turbulent world in a redemptive flight to a serene, transcendent afterlife.

Yet as scholars and theologians explore environmental ethics, religions are starting to find their voices regarding the environment. The monotheistic traditions of Judaism, Christianity and Islam are formulating original eco-theologies and eco-justice practices regarding stewardship and care for creation. Hinduism and Jainism in South Asia, and Buddhism in both Asia and the West, have undertaken projects of ecological restoration and tree planting. In China there is a movement called Ecological Civilization drawing on the traditions of Confucianism, Daoism and Buddhism.

Indigenous peoples bring to the discussion alternative ways of knowing and engaging the natural world. Their perspectives of kinship with Mother Earth are being appreciated around the world. Moreover, they are pressing forward with the Rights of Nature as can be seen in the Universal Declaration of the Rights of Mother Earth. In North and South America, native peoples are speaking out on the negative effects of resource extraction and oil pipelines.

All of those religious traditions are moving forward to find the language, symbols, rituals and ethics for encouraging protection of bioregions, species and vulnerable communities. Religions are beginning to generate the energy needed for restoring the Earth in such practices as forest preservation and tree planting as well as water protection and river cleanup. A major Interfaith Rainforest Initiative (www.interfaithrainforest.org) was launched in Oslo in June 2017 at a conference sponsored by the United Nations Development Program, the Norwegian government, the Yale Forum on Religion and Ecology and many other religious organizations. This initiative especially honors the voices of Indigenous peoples in rainforest protection.

Some of the most striking examples of the intersection of religion and ecology have taken place in Iran and Indonesia. In June 2001, May 2005 and April 2016, the government of Iran and the United Nations Environment Programme sponsored conferences that we attended in Tehran, which focused on Islamic principles and practices for environmental protection. The Iranian constitution identifies Islamic values for appropriate ecological practices and threatens legal sanctions against those who do not follow them. In Indonesia projects of tree planting and restoration draw on the Islamic principle of maintaining balance (*mizaan*) in nature. Students in Islamic boarding schools are taught such principles and are encouraged to apply the Islamic doctrine of trusteeship regarding the environment.

In the United States, the greening of churches and synagogues has led religious communities to search for sustainable building materials and renewable energy sources through Interfaith Power and Light. Many religious leaders, including some evangelicals, are focusing on climate change as a moral issue that will disproportionately hurt the poor around the world. Greenfaith and the Green Seminary Initiative have been working effectively with Jewish and Christian organizations to promote environmental awareness and climate justice.

The Sisters of Earth, a group of Roman Catholic religious women, sponsor a variety of environmental programs drawing on the ecological vision of Thomas Berry and Brian Swimme, who describe the story of the universe in both sacred and scientific terms.

The Greek Orthodox Ecumenical Patriarch Bartholomew has written books and led several international symposia on religion, science and the environment. Pope Francis's stirring encyclical, *Laudato Si*, is one of the most significant contributions with its call for an integral ecology that responds to "the cry of the Earth and the cry of the poor." Together Francis and Bartholomew issued a call to action on September 1, 2017.

## Journey of the Universe

We also brought the *Journey of the Universe* multimedia project to Schumacher. The *Journey of the Universe* film and book narrate the 14-billion-year story of the universe's development. It begins with the great flaring forth at the universe's inception to the emergence of simple molecules and atoms. It proceeds to the evolution of galaxies, stars and solar systems. It then describes planetary life that evolves toward greater complexity. Ultimately this results in reflexive consciousness in the birth of humans.

The story is told with attention to the earlier cosmologies of the world's religions, especially Indigenous traditions. The sense of kinship with all of life in native religions, the experience of interdependence in Buddhism, the life-generating Dao in Daoism and Confucianism and the attention to the sacredness of Creation in the Abrahamic religions—all of these are woven into this epic universe story. Such a cosmological perspective is both ancient and modern—embedded in certain aspects of world philosophies and religions and revealed anew in the scientific story of the universe.

*Journey* does not rely on reductionist scientism, which tends to see the universe and Earth as simply composed of mechanistic processes. *Journey*, however, recognizes that evolution is governed by natural laws discoverable by scientific methods and empirical observation. The self-organizing dynamics of evolutionary processes are part of the remarkable creativity of evolution, which humans are discovering. While humans are gifted with the creativity of symbolic consciousness, we know that different kinds of self-organizing creativity abound in the universe and Earth—the formation of galaxies and stars, the movement of tectonic plates, the chemistry of cells, the biological complexity of photosynthesis, the migrating patterns of birds, fish, turtles and caribou.

This, then, is a story that inspires wonder as we begin to understand such complexity through science and appreciate such beauty through poetry, art, history, philosophy, spirituality and religion. It also awakens us to the dynamic processes of evolution that are chaotic and destructive, as well as creative and life-generating. It shows us how we have arisen from these processes and how Earth systems have maintained a self-regulating context for life to continue. James Lovelock and Lynn Margulis have named this Gaia and Stephan Harding has called it the Animate Earth. As *Journey of the*

*Universe* suggests, awareness of the livingness of the Earth draws us into an ever-deepening sense of wonder that evokes appreciation and gratitude.

*Journey of the Universe* is, however, more than an awe-inspiring story; it is a functional cosmology, as Thomas Berry suggested. This is because it harnesses the energy of awe and wonder for the multiple efforts of humans to contribute to the flourishing of the Earth Community. This is what Berry called the "Great Work" in which humans will become a mutually enhancing presence for Earth's ecosystems and societies.

He felt this work would assist in the transition from the Cenozoic era to what he termed a life-sustaining Ecozoic era. There are hundreds of thousands of people around the planet who are participating in this transformative work for the environment, energy, agriculture, economics, education, the arts, sustainable cities and improved racial and gender relations. Many of these specialists are inspired by the comprehensive perspective of *Journey of the Universe*, and some are interviewed on their work in the twenty-part podcast series of "Journey Conversations."

A conviction is emerging that we need a new "species identity" to rally humanity to a stronger sense of solidarity than nationhood, clan or family can muster. This implies coming to understand our place within this vast field of force we call Gaia and the deep time we call evolution. Such a perspective invites us to embrace a new universe story, one that evokes responsiveness and responsibility, and inspires humans to help shape evolution in benign directions. This is the invitation of the *Journey of the Universe* project.

## Conclusion

As these examples illustrate, around the planet a new story is emerging along with a new alliance of religion and ecology. Religious and spiritual attitudes are being reexamined with concern for a vibrant future for the whole community of life, not just humans. A universe story is emerging in many languages. The urgency of these efforts for the future of life cannot be underestimated. Indeed, the flourishing of the Earth community may depend on it. For thirty years Schumacher College has held a similar vision as central to its mission—namely the comingling of ecology and spirituality within the dynamic living context of Gaia. For this we are immensely grateful and look forward to further partnership.

 MARY EVELYN TUCKER is the Director of the Forum on Religion and Ecology at Yale University.

ENGAGED ECOLOGY

# A Learning Arc

*To be native to a place
we must learn to speak its language.*
— ROBIN WALL KIMMERER

I came to Schumacher when my life had reached a crisis point. I'd been teaching as an associate lecturer in the Study of Religion at Oxford Brookes University for a decade. Rolling contracts. No security from one year to the next. No work from May to September. Ever increasing and unfeasible workloads. Students who seemed not even vaguely interested in the subject. I was approaching burnout.

My urge, my need, was to go home, and so in 2013 my family and I dropped everything and moved back to Devon, not to the South Hams of my childhood, nor to Exeter where Nomi, my wife, was raised but to Chagford on the Moor. The land there is magnificent, with the community of artists, puppeteers and shamans doubly so. It was a good place to put our lives back together and to unpick how on earth to eke out a living.

Just then I was told that Schumacher College was looking for a teacher and that I ought to send off my CV. To my happy surprise I was invited to lunch with John Rae and Rachel Fleming, and to my even greater surprise I realized, halfway through my first bowl of famous Schumacher soup, that I was being *interviewed*. In the end I was invited to teach the very first module of the new master's program in Ecology and Spirituality, and eventually to run it as program leader.

The Ecology and Spirituality program, run in partnership with the University of Wales, Trinity St. David, was created to ask to what extent the ecological crisis was underpinned by a spiritual crisis. In that questioning, it was expressing something that is fundamental to Schumacher and indeed to the wider Dartington experiment: the importance of spirituality. Rabindranath Tagore would have welcomed it, as would have the many spiritually inclined thinkers and seekers that visited the Elmhirsts, from Gerald Heard to Aldous Huxley.

## What Is Spirituality?

Legion are the arguments amongst scholars of religion as to what, exactly, spirituality is, how it may be defined and what its role is today. Some point to the decline in traditional Church attendance and the growing secularization in the northern hemisphere to suggest spirituality has no part to play in the modern world. Others point to a growing sense of ennui, a crisis of meaning that's led to the swelling numbers of millennials identifying as "spiritual but not religious." Yet others critique the marketization of spirituality as an expression of, rather than a counter to, neoliberal capitalism. And so on, and so forth.

For myself it has always seemed a very credible suggestion that our being out of kilter with the wider ecological world is mirrored, if not caused by, our being out of kilter with ourselves. If, as the mystics tell us, the world is a great song, then modernity adds little but stridency, noise, inchoate rhythms and jagged harmonies. The explicit focus on spirituality at Schumacher, as expressed through the daily rhythm of meditation, morning meetings and work groups, stills the mind and silences the machine, allowing us to add our voices more sympathetically to the song. It shows us experientially how to *be* in the world, even as in class we grapple more abstractly with the problems of the day.

The Ecology and Spirituality program is no longer running, due to the unforeseen administrative difficulties thrown up by running a program across two institutions. The few students that remain are now writing their dissertations with impressive results. As a teacher it's heartening to see how much they've learned and how motivated they now are to use their skills in service of a better world. They leave the program fortified.

## Engaged Ecology

However, I'm delighted that a new master's program has arisen, Engaged Ecology, which takes many of the themes of its predecessor but allows people to explore them in a fully residential and experiential manner. Engaged Ecology inverts the usual dialectic of theory and practice to privilege the latter. Students get to *do* things and then to think about them later, all within a learning arc that invites them to consider how they will act in the world upon graduation.

Let me give you an example. This morning I opened the back door and engaged with ecology by stepping into the garden and listening to the dawn chorus. There are many different ways I might have done this. I could have used phenology, the study of cyclical or seasonal phenomena, to listen for the arrival of blackcaps, chiffchaffs and warblers, all summer visitors from Africa. By comparing the date of their arrival with previous years, I could see how climate change is affecting the onset of spring (getting palpably earlier each year, I regret to say). Or I could have counted the different bird species, measured how long they sing for and with what intensity, to try and draw out some quantitative ecological patterns that might explain why birds sing at dawn (an as yet unanswered question). I could have meditated, stilling my mind so as simply to receive the sound as pure unmediated experience. I could have used Indigenous methods of relating that allowed me to interpenetrate deeply with, say, the spirit of a blackbird. I could have prayed to the dawn, performed a puja, sung an improvised praise poem.

Each of these modes of engagement come with assumptions about how the world is and what our place within it might be—an ontology, we would say—and the correct means of deriving information about it—an epistemology. By trying each of these methods, we get to experience them firsthand. Then we can think through their implications, assess how they sit with us, their relative merits, the different ways in which they distance or interlock us with the world, what they include and preclude. Thus, we can develop a toolkit of experiential and intellectual skills that allows us to intensify our relationship with place, a toolkit we can then take out beyond the college into a life of service.

We have other exciting things planned, such as inviting students to weave a piece of linen cloth that they have grown from seed and prepared by hand (there's an obvious nod to Mahatma Gandhi here), or asking them to carve by hand a cup and a spoon that they use for the duration of their studies. How is our relationship to things changed when we have crafted them by hand at every stage of production? As with Ecology and Spirituality, we will question what we mean by spirituality and what role it has in addressing the ecological crisis, but also ask how best we can live together in community, without excluding people by gender, race, sexuality and ability. And we will read a lot too, gleaning the best from the world of thought within the burgeoning discipline of environmental humanities in which this program sits.

My hope is that this program will build on the deep roots of experiential inquiry that have grown here at Schumacher College over the last thirty years, but add something fresh and contemporary that's relevant to a new generation of people wanting to act in the world. Above all I want students to experience firsthand the magic of living and learning together in the Schumacher community. For there isn't a day that goes by without me pinching myself to make sure I'm not dreaming.

But maybe I am. Before I left Oxford, I literally had a dream. I was in the famous quadrangle of the Bodleian Library, a building where I had spent many happy hours, only in my dream it had been magically and elastically expanded. Now, instead of cobblestones and a reverent hush, there was a garden with lawns and charming bridges over rolling streams. I looked and saw groups of students discussing weighty issues in the shade of great trees. Elsewhere there were people doing yoga, tai chi, meditating. It was a vision of a different kind of education, where book knowledge was complemented by something more direct and experiential. It never occurred to me that it was a kind of foretelling of what was to come.

I have certainly been changed by being at Schumacher. Yes, I've become even more ecologically aware. I've encountered some new and radical ideas. But most importantly I've been asked to show up, not just as "Dr." Andy Letcher, the teacher, but as a whole person. I'm learning, still, to speak not just from the head but from the heart and the belly too. No matter what people come to do—to volunteer, to do a short course, to garden, to do a master's, to teach—there is a subtle magic that calls people to be fully themselves. I'm delighted that so many have been changed by being here over the last thirty years, and I look forward to facilitating that change in others as they come to engage creatively with ecology.

 Dr. Andy Letcher is a Senior Lecturer at Schumacher College with a particular interest in the intersection of ecology and spirituality. He has a DPhil in Ecology from the University of Oxford, and a PhD in the Study of Religion from King Alfred's College (now the University of Winchester). He is also a folk musician.

ECOLOGY AND SPIRITUALITY

# A Sense of The Sacred Earth

MATTHEW FOX

*Revelation comes in two volumes:*
*Nature and the Bible.*
— ST. THOMAS AQUINAS

I have always felt at home at Schumacher College. First, because E. F. Schumacher's classic work *Small Is Beautiful* hit home deeply with me when I first encountered it in the seventies. Indeed, I cited Schumacher on the very first page of my foundational book, *Original Blessing*: "The late E. F. Schumacher believed that there are two places to find wisdom: in nature and in religious traditions." And I put the question: "In our quest for wisdom and survival, does the human race require a new religious paradigm and does the creation-centered spiritual tradition offer such a paradigm?" That I began my pivotal work with a quote from Schumacher hints at the alliance I have always felt with his work and its reincarnation in the work of Schumacher College under the vital leadership of Satish Kumar.

Schumacher's book on *Good Work* also played a meaningful role in my book on *The Reinvention of Work* in 1994. Clearly our values were and are deeply aligned.

It was special to me to be invited to speak at the Schumacher Lectures in Bristol, England, in autumn 1992, where I followed Lester Brown who ended his lecture by naming the "number one obstacle to the environmental revolution" as "human inertia." That was a perfect lead-in to my presentation since inertia is a spiritual problem, one of the seven "deadly sins" which we sometimes call "sloth" but in fact is *acedia*, which Thomas Aquinas defines as "the lack of energy to begin new things." In other words, inertia is apathy, depression, despair, boredom, not caring. Aquinas's medicine for such a condition is "an intense experience of the beauty of things."

Schumacher's journey into Buddhism as well as Christian wisdom affirmed my interest in the deep, creation-centered mystics of medieval Christianity including Hildegard of Bingen, Thomas Aquinas, Meister Eckhart, Mechtild of Magdeburg and Julian of Norwich.

In addition, I have always enjoyed my visits to teach at Schumacher College, where I met many committed seekers including the Dutch philanthropist Fred Matser who subsequently helped support my University of Creation Spirituality. I will always be grateful to the many persons I met as students, as well as fellow faculty at Schumacher College. For my most recent visit, a few years ago, I brought with me a friend who is a movement instructor but also a long-time dancer in the deep and demanding Sundance of the Lakota people. Meschi Chavez sat in on my teaching in the morning and then led students in the afternoon in putting the concepts from the morning seminar into the body. It was a dynamic learning experience. So too was a public evening lecture which Meschi opened with powerful singing and drum playing from the Lakota tradition.

At Schumacher College there is a tradition of what I call in my pedagogy over the years *art as meditation*, and that is what Meschi brought to the class in the afternoons. By engaging in art as meditation—whether gardening, working with clay, movement or body— one is bringing ideas home into the body where they belong instead of just swimming around aimlessly in our heads. Art as meditation has been called by psychologists Claudio Naranjo and Robert Ornstein "the way of the prophets." And so it is.

Another dimension to Schumacher College is the experience of community—people doing everyday tasks together and also sharing in a heartfelt way over meals. I was struck, in my most recent visit, listening to the stories of students attending the school who came from various European countries—Italy, Germany, Poland, France, Holland—as well as Brazil. Most shared a common frustration with education in their countries which they found far too rational and heady. They appreciated Schumacher College's balance of intellect and intuition, an integration of head, heart and hands, that was missing on the continent.

This concern parallels very strongly the critique I made of American academia some forty-five years ago when I consciously rejected the inherited version of education in favor of an experience that balances both intellect and intuition, thus seminars in art as meditation and body prayer were integral to our educational model for creation spirituality trainings for the past forty-five years. And not just for adults but also for inner-city youth where boredom often drives young people away from school.

For all these reasons and more, I celebrate Schumacher's 30th anniversary and repeat my long-time appreciation for the values it stands for and the value questions it raises about education but also about society and culture. I can only imagine how richly the graduates of Schumacher have contributed to a healthy culture over the decades on returning to their respective countries and professions!

Since both Schumacher's goal and my own have been to create a wisdom school in contrast to the knowledge factories that have ruled academia for too long and whose shortcomings are on display for all to see today as we undergo the rapacious exploiting of our planet, I feel very pleased to be asked to contribute to this volume in celebration of the Schumacher vision and of the life work of Satish Kumar. Satish has been a supportive friend not only to me and my work but to so many change agents of my generation. And he leads by example—a joyous example—and critical thinking such as emerges in *Resurgence* magazine. So, I truly want to congratulate and salute Satish as well.

## A Current Project: The Order of the Sacred Earth

One of my projects that I sense resonates deeply with the values and vision of Schumacher College is the Order of the Sacred Earth that I launched with two young people, Skylar Wilson and Jen Listug (32 and 29 years old respectively when we launched two years ago).

Our vision is this: In a time when organized religion is often being abandoned, and Earth calls out for action and strong hearts to defend her from the onslaught of extinction spasms, wild fires, seas rising, wild tornadoes and hurricanes, fierce temperature increases (Antarctica last year posted unheard of temperatures of 75 degrees Fahrenheit), melting of glaciers and ice, extinction of species and the rest, it is time to gather our human energy to heal the planet. Which begins with healing ourselves and creating communities where we can become our best and most generous selves.

If one looks at the history of religion in the West, often when religion was on a downslide (as it is today), a new order sprang up. This happened in the third century when the Christian church was flirting with the empire—the movement we now call the desert fathers and mothers was a movement of young people who left the cities to live a more authentic life in the desert. In the fifth century, after the Roman Empire and the church married, Benedict and his sister Scholastica launched the Benedictine Order that supported much needed education, agriculture, art and the rest for hundreds of years. By the late twelfth century, the monastic orders had become too aligned with the feudal powers and privileges, and the result was considerable laziness and lack of service by those complacent institutions.

Thus, St. Francis and St. Dominic came along to launch their movements to serve the new generation that was fleeing the countryside to attend new universities in rapidly burgeoning cities. The Beguine movement too in the thirteenth century offered women an alternative to being cloistered nuns or married women.

In the sixteenth century, another low point for religion, we had the rise of many Protestant denominations that can be viewed, in my opinion, as lay orders led by certain charismatic persons such as Luther, Calvin, Knox, etc. Ignatius of Loyola also launched his new Jesuit Order in response to the corruption in Rome at the time.

But today? Religion is on a downturn, but few healthy alternatives have arisen. Why not a new Order, one that is not beholden to any one religious tradition but invites all wisdom traditions to band together in a light sense of community (often conducted online) to address the Number One Moral Demand of our time: The survival of the Earth as we know it. The common goal of this Order of the Sacred Earth is grounded in a common vow: "I promise to be the best lover of Mother Earth and best defender of Mother Earth that I can be."

At our first vow-taking ceremony, held at a Buddhist center in Berkeley, California, on the winter solstice two winters ago, eighty people showed up of diverse traditions: Buddhist, Christian, Jewish, Indigenous, Sufi and at least one atheist. Together we shared discussions of the vision and took the vow. Today we count about two thousand people and sixty-five "pods" or local groups in North and South

America and Australia who are participating in this new Order of the Sacred Earth.

One twenty-six-year-old told me: "This is exactly what my generation needs. We are so dispersed and distracted by social media that we need a common focus—and what issue is more important than the Earth's demise?"

It is this recovery of *the sense of the sacredness of the Earth* that is so important in the next stage of planetary struggle. As Thomas Berry puts it, "An absence of a sense of the sacred is the basic flaw in many of our efforts at ecologically or environmentally adjusting our human presence to the natural world. It has been said, 'We will not save what we do not love.' It is also true that we will neither love nor save what we do not experience as sacred...Eventually only our sense of the sacred will save us."

A second current project that shares values and vision with Schumacher College is my most recent book, *The Tao of Thomas Aquinas: Fierce Wisdom for Hard Times*. This spiritual handbook for activists is built on the substantive teachings of Thomas Aquinas, one of the greatest spiritual, intellectual and scientific geniuses of Western civilization.

Several years ago, I wrote an article on Aquinas as a green prophet, entitled "Thomas Aquinas: Mystic and Prophet of the Environment." I also wrote a major study of Aquinas called *Sheer Joy: Conversations with Thomas Aquinas on Creation Spirituality* in which I de-scholasticized him by interviewing him (this could not have been accomplished without the invention of the Apple computer, which was new at the time, since every sentence from him had to be footnoted). In that book I also translate for the very first time many of his works which had never before been translated into English, French, German or even Italian. This included many Biblical commentaries from both the Hebrew Bible and the New Testament but also his very first work written when he was twenty-eight years old, his "Commentary on Denis the Areopagite."

Father Bede Griffiths assisted me with my translations from the Latin, rendering them in a version that was more true to the Queen's English, and he wrote an afterword to the book, and Rupert Sheldrake penned the foreword. After graduating from Oxford University, as a young man Bede Griffith identified himself as an atheist, but on picking up Aquinas's *Summa Theologica,* he was awakened to the Christian path and became a Christian and then a Benedictine monk. So, he was very excited to assist my endeavor on Aquinas. Father Bede lived in a Christian ashram in southern India for over fifty years and was a pioneer in religious ecumenism. Indeed, in a dialog we shared in Oakland, California, close to his death, he declared that "Matthew Fox's Creation Spirituality is the spirituality of the future; and his theology of the Cosmic Christ is the theology of the future."

In the *Tao of Thomas Aquinas,* I gather some of Aquinas's wisdom to sustain eco-activists and social activists in our critical times. I can think of no more substantive teacher to ground us in a deep but activist spirituality at this time. As Aquinas puts it, "Wisdom is able to direct us not only in contemplation but also in action."

Each of the thirty-one chapters of the book bears the title from a sentence from Aquinas—sentences which hold the energy to wake people up and ground a post-modern consciousness. In each chapter I offer fuller reflections on each theme from Aquinas. Such titles as these are at play:

"Revelation comes in two volumes: Nature and the Bible."
"A Mistake about Creation results in a mistake about God."
"They shall be drunk with the plenty of they house, that is the Universe."
"Joy is the human's noblest act."
"The first and primary meaning of salvation is this: To preserve things in the good."
"The greatness of the human person consists in this: That we are capable of the universe."
"We ought to cherish the body [and] celebrate the wonderful communion of body and soul."
"Every truth whoever utters it comes from the Holy Spirit."
"Revelation has been made to many pagans...The old pagan virtues were from God."

One sees in these themes how he turned his back on centuries of dualistic theology derived from Plato and neo-Platonist church "fathers" in favor of the new science of his day, arriving in Europe by way of Islam and Aristotle. He tells us why he wrote twelve books of commentary on Aristotle—and not one on Plato: because "Aristotle does not denigrate matter." Aquinas got condemned three times after his death for his insistence on non-dualism or the "consubstantiality of body and soul." His prophetic and warrior self stood up for truth in spite of the costs. He is truly a wise and courageous guide for our times.

The latest book by MATTHEW FOX is titled *The Tao of Thomas Aquinas: Fierce Wisdom for Hard Times*, published by iUniverse. matthewfox.org

# Experiencing Gaia

PETER REASON

*The universe is a communion of subjects,*
*not a collection of objects.*
— THOMAS BERRY

The master's degree in Responsibility and Business Practice was established at the University of Bath in 1997 by Judi Marshall, Gill Coleman and myself, with support and encouragement from Anita Roddick, founder of the Body Shop and pioneer in ethical business. It ran for thirteen years after which a version of the program was run from Ashridge Management College until quite recently. From the beginning we considered how to design such a degree as a radical participatory educational venture within a prestigious business school. We were adamant that it attend to questions of meaning, value, spirit. In particular we wanted students to study Earth's ecology, to be exposed to radical thinking about the nature of the planet Earth as the originator of all human and non-human wealth. We wanted to explore deep ecology and Gaia theory, within the overcrowded British Isles, offer students a wilderness experience, an opportunity for a direct experience of the wildness of the natural world.

It soon became clear that Schumacher College in Devon was the place to go; at an early meeting with Satish Kumar, Anne Phillips and Stephan Harding, we realized the extent to which our educational practices were aligned. The college is located within Dartington Estate, in an area where there is both extensive agriculture and open countryside—the River Dart and Dartmoor in particular—although of course there are no places within the British Isles untouched by humans. Anne Phillips, director of the college at the time, was keen to introduce the underlying philosophy of the college, explaining how the day-to-day program fostered a community of learning, in which participants learned about how to live lightly but still comfortably, including the sourcing of sustainable, healthy food. Everyone joined with staff in the everyday tasks of cooking, under the direction of Julia Ponsonby, and joined the volunteers cleaning the public areas. All these activities contributed to the development of our own community of inquiry within the course. Satish Kumar told me when we first met that the best way to build good relations in a group was for people to cook together. I will never forget the look on one participant's face when he told us he had never before cleaned a toilet bowl!

In collaboration with the Schumacher teaching staff, we designed a week-long experience which included lectures on deep ecology, Gaia theory and the state of the natural world. Later, when Brian Goodwin joined the Schumacher faculty, he contributed sessions on complexity theory. Once the Schumacher master's in Holistic Science was established, there were many fruitful discussions between the students on the two programs. And the Schumacher College library was an invaluable resource; participants would spend stimulating time browsing the shelves.

But a lot of time was spent outside. We took participants on a night walk through woodland and spent an afternoon meditating by the River Dart. We summoned the Council of All Beings, the ceremony developed by John Seed and Joanna Macy, in which participants come to the council circle to speak as many diverse beings of their concern for the state of the world. And we spent one whole day in a hike along the upper reaches of the River Dart, along what must be one of the last remaining stretches of wilderness in England. On this walk we left the footpaths and scrambled over rocks and under branches; we helped each other through bogs and over torrential streams. And under Stephan's guidance, we experimented with deep ecology exercises which shifted our experience of the more-than-human world, helping us directly understand the interconnectedness of all things.

## Wilderness Experience

The River Dart thundered down from the moor toward the sea. It was full after recent heavy rain, the water so high that it lapped over the banks, swirling around the roots of trees and making soggy patches in the grass. In dryer weather the water rushes between the rocks scattered across the riverbed in little cataracts, but on that day it poured over them in smooth torrents, pounding into the pools below with a deep roar. We had to shout to hear each other over the noise.

We stopped to inspect a chunk of granite that stuck out from the ground by the side of the path with a green luxuriance of moss growing over the top and hanging down each side. Its surface was pitted like a sugar lump, light grey decorated with patches of black lichen. Embedded fragments of quartz, harder than the surrounding rock, protruded slightly and sparkled in the dappled sunlight. A deep fissure ran vertically down the front face of the granite; over time the crack had filled with organic debris marking a dark line, dividing the surface into two planes. The rock leant back into the bank, surrounded by young bramble shoots and bracken with its rear side underground and hidden from our view. Its shape was evocative. A face kept peering out, suggesting itself to me: the fissure, a nose; two blobs of lichen formed eyes; the moss a head of hair. A troll, maybe?

But granite is alive in a more fundamental sense. This rock had broken off from the dome of granite that erupted from deep in the Earth some three hundred million years ago to form Dartmoor. The pitted surface and the fissure down the middle were signs of weathering over geological time. It had been tumbled down the valley. Rain had washed over it. Ice had fractured it. The roots of the moss now found their way into hairline cracks, forcing it further apart physically, and secreting acids that helped break it up chemically. As the rock fragmented, exposing new areas to the rain, it gradually dissolved: carbon dioxide from the atmosphere split calcium from the silicate in the granite and combined with it to wash away in a chalk solution, calcium bicarbonate. Some of this we could see, some we knew from our classroom studies prior to the field trip.

I looked around. Everything in the woodlands along the banks of the Dart was part of this process of turning granite into chalk. Small rocks and gravel tumbled against each other in the torrent. Trees seeded clouds, brought rain, keeping the ground and undergrowth damp. Roots broke up and dissolved the granite. Insects and animals pollinated flowers and transported seeds. Bacteria turned vegetable matter into humus, and fungi grew in symbiosis with the roots of the trees, making nutrients more readily available. The river collected the chalk solution and carried it down to the sea.

Stephan asked us to recollect the rest of the story in our imagination. Once in the sea the chalky water was taken up by tiny creatures called cocolithophores. Along with other animals like crabs and molluscs, they precipitated solid chalk to form their hard skeletons. When they died, they fell to the bottom of the sea and formed a chalky layer, compressed over time into solid chalk rock. So, when we look at the white cliffs of Dover, we are actually looking at solidified atmosphere. This is a continual self-regulating process through which the carbon dioxide that is spewed out of volcanoes thousands of miles away is locked up in the geology of the planet.

Carbon dioxide is, of course, one of the greenhouse gasses which traps heat. If too little is present in the atmosphere, Earth will freeze. Too much, and the planet will heat up. Either way, it will no longer support life as we know it. We had learned in the classroom that plant life accelerates the physical weathering of granite by up to a thousand times. When it's warmer, this biologically assisted rock weathering goes faster; when it is cooler, slower. This self-regulating cycle keeps the temperature of the planet at levels suitable for life.

It was at this point that Stephan bent down, scooped up a handful of granite granules from the side of the path, held them out to us and asked, "Do you realize that these rocks are participating in life on Earth?" As we stared at the fragments—bits of black, shades of grey, white quartz, glistening fragments of mica—the classroom theory took on a deeper meaning. Now we felt the presence of Gaia directly; on our pulse, as poet John Keats puts it.

Gaia theory draws together the disciplines of biology, physics, chemistry and geology. It offers a view of the Earth as an interacting process, a co-evolution of living things and their environment. The hard line drawn between living and non-living things becomes blurred: we can see that while the granite we were contemplating is not "alive" in the same sense as a living animal or plant, it is nevertheless participating in life on Earth.

We reached the end of our walk, footsore and weary, happy to climb into the bus for the trip back through the narrow Devon lanes to Schumacher College. As we had been out all day, we had not been able to contribute to preparing the evening meal. Nevertheless, we were welcomed to steaming vegetarian food prepared by the staff and volunteers. Everyone slept well after the walk down the River Dart.

Embracing Gaia evokes feelings of amazement at the mystery of it all with no need for belief in a transcendental designer god. The Schumacher experience nurtures a wonder that links scientific understanding with a spiritual response, a sense of sacredness immanent in the whole. For many of our participants, this was literally a life-changing experience.

PETER REASON seeks to link the tradition of nature writing with the ecological crisis of our times, drawing on scientific, ecological, philosophical and spiritual sources. This essay is adapted in part from *Spindrift: A Wilderness Pilgrimage at Sea*, published by Jessica Kingsley Publishers, 2014. His most recent publication (with artist Sarah Gillespie) is *On Presence: Essays | Drawings*. peterreason.eu/OnPresence.html.

# Sacred Activism

### STARHAWK

*There can never be peace between nations
until there is peace within the human soul.*

— BLACK ELK

I'll never forget the first time I arrived at Schumacher College. Tired after a long journey, I was delighted to be welcomed into a beautiful old parsonage that could have come straight out of an English novel. I took a walk through the beautiful woodlands that surround the institute, taking a peak into the Agroforestry Research Trust grounds that have done such important work on models for food forests, and into the woods. Looking up at the trees, I stopped for a moment in astonishment. Surely that tall, stately, red-barked conifer was a redwood—but what was it doing in Devon? Was I losing my mind? Or was it there to give this California girl a feeling of being at home?

It was indeed a redwood, in a small grove of them planted by the owners of the estate long ago. To me, it seemed emblematic of what I think of as the spirit of Schumacher—a sense of welcome and home.

That welcome is the core of Schumacher's educational approach, which is wide-ranging and eclectic. The warm, accepting atmosphere within the college fosters confidence, learning and intellectual and spiritual risk-taking. When people feel that their whole self is welcome—not just the mind but body and spirit as well—when they feel seen and cared for, they are free to learn and explore. The Schumacher model of core class sessions, cross-pollenization with other programs running concurrently and small-group discussion sessions creates fertile ground for exploration.

In permaculture, we often speak of edges—the places where two systems come together and create more diversity and dynamism than either system alone. Schumacher's educational approach creates those fertile edges, where change is generated.

The subject matter I've taught at Schumacher is itself an edge—Spiritual Activism. How do we bring our spirituality, our deepest core values, into alignment with our actions in the world? How do we root movements for change and justice in the heart?

## Core Values

Spiritual activism encompasses a number of core principles and understandings. The first is that mind, body and spirit are one. When we act to bring about change, we can't compartmentalize ourselves into strategist, foot soldier and chaplain. We must be all three at once. We need our thinking mind, to discern what is the most effective use of our resources and find our opponents' vulnerabilities. We need action—not just talk, not just Twitter wars or Facebook face-offs, but creative campaigns to marshal power and influence decision makers, to directly interrupt systems of oppression and/or to build alternatives. And our strategies and actions need to be grounded in our deepest core values, values of interconnectedness and compassion that transcend any given political moment.

Another term I like for spirituality is "magic," and my favorite definition of magic comes from nineteenth-century occultist Dion Fortune: "Magic is the art of changing consciousness at will." That is also my favourite definition of spiritual activism. We need to change more than who holds power—we need to change the consciousness that supports systems of unjust power and engage our collective imagination to envision something new.

To shift consciousness, we need to understand that people are not just rational actors, but emotional beings who are moved by deep needs and complex forces. Spiritual activism attempts to address those needs. Three of the core needs I see are:

- People need to belong, to feel that they are part of something bigger than themselves.
- People need to be seen and valued for who they are.
- People need to make an impact on the world, to make a contribution.

When those needs go unmet, people may attempt to meet them in extremely destructive ways. They may join white supremacist groups that create a sense of belonging by excluding and dehumanizing others. They may demand endless, unearned adulation. They may shoot up a shopping mall or a synagogue to feel a desperate sense of power and impact.

But a movement rooted in spirit meets those needs in positive ways. It maintains an open, welcoming attitude that brings in newcomers and creates belonging through positive attraction, not exclusion. It uses language that everybody can understand, not abstract academic terminology or in-group jargon. It creates many ways for people to get involved, at differing levels of skill and risk. And it may create entry rituals or trainings to help people consciously enter in.

A positive, spiritual activist movement creates a culture of appreciation and value. Like an ecosystem, it has a niche for a broad diversity of people. It values those from groups who have historically been devalued and oppressed and recognizes their contributions. And it also sees the value in participation from those groups who hold privilege, acknowledging that they, too, can perform important roles. Most of all, it strives to create a culture where people can be seen for the full complexity of who they are, not for the categories into which they fall.

A spiritual activist movement provides a wide variety of ways that people can make a contribution. Some may be low-risk, like joining in prayer or meditation, or writing letters to officials. Some may be high-risk, like risking arrest to blockade a pipeline. Some may require great physical strength, like climbing a two-hundred-foot redwood to prevent it being logged. Others may require mental agility, like facilitating a big meeting, or organizational capacity, like arranging transport and communications, or simply being able to cook a tasty meal for a large group.

## Activism as a Prayer

I can't think of a better example of spiritual activism in practice than what I experienced during the weekend I was privileged to spend at Standing Rock in the autumn of 2016. The Dakota Access Pipeline, bringing dirty oil across the lands of the Standing Rock Tribe of the Lakota, was being built across sacred land and the graves of Lakota ancestors. It endangered the life and health of the people, the land and the rivers. Indigenous tribes came together in a historic gathering that began in the spring of 2016 and continued on into the winter. More than a hundred tribes came together to support the blockade, and non-Indigenous supporters also came by the thousands.

Because of complex factors in my own life, I wasn't able to come until Thanksgiving weekend at the end of November. When I arrived at the front gate, I was greeted by a sign that said, "You are entering a place of prayer and ceremony."

For forty years or more, I'd been participating in activist movements, always maintaining that we needed to bring spirituality and activism together. Now, I almost wept to see them so powerfully united.

The encampments at Standing Rock were very powerfully held as Indigenous space. After arriving and settling in, I attended a training required of every newcomer that served as an entry ritual, to orient non-Indigenous folks to the customs, traditions and protocols that were expected of us. We were asked not to speak at the Council Fire without first requesting permission from an elder, to make sure that Indigenous voices were the primary ones being heard. "We love music," the trainer said, "but we ask you not to strum your guitars or sing your songs, so our songs can be the ones we hear."

The language used by the activists was poetic, powerful and spoke of positive values. "*Mni Wiconi*—Water is sacred, water is life," was the message. Activists did not call themselves "protestors," but "water protectors." Spiritual activism speaks not just of what we are against but of what we stand for. It uses language that calls to the heart. And, while anger is always a motivation in activism, for anger is the life-force emotion that arises when we are threatened, spiritual activism is profoundly moved by vision and imagination.

The activists at Standing Rock had withstood violent attacks by the police. They'd been sprayed with water cannons in freezing weather, arrested and held in dog kennels, beaten and teargassed. But the weekend I was there was a relatively peaceful one. I attended trainings, sat in a global meditation for peace and was invited to participate in a women's sweat poured by Dineh singer Lyla June Johnston. I stayed in a crowded yurt in Sacred Stone Camp, made new friends and, as a grey-haired elder, was treated with so much respect and consideration I almost felt guilty. I was also asked to do a nonviolent direct-action training for a Women's Action and to participate in it.

## Power of the Human Spirit

The action, for me, was the moment I felt most deeply the embodied power of spirit. We marched to the police line, where not long before the police had brutally attacked protestors. The police stood behind a barricade, and a few elders moved forward to confront them. I stood behind elders Cheryl Angel and LaDonna Brave Bull Allard and listened to them speak. It was one of the most powerful moments of nonviolence I have experienced in a lifetime of activism.

"We are doing this for you, as well as us," LaDonna said. "We are your neighbors, your community. We went to school together. We are doing this out of love."

I watched the face of a young policeman across from me—first blank and closed, then a slight nod, a softening, a turning...

In the end, the elders were able to go down to the river without being attacked and make a water offering. It included a small amount of our Waters of the World—water that comes from sacred places, rituals and actions all over the world that myself and a group of sacred activists have been collecting and offering for almost forty years.

There were arguments and conflicts at Standing Rock. Relations between Indigenous folks and non-Indigenous supporters were sometimes rocky. Even the Women's Action was contentious. But underlying it all was this strong commitment to act in accordance with spirit. The encampment finally had to end with the winter blizzards. The pipeline was stopped—then given the go-ahead when the Trump administration took power, then stopped again by a judicial action. But the success of the movement cannot be measured just by its impact on the pipeline. It galvanized and educated thousands of people who came to the encampment, and tens of thousands more who supported the actions. It provided an inspiring model of Indigenous leadership and spiritual activism. And it sparked actions and movements around the world.

A year later, I was teaching in Germany. Our German translator told us how, in her village, they had formed a group to support

Standing Rock. "And then one day, we looked around and we asked ourselves, 'What about our own river? Shouldn't we also be water protectors?'" They formed a group to protect their river.

And that is the power of spiritual activism!

I write this in the midst of a global pandemic, when the COVID-19 virus has forced people all over the world to self-isolate and cancel all gatherings. In this moment, the immense privilege of teaching and learning at Schumacher seems like a beautiful dream—to be able to meet together in person, eat together, hold a long discussion over a pint in the evening, wander through the grounds or along the path to town. I hope those days will return, and that I can come back to Schumacher again. But as we negotiate this challenging moment and the challenging times that surely will follow, I know that the lessons taught at Schumacher will be more than ever important.

Schumacher's model of learning rooted in spirit, compassion and engagement with the world can help us envision a different way to live, so that we do not return to an unsustainable "normal," but create a world more just, more balanced and more infused with kindness and love.

STARHAWK is a writer, activist, permaculture designer and teacher. She is the author of thirteen books. Starhawk holds a double diploma from the Permaculture Institute of North America. starhawk.org

# A Quincentenary in the Old Postern

CHARLENE SPRETNAK

*We are all bound by a covenant of reciprocity:*
*plant breath for animal breath, winter and summer, predator*
*and prey, grass and fire, night and day, living and dying....*
*The moral covenant of reciprocity calls us to honor*
*our responsibilities for all we have been given,*
*for all that we have taken.*

— ROBIN WALL KIMMERER
Potawatomi Nation:
Great Plains, Upper Mississippi, Western Great Lakes

Our sense of being is continuously sculpted by every experience we have and every response we make—to humans and to the more-than-human world. Some of these experiences remain luminous in my memory even decades later because they immersed me in a wondrous gestalt, an extraordinary mix of qualities and energies coalesced in a way that has always resisted analysis. One such cluster in my life comprises the three times I was invited to teach a short course at Schumacher College as scholar-in-residence: in 1992, 1997 and 2003. All three courses were memorable for me because of the truly interesting participants Schumacher College attracts from all over the world. As teachers know, though, it is the first course we teach in an institution that remains most vividly in our memories.

That first course took place on 28 September–15 October, 1992, when Schumacher College was only in its second year, but Satish Kumar's vision for holistic, communal and engaged education had been brought to full fruition. And what a setting! The spacious and elegant fifteenth-century hall house, known as the Old Postern on the verdant grounds of the Dartington Hall estate, cocooned us in a blessing made of stone, timbers and glass, capped with a sturdy slate roof.

The title of the course was Reclaiming the Wisdom Traditions: Spirituality and Eco-Social Change, based loosely on my book *States of Grace: The Recovery of Meaning in the Postmodern Age* (1991). The thesis of the book is that deeply pragmatic approaches to addressing many of the crises of modernity can be found in the last place modernity would look for them: the core teachings and practices of the great spiritual traditions. While each tradition does engage with the whole of human life, each places much of its attention on one particular aspect. Who has gone further into the nature of mind than the Buddha's teachings on insight meditation? Who has gone further into the relationship between nature and humans than Indigenous cultures? Who has gone further in honoring the female bodymind and the Earthbody than contemporary Goddess spirituality? Who has gone further in a focus on social justice and community than the Abrahamic religions: Judaism, Christianity and Islam? In each of these four areas—mind, nature, body, community—the core spiritual teachings of the wisdom traditions provide antidotes to the meaninglessness inherent in much of modern life and also constitute paths of convergence between spiritual awareness and the emergent Green (ecological plus social) politics.

The orientation that was particularly on my mind that fall was Native American spirituality, unique to each culture yet with much in common across the nations. The Quincentennial anniversary of European contact with the Indigenous peoples of North, Central and South America was about to be observed on 12 October 1992, while my course at Schumacher College would be in session. The Quincentenary was much in the air in Green-oriented circles of alternative politics in the United States that summer and early fall. As it happened, I was a participant in the Elmwood Institute's Native American Symposium, hosted by the founder, Fritjof Capra, in Mendocino, California, only a month before I was due at Schumacher College. After the symposium I asked three Native American participants if they would be willing to record a message for my students at the upcoming course. Each of them kindly agreed, and I carried that audiotape with me to England. I also asked one of them, Jeannette Armstrong of the

Okanagan Nation in southern British Columbia, if she wouldn't mind my using a slight variation of the structure of four societies she uses for organizing participants for discussions: Youth, Cultural Mothers (not necessarily biological), Cultural Fathers (not necessarily biological) and Wise Elders. She smiled and said that would be fine.

On the first day of the course at Schumacher College, we introduced ourselves and then divided into the generational groups, or societies. The fifteen participants sat with their groups during all class sessions, with the result that they felt freed to speak deeply from their perspective framed by the stage of life they were in, rather than holding back because they were aware that other generational views need to be taken into account and that others see things differently. Instead of trying to present a universal perspective, each participant knew the other groups would speak from their own experience, analysis and vision so he or she was encouraged to do the same.

We began the course with an overview of the historical roots of the modern worldview and the ways in which its premises and assumptions have led to the problems of modernity. For two weeks we delved into the four wisdom traditions sequentially, immersing ourselves in spiritual orientations that conceived of nature, mind, body and community in ways that challenge the modern mechanistic worldview and can potentially reorient modern thinking to recognize interrelatedness as the ground of being. Native American spirituality, or their worldview, in all its variations, demonstrates that we are continuous with nature, not apart from it. Buddhism provides techniques of meditation by which we see that everything that arises and passes away in the mind can be observed with calming and centering equanimity, rather than clinging and craving or aversion. Goddess spirituality today is a quest to discover women's authentic spiritual experience and to draw from the history of Goddesses, women and entire cultures embedded in the cosmic rhythms of nature. The Abrahamic traditions emphasize community as spiritual practice: *Tikkun* (to heal and repair the world) in Judaism; the social gospel of Christ; and the brotherhood of Islam as well as *Tawid* (the divine unity of the cosmos), the grand community.

On the evening of 12 October 1992, we created a ritual observance of the Quincentenary of European contact with the Indigenous peoples of the New World. We gathered in the central hall, now the library, of the fifteenth-century building to mark that momentous fifteenth-century event. At the threshold someone held a softly smoking bundle of sage and passed it over our heads and down the front and back of our bodies, purifying us for the ritual space. We formed a circle around a cloth laid in the center of the carpet on which students had created a beautiful altar with candles and arrangements of flowers and greenery and seeds and stones, representing all the life forms on Earth. We listened to an audiotape I had brought of a prayer-song from the Lakota Sioux nation (South and North Dakota) chanted in a deep register by male elders. We called in the spirits of the four directions. Someone from the Youth society called in the spirit of the East with a poetic invocation as we all faced in that direction. Someone from the Cultural Mothers society called in the spirit of the South. Someone from the Cultural Fathers called in the spirit of the North. Someone from the Wise Elders called in the spirit of the West. We sang the chant *The earth, the fire, the water returns, returns, returns, returns.* Then we sat down and listened to a flute composition from the *Echoes of Time* album by Carlos Nakai (Dineh/Ute, Arizona).

In sequence each participant around the circle who was from the Americas described the bioregion in which he or she lived and told us the name of the Indigenous people who had lived, and perhaps still do, on that land, as well as what happened to them historically. (Every single participant knew this history because the sort of people Schumacher College attracts are aware, informed and engaged.) We sang the song *We Are One in the Spirit.* Then I read aloud short passages from the journal accounts by Christopher Columbus that were sent to King Ferdinand and Queen Isabella after his three small ships had sailed for five weeks from the Canary Islands to the Bahamas, where he dropped anchor off an island and was soon visited by the inhabitants in dugout canoes.

> 12 October: *They should be good servants and very intelligent, for I have observed that they soon repeat anything that is said to them, and I believe that they would easily be made Christians, for they appear to me to have no religion.*
> 14 October: *I do not, however, see the necessity of fortifying the place, as the people here are unskilled in arms, as your Majesties will discover from the seven whom I have caused to be taken and*

*brought aboard so that they may learn our language and return.*
*However, should your Majesties command it all the inhabitants*
*could be taken to Castile or held as slaves on the island, for with*
*fifty men we could subjugate them all and make them do whatever*
*we wish.*

I then read a response to these passages that describe the meeting of two civilizations. The American historian Frederick W. Turner notes in *Beyond Geography: The Western Spirit Against the Wilderness* (1980) that the "discovery" of the "New World" could have been embraced as a new, regenerating chance for a civilization "enervated by its commitment to a history that precluded genuine renewal": "What secrets, what unforethought-of initiations waited here amongst these islands, their flowers and trees and generous, trusting inhabitants? What entrances into mystic groves, cycles of simple contentment? Prelapsarian visions hovered like tropical clouds—and like tropical clouds were dispersed by the burning, relentless sun: gold. Where was it?" (p. 130).

To complete this part of the ritual, I read one more sentence from Turner's book summarizing Columbus's view of how it all turned out: "Columbus was wholly sincere, believing to the end of his days that the enslavement, exploitation, and extirpation of these naked ritualists conferred strength and new vitality upon Christian civilization." (p. 134) The confiscated gold enabled the enlargement and aggrandizement of the culture of the High Middle Ages as well as the Commercial Revolution of the sixteenth century and beyond. The genocidal consequences in the Americas counted for nothing.

Previously formed geographic groups in our class then gave brief accounts of what was done during the colonial era to the Indigenous peoples of Africa, South America, North America, Australia and New Zealand. We sang *We Are One in the Spirit*. Then I played the recorded messages for our class from the three Native Americans: Jeannette Armstrong (Okanagan, British Columbia); Jim Dumont (Anishenaabe, Minnesota/Wisconsin); and John Mohawk (Seneca, New York State). They each felt that the celebratory nature of the Quincentennial commemoration in the United States was insulting, as the event marks the beginning of a history of violence, aggression and the destruction of Indigenous cultures. The invaders' attitude of superiority never allowed for any possibility of brotherhood, only domination. The real miracle, they said, is that they have survived and are now focused on sustaining their cultures. They added that the descendants of the genocidal countries, whether in Europe or North America, bear responsibility for what was done and is still being done to Indigenous peoples. After a long silence, we passed the Talking Stick and listened to each other's reflections on what we had heard.

We passed around a basket with cuttings of wildflowers and herbs from the garden to be kept and pressed, if desired. We stood and recited the Dineh prayer "Beauty Is Before Me" four times. We heard from the four societies about our time together that had brought us to this point. Someone led us in a circle dance. Someone read a poem. We sang a song. Someone from each of the four societies led us in releasing the spirits of the Four Directions. Our recessional hymn as we walked from the circle was a Lakota prayer chanted by male elders.

Thirty years ago? That evening seems like yesterday to me. I believe we were all changed by it in some way. When I look at our class photo taken on the grounds of the college, it almost seems that we could become animated at any moment within that frame and turn to those around us in convivial conversation. We all felt so alive, energized by learning and exploring and speaking from our heart-minds together for the previous eighteen days. As for my own life experience, it would have been diminished without Schumacher College. Thank you, Satish. Thank you all.

 CHARLENE SPRETNAK is the author of eight books, including *The Resurgence of the Real*, *Relational Reality* and *The Spiritual Dynamic in Modern Art*.

# Creating a Core New Myth

COLIN CAMPBELL

*We lose our souls if we lose the experience of the forest,*
*the butterflies, the songs of the birds,*
*if we can't see the stars at night.*
— THOMAS BERRY

Congratulations to Schumacher College for reaching such an important milestone and celebrating its 30th anniversary. For the past ten years, I have had the pure pleasure of teaching at Schumacher College. I, together with students and participants from many countries, have been on a journey of learning and sharing the Indigenous Wisdom and Power of Ritual to discover their relevance in our personal lives and in the life of our precious Planet Earth. But, before I go into how I discovered Schumacher College, let me share with you, my dear readers, a brief story of my own journey of life and how Schumacher College became an important part of my life.

## A Story of Origin

Some things in our experience of being human have remained the same for a very long time. Among the most consistent, and perhaps the oldest of these, is both the fact and the general nature of our birth. We are ejected from the amniotic universe into a seeming assault of elemental forces of which, as yet, we have no understanding or experience. The rest of our days in this physical embodiment will be spent gathering that experience, and for many, or even most, the search for a rationale that explains and potentially gives existential meaning to that monumental initiatory event.

Yet search though we may, and historically have, the ultimate meaning of it all remains mysterious. Where we were before our birth and where we might be after our death is as perplexing a question as why we exist at all.

In *Mysterium Coniunctionis* C. G. Jung writes:

> Any renewal not deeply rooted in the best spiritual tradition is ephemeral; but the dominant that grows from historical roots acts like a living being within the ego-bound man. He does not possess it, it possesses him.

We are surely pressed to question in this time of ecological and social crisis just what "dominant" it is that possesses us. The story recited in the current history of our collective past focuses almost exclusively on our disputes over who owns and presides over what portion of the earth. Such ownership amounts primarily to arguments over who has the sovereign right to utilize the raw materials that fuel our voracious human industry.

That history is the framework of our collective story of origin in the contemporary occidental world. It is a story that places us humans in the position of ownership in relation to all that is other than human and ultimately to the earth herself.

We might refer to the narrative around which a culture or greater human collective coheres as a core myth. Jungian analyst and writer Edward Edinger points out that history and anthropology teach us that a human society cannot long survive unless its members are psychologically contained within a central living myth. Such a myth, he asserts, provides the individual with a reason for being, and further, it is evident to thoughtful people that Western society no longer has a viable functioning myth.

There is much that is unclear about the condition of our present predicament as a human collective. What has become profoundly clear, however, is that we, as the apparent prime cause in the sixth great extinction, cannot continue living as we currently do without potentially catastrophic consequences not only for ourselves but for all life on this planet.

I had the great fortune of growing up in the wilderness of Southern Africa. During those years I traveled extensively within my home country, Botswana, accompanying my father who was an ecologist, anthropologist and archaeologist. He was a passionate researcher working to help find ways in which the country could be helped as the mounting waves of globalization took their toll on that extraordinary land and its huge diversity of living inhabitants.

## Seeking Answers to the Unanswerable

As far back as I can recall, I have been plagued by the core existential questions pertaining to my existence along with the equally perplexing question of what will become of it at my death. As I grew up, I learned that these questions were by no means mine alone. They are questions that have been at the heart of our human endeavors since the dawn of cultural history. It is in large part our response to these questions that gave birth to the cultural myths and creation stories of our ancestors.

For millennia our core narratives, our stories of origin that both give meaning to our existence and sustain that meaning, firmly cohered around a deeply symbiotic relationship with the natural world. It is only very recently in the grand scheme of our human history that this relationship has begun breaking down with increasingly dire consequences for all life on this planet.

Through the course of my life so far, I have been witness to the devastating impact that globalization has had on both the biodiversity and the cultural diversity of Southern Africa. As I moved from childhood through adulthood into middle age, the external environmental and cultural crisis has become an increasingly intense personal inner existential exigency. This condition has resulted in a kind of inner impasse where I find myself deeply questioning the core notions of what being human means in just about every possible sense. The questions abide within a psychospiritual malaise at the heart of which is an unbearable feeling of loss.

Much of my childhood dialogue with my parents was driven by an almost continual barrage of existential questions as I feverishly searched for answers to the seemingly unanswerable. By way of standard response, my father, at whom the majority of my questions were directed, merely tilted his head to one side with a wry smile as if to say, you will have to figure all that out for yourself. One day, during a particularly fervent bout of questioning when I was about seven years old, he finally said that he simply didn't know the answers to these particular questions. Sometime later, however, he partially relented by offering that perhaps he could help me find someone who could.

And true to his word, over the remaining years of my childhood, he arranged almost all his field trips around my school holidays so that I could venture with him into the wilderness of Botswana in search of answers. He introduced me to elders from a diverse range of cultures and traditions who would become my mentors, teachers and initiators into the spiritual and magical knowledge of traditional Southern African Indigenous people.

The questions remain unanswered. Yet I gradually came to realize that their essentially unanswerable nature carried a tremendous invitation to potent creative engagement and continuing exploration. The nature of both the engagement and exploration was guided and facilitated by the teachers who, just as my father had, firmly pointed out that I would have to find such answers for myself. They could show me what to do, where to go and how to engage within the framework of both the cognitive system and the places within which they resided. The rest, I was told, was between me and the ancestors.

## The Great Work

In the years since leaving Botswana at the age of twenty-one, I continued to visit regularly as my learning and related initiation processes unfolded, ultimately bringing me into full initiation as a practitioner of African medicine in early 2000.

After a period of study at the University of Cape Town in the early 80s, I made my new home at the tip of Southern Africa on the slopes of Cape Town's Table Mountain from where I have based my practice up to this day.

Then in mid-2001 a tremendous turning point in my work occurred. It began with the arrival in my life of a book, *The Great Work*, by cultural historian and theologian Thomas Berry, who has been a teacher at Schumacher College.

In this seminal environmental writing, Berry advocates the vital role of Indigenous knowledge in the forging of a way forward in response to the ecological crisis. This was the first time I had encountered the acknowledgement, on the part of a seemingly very small sector of the Western environmental movement, of something I had strongly believed for many years. I felt a prickling of movement within me. Something of a tiny life-bearing upsurge amid the deepening despair about the way both environment and Indigenous culture were faring as globalization plunged into the innermost and wildest sanctums of the Southern African wilderness.

The impact of reading this book had tremendous influence on the direction of my public work. From that point on, the focus of my work as a practitioner of African medicine began to broaden to encompass work of a more general environmental nature within a matrix of cross-cultural psychology, thus laying a path towards creating a core new myth.

## A Broader Vision for My Work

Between 2001 and 2019, my brother and I had collaborated with Liz Hoskin, co-founder and director of the Gaia Foundation and a long-standing supporter of Schumacher College, in the creation of wilderness immersion trainings convened in the wilderness of South Eastern Botswana. Drawing on a combination of Indigenous cosmology, contemporary psychology and environmental philosophy, the training processes focused on the further visioning and practical development of Berry's ideas in what he termed the new Earth Jurisprudence. We believed that the undergirding task within these trainings was the re-examining and revisioning of the current core myth at the heart of modern industrialized culture.

The trainings drew lawyers, governmental policymakers, environmental activists, Indigenous elders and many others who were responding to the urgent call to action in the face of the deepening global environmental and cultural crisis. Indigenous elders from many traditions came seeking outside help in the battle to restore their traditional knowledge systems. They additionally sought help in rescuing from the ravages of industrial globalization the natural world within which those traditions had existed. Among the most pressing concerns addressed within the programs was the restoration of the broken relationship between our human collective and the rest of the living world.

In 2009 the Gaia Foundation in collaboration with Schumacher College convened a gathering of colleagues and associates who had been working together on the development of the Earth Jurisprudence trainings. The meeting was held at the college over seven days and included discussions, visioning processes and some of the wilderness immersion processes drawn from the trainings in Botswana.

Though I had been to Devon many times before, this was my first visit to Schumacher College. I had heard much talk of the college from many of the people I had worked with over the preceding decade. Most had attended courses there, both short and longer term. The reports glowingly recounted time spent at an extraordinary school rooted within the rigors of modern academia that was courageously developing and offering a range of training processes within a new and profoundly different holistic pedagogy.

To my delight, many of the core precepts that cohered the work we had been doing in Southern Africa were also strongly held beliefs and principles at the college. As a first gathering of this kind outside Southern Africa, the 2009 process at Schumacher College heralded another era of our work, bringing it to the vast global community that the college serves.

Anchored within the potent foresight and original visions of its founder, Satish Kumar, the college draws on a wide variety of different cultural, spiritual and philosophical paradigms. These are brought into an extraordinary synergistic interweaving housed and operated within the very heart of contemporary Western industrialized culture. I experience the college as one of a growing number of oases within our contemporary world. These are places where groups of people are germinating, nurturing and spreading the seeds of a profound and potent new vision for the healing and recovery of our world.

Over the last ten years, I have collaborated extensively with the college in the development and presentation of a number of different training programs both academically accredited and non-accredited. All have been created within an environment of wild and bold experimentation I find unequalled in other academic institutions I have encountered within the contemporary academic world.

I cannot sufficiently express how tremendously fortunate and privileged I feel to have had the opportunity of working with Schumacher College. I hugely appreciate the extraordinary community of brave and visionary individuals who introduced me to the college and whom I have continued to meet during my years of teaching there.

 COLIN CAMPBELL is an artist, musician and co-founder of a training school in Botswana for Indigenous doctors, and he himself is a practitioner of traditional African medicine.

# PART 4

# Education of Hands

NATURE AND ART

# The Big Picture

SUSAN DERGES

*I have nature and art and poetry,*
*and if that's not enough, what is enough?*
— VINCENT VAN GOGH

For me Schumacher College is like a large family where ecology and art can meet like siblings. That in itself is unique. I feel the college is a place that attracts people from across various fields of concern. Because of the small size of the college, there is this possibility of communication between different fields that organically happens in the courses and day-to-day life of the place.

In a similar way to how things unfold in the natural world, something can organically emerge and find its way into "being" in this kind of environment, which rarely happens in a big university.

I have been inspired by a number of the teachers at the college, some of whom have shaped my thinking and working, particularly the late Brian Goodwin, Fritjof Capra and Satish Kumar.

I greatly admire how the college encourages all of its participants, including the facilitators, to not passively receive information, but to go out and explore for themselves what nature and the world means to them. I see imagination, play and creativity combined with observation and analysis, as valuable teaching tools for this time. The college plays an important role in teaching differently. Going forward, I hope that the college continues to live a long and healthy life, and yet can stay small enough to provide this intimate atmosphere from which new possibilities can emerge.

I have felt a deep connection and longing to be in nature ever since I can remember. My parents always had a passion for the sea, and I spent a lot of time outdoors on occasions with my mother, who enjoyed painting the landscape around our home in Hampshire. At some point early on, nature became fused with the idea of mother, and consequently the notion of Gaia and the earth as a living being has never felt that strange to me.

Later, when I went to art school, I became fascinated with Japanese art, where I saw expressions of the natural world combining an intimate understanding of nature with a spiritual essence. This curiosity took me to Japan as part of my postgraduate studies. After a year at Tsukuba University, I decided to live outside Tokyo in a small fishing village, and it was only after six months of being there, after the first typhoon of the season, that Mount Fuji appeared above the sea's horizon, having been obscured by the smog of Tokyo throughout the summer months. The sea was heavily polluted at certain times of the year as well, and my awareness of our impact on the environment began to dawn in a more visceral way than just through the information around at that time. From then onwards I started seeing human behavior towards the environment differently. To this day, my work is concerned with deepening my own and others' connection to nature.

When I came back to England, I moved to an organic small holding on Dartmoor, which informed an understanding of what was involved in maintaining the land and animals that depended on it. Also Dartmoor was, although not a wilderness because of the deforestation and heavy grazing there, a very ancient and elemental environment to live and work in.

I pursued art in relation to this environment by abandoning the camera that I had previously been using, in order to attempt a deeper connection and to avoid the distancing that can often come between the one behind the lens and that which is before it. I decided to take a more participatory approach where I would be immersed in the elements of the land or water rather than outside it, by methods like exposing paper that was immersed just below the surface of a river at night and exposing all that to light. The flow forms, vortices and undergrowth were all revealed in great detail by this simple process.

Previously I had been interested in the phenomenon of sound vibration as a means of exploring more subtle, hidden aspects of the natural world and at that time came across Fritjof Capra's *The Dao of Physics* and *Spirals in Nature and Art*, edited by Jill Purce as part of her Thames and Hudson series on Art and Imagination. I worked with liquids, mercury and sand to generate patterns, often called Chladni patterns, and other visualizations of sound through vibrating surfaces with sound frequencies and making prints of the results. This curiosity around vibration and form led to working further with the nighttime landscape by including moon, stars, the trees and the rivers Taw, Dart and Bovey.

I think artists and scientists are both interested in exploring what it is that brings something into being. Both are curious about observing, studying and understanding the world, but we do it through different lenses.

I think we need to reconnect with our innate pleasure and ability to play, imagine and create as well as to tap into stillness to cultivate the kinds of insight that might help a deeper understanding of ourselves and the world.

At the short course at Schumacher College, I took my students out to the moor at night to create a collective "print" of the river Taw with photosensitive paper. The resulting image alone is not what changes our perception of the world, but that in order to create the work, each of the students had to deeply familiarize themselves with the environment to a level of detail and depth they hadn't experienced in quite the same way before. We worked very slowly with the intention of sensing the many different qualities of the light and darkness of the night sky, the wind, sounds, smells, flora and fauna of that particular stretch of the river. It was an invitation to meet something extraordinary in the silence of place and imagination, and that, I hope, made a profound impact.

So many of us are overwhelmed or paralyzed by the dismal scenarios and messages circulating in the media environment. Regardless of the content, how can we be effective in the world if we are continuously bombarded with information, every day? This overload and fear kill imagination, which is unhelpful in facing highly complex problems.

The solutions to the many challenges we face are not going to be simple. In a culture where particular specialisms and expertise are valued above the interconnected web of connections between things, we are missing out on the bigger picture and an understanding of how the whole might function. Therefore, the work of Schumacher College is vitally important. At the college the big picture is always kept in mind.

 SUSAN DERGES is a Devon-based nature artist who specializes in camera-free photographic processes, working with nature's landscapes. She is represented by Danziger Gallery, New York, and Purdy Hicks Gallery, London.

NATURE AND ART

# Web of Connections

CHRIS DRURY

*I am not grumbling that roses have thorns,*
*I am grateful that thorns have roses.*

— ALPHONSE KARR

Schumacher College is a wonderful place to be and a very special place to teach a course on Art and Nature. It is place where the nature/culture divide is blurred, and it is set within the wider community of Dartington and Totnes, with its links to rural Devon, the sea and Dartmoor.

The sharing of food and community is the main experience of anyone who comes here, so it is always a joy to teach in such surroundings as it gives rise to a wider conversation about our place in the world and how we might imagine a future within a troubled world. There is always the space here for discussion with people from all walks of life and ethnicity.

All that said, it is my practice to encourage students to get out and walk in the surrounding countryside—explore the river, fields, woods; immerse themselves in the physicality of place with no thoughts as to what art to make, where or how. Three days is a short time, but a day doing just this, whether the sun shines or it rains, is cathartic. Students are eventually encouraged to find a place and, using materials to hand, make something which speaks to them of place. This might use the daylight, or it might also explore the experience of dusk and dark, or of light moving from dawn to dusk. It may take into account encounters with other species—birds, mammals, fish and insects; the large and the very small. It may look at trees and plants or micro-organisms within the earth. It might look at the whole and the part and the relationship between the two. This is an art that is born of instinct, which arises in the body and moves to ideas of the intellect.

So, students may use the outside as a place of encounter, of ritual, of making, of making use of what is there. The emphasis is always on the outside, which may bring forth what is on the inside, without an emphasis on ownership. An aspect of what is encountered outside may be brought inside and explored further as both material and idea. It might even form the basis of a life's work connected to who we are in a wider web of interconnections.

CHRIS DRURY attended Camberwell College of Arts. He was awarded the Lee Krasner Lifetime Achievement Award in 2018. His book, *Silent Spaces*, is published by Thames and Hudson. chrisdrury.co.uk

# The Magic of Making

LOU RAINBOW

*We've tried getting wrecked, we've tried hard capitalism,*
*we've tried social media, and they're not making us happy.*
— BARNABY CARDER, spoon maker

The Craft Revolution is like alchemy. Its learning program is a unique combination of Schumacher College's model of a deeper ecological learning experience, promoting mindfulness and community spirit with almost a hundred-year history of craft and making at Dartington. This unique blend of education has created a vibrant hands-on learning space where people can interact and flourish. One of the greatest influences on our program comes from the depth of ecological learning at Schumacher College; it is spiritual, philosophical and practical.

Inspired by Nobel laureate Rabindranath Tagore's vision, Schumacher College uses head, heart and hands to teach its student body not only knowledge but wisdom by encouraging creativity and service. We offer the hands and creativity that embody this learning experience.

The influence of Schumacher College's teaching practice is that we place nature at the heart of all of our courses; a bench making course begins in the woods with a tree identification, a cool interiors wool course starts with shearing the sheep. Our Ocean woodblock printmaking celebrates the diversity of our oceans and the need to protect them through our fight against plastic pollution.

Basically, we teach the how and where and why of craft, and we program courses that promote "well-doing"—the perfect antidote to modern times. Satish Kumar is a huge champion of craft. He is a strong believer in the transformational nature of making. He has a love of all things handmade and deeply connects with the spirit of the material. Satish has often reminded me that the Greek definition for the word poet is "maker"—a person who is especially gifted in the expression of the beautiful. This is true. To make something from your heart is essential and meets every need of being human.

Five years ago, we launched the Craft Revolution at Schumacher College, Dartington, in Northwoods with a long weekend course, wild camping and spoon making, and we invited the now legendary Barnaby "Barn the Spoon" Carder. Today he is known as the Spoon Prophet.

On reflection, Spoon Camp, back in 2015, was a humble beginning where we created ideas that have formed the bedrock of a profound movement about making here at Dartington over the past five years.

## Craft with Human Heart

*The chief characteristic of craft is that it maintains by its very nature a direct link with the human heart...*

— SOETSU YANAGI

In fact, knowledge is firmly rooted in tacit learning. It is knowledge that cannot be adequately articulated into words. It is a feeling—of being transported, of being at one with yourself. It is empowering and self-actualizing. It is the motive to realize your own full potential.

Basically, to make is pure freedom of expression.

So, we believe that making is vital to a well-rounded life. When we explore knowing-how or embodied knowledge, it does not explicitly rely on rules or principles. We like this. This is the feral side of making, where the magic happens. The Craft Revolution helps us connect with making as a practical expression and manifestation of ecological, imaginative, creative and good living.

We offer a diverse range of making courses from spoon carving to soap making, from building a tiny home where all of its contents are handmade to brewing beer to making your own clothes; from foraging to fermentation, carving to canoe making. In short, a range of courses where you can see craft created from the heart that has purpose, uniqueness and love channeled into it.

The Craft Revolution aims to enhance craft and community by providing creative and cultural experiences that enrich people's lives. We are a part of a sustainable, resilient and regenerative economy. It is no surprise that craft is the UK's fastest growing creative industry.

*Have nothing in your house that you do not know to be useful,*
*or believe to be beautiful.*

— WILLIAM MORRIS

Founded in the 1920s, and believing in "progressive forms of education including the arts and craft to be the foundations of human flourishing," Dartington has a long tradition of craft and making. Dorothy Elmhirst, the co-founder of Dartington, was deeply influenced by William Morris and John Ruskin, and one of the first artists that she invited to Dartington in 1926 was the eminent potter Bernard Leach, arguably one of the greatest British potters of our time. Leach's former assistant Sylvia Fox-Strangways installed a kiln at Dartington and felt it was her duty to bring art and craft to everyone on the estate from "children to bricklayers."

We are striving to honor and regenerate and innovate a great tradition of craft here on the Estate. Dartington Printmaking Workshop celebrates over forty years here, and Mary Bartlett's bookbinding workshop continues to inspire people both locally and across the globe.

In the past five years we have created a thriving studio space. The Shippon Studios, with eight makers and artists, has two thriving potteries: Studio 45 and Mad About Clay. We have a rolling program of a hundred courses a year, residential and non-residential. We host a range of community events, national Makers Markets, talks, shared meals, events, performances, educational workshops and other public programs to encourage interaction and participation.

## We Work in Partnership

In 2017 we began an exciting three-year collaboration with Plymouth University architecture students and local eco-build company Terraperma in Totnes. Each year the 120 students were given a brief to design and cost and plan and build something on the estate.

They learned about the diverse architectural history on the estate, woodland management, systems thinking, local sustainable materials, scenario planning, eco-building and working as a team from drawing to building. They have built a tiny house on wheels; a bird hide; and this year The Big Tent—a communal shelter/space, designed to be used on a campsite, that is flat-packed and movable. This is a unique co-lab where students enjoy a break from their drawing boards and computers and come onto the estate for hands-on learning.

## Craft Can Save Us

When we ask our participants, "How does craft make you feel?" there is a universal vibe.

"Totally in the moment."

"Craft brings me back to life."

"It fills me with energy and love and makes me very happy."

"Empowered, energized and excited."

"It calms me, nourishes me, it feels like that's what I was made to do, not sit in front of a computer."

Craft is an involvement of head, heart and hands. The whole process from idea to realization is fascinating and all-consuming.

Our vision is that everyone should have the opportunity to discover their practical abilities, develop their creative talents and become a maker of the future. This vision is rooted in the knowledge that craft skills lead to diverse careers and creative satisfaction throughout life.

The world is changing. We are waking up to the universal truth about the connection between "well-doing" and well-being.

The continual rise in popularity of shows such as Pottery Throw Down, Repair Shop and The Great British Bake Off could create a seismic change in future career choices.

Today, instead of staying in careers for life, people are choosing to leave jobs that they are unhappy in, to pursue more meaningful ways in which to earn a living. They want to find their right livelihood driven not by money or status but by satisfaction.

Schumacher College keeps the legacy of progressive learning alive today through its innovative model for transformative education and a growing range of courses designed to advance the transition to a society in which all can thrive within ecological limits.

It is a unique place where we offer the opportunity to explore these worlds and to find new, meaningful directions.

Here at the Craft Revolution, we offer an opportunity for individuals to connect with their creative expression and provide a tangible reminder that we are more than consumers, more than useful data to be sold to advertisers.

A chance to find happiness in the making.

 Before joining Schumacher College, LOU RAINBOW worked for the Arts Council, England, specializing in visual arts and literature. lou.rainbow@ schumachercollege.org.uk

GAIA'S KITCHEN

# A Rich Mix

Julia Ponsonby

*One can not think well,*
*love well, sleep well, if one has not dined well.*
— Virginia Woolf

*It is my great pleasure to invite you to a feast. A delicious meal with*
*four courses: an hors d'oeuvre, entrée, dessert and, perhaps, a little*
*digestif...just to round things off.*

Every meal is a journey, usually short, but almost always looked forward to and consisting of different stages. In the case of this feast—the feast of the evolution of the Schumacher College Kitchen—we are taking a journey over time from the moment the first meal was served up on the first evening of the first five-week course back in 1991 to another meal some thirty years later.

For starters, we will explore how the food looked back at the beginning on that first Schumacher course (which happened to be one on Gaia Theory with James Lovelock). What were the flavors, inspirations and responses? For the main course, we will look back at the influences, improvements and benefits of the enduring way we do cooking at the college; this will be something to really get our teeth into! Then, a little entertainment while the dessert is brought on—let's invite some of the wonderful Schumacher characters on to the floor and see how the people of this place interweave and make such a difference. Then, to sweeten our palates, let's look at all those extra practices that complement our everyday cooking and which are for many people the favorite part of every day's repertoire. After that, it only remains to round off our journey through the life of the kitchen with a reflective sip of this or that.

Going back to the beginning. *Please take your seats! There are no place names, you may sit wherever you like, perhaps next to a friend or someone you have never met before (and who may well turn out to be a kindred spirit). But! Hang on a moment! There is no waitress service here, so please go to the serving table—that abundantly filled table over there where pottery dishes are laden with colorful culinary concoctions. Fill your plates before you sit down and don't forget your knife and fork!*

Right from the start, the menus at Schumacher College have been entirely vegetarian—no meat or fish or chicken, not even any insects. The food has always been lacto-vegetarian, with some meals entirely vegan and others including cheese and eggs. Perhaps it is because one of our founders had been a Jain monk earlier in his life, or perhaps because we want to respect animal welfare and the intrinsic right of animals to live a happy life; perhaps because we want to conserve ecological domains from overfishing or deforestation; perhaps to reduce the risk of food poisoning, and so we can open our kitchen to a wide range of untrained students and enjoy cooking together. Or perhaps, as I like to think, because *all* of these reasons are important and point in the same direction—to a healthy vegetarian diet that includes the dairy produce so abundant in Devonshire.

Our food has always been vegetarian, as local and seasonal as possible, as free from additives and packaging as possible (to minimize our carbon footprint). We've always opted for whole foods and have preferred organic ingredients—fairly traded when reaching abroad for those items people don't seem quite ready to give up (bananas, chocolate, coffee). However, at the beginning, we were following a much more Californian-fusion style of cooking, and this brought in more unseasonal produce. So long as we had no access to abundant local organic produce, this was not a big issue, and it didn't therefore seem inconsistent with our deeper ecological values.

In fact, some of the recipes we launched the college with remain among the time-honored favorites. These recipes were selected by Helen Chaloner, our first head of catering, who had come to Dartington hot-foot from the inspiring Tassajara Zen Centre at Green Gulch in California and from eating the food of Ed Espe Brown the chef, Zen priest and cookery writer (who subsequently taught cooking and meditation at the college on several occasions on a course called The Zen of Cooking). Mollie Katzen was another great influence. When I tasted her classic broccoli and tofu in a spicy peanut sauce served up with brown rice as a participant on the first course, I felt I had at last come home. It was the first time I had experienced such delicious vegetarian cooking, and as a vegetarian I was hugely impressed and keen to learn.

## Students' Participation

Right from the beginning, we have been getting students involved in cooking, helped by a bit of careful planning and gentle structure. One of the enduring practices that has worked well to anchor the college day in its own particular context right from the start is the 8.30 a.m. morning meeting. During this time, everyone gathers together to share a reading, share insights into the forthcoming day's rich blend of activities and perhaps enjoy a loosening up activity (which could be hilarious!).

After this everyone divides into small groups to accomplish an essential task. This could be gardening, cleaning or cooking. Thus, groups of four to six people join us for morning food preparation in the kitchen once a week and cook the evening meal with a chef— also once a week. This means that from Monday to Friday we have the amazing assistance of enthusiastic people who have come to the college to learn something particular—but also to learn through participating in community life. It is a double blessing: we the chefs get to know people and hear what is going on in the classroom, and we get all the vegetables for our soup scrubbed and chopped at the same time. On the other side, our students get to talk to us and each other and have a real feeling of contributing to the nurture of their fellow members of the pop-up learning community they have become a part of.

Together in the kitchen, our students find an opportunity to fine-tune their teamwork skills with respect to a very specific goal. The meal must be served on time and has two hours to manifest. This means everything being prepared in the right order using the appropriate tools and techniques. There needs to be awareness of the sensitivities and strengths of others in the team; for example, someone might respond to onions more violently than others, so there could be some task swapping. Perhaps someone with contact lenses could take over the onions. Because everyone gets to work in the garden on other days, the food preparation experience at Schumacher College really helps to embed the learning around food—how and where it grows and what you need to do to make it taste good. There is nothing as powerful as seeing a plant grow from seed to supper to underline the sheer awe-inspiring magic of creation. This is ecological learning in action!

## Volunteer Program

To start with we didn't have a team of volunteer helpers supporting the kitchen, and we didn't have our own vegetable garden for growing vegetables. Though all participants on the first course weeded and learned about permaculture in a very hands-on way, the beds were not tended once the course was over.

The volunteer system evolved organically as participants on the first course, noticing that Helen could really do with a bit more help in the kitchen between eleven and one, offered to stay on and help prepare lunch and do the laundry. Within a few months, we had about six eager volunteers—people who were extending their experience of learning in the Schumacher oasis by staying on and helping in return for board, lodging and access to the occasional talk. Our volunteers manage a lot of the "front-of-house" activity for staff and usually stay for about three months—long enough to learn the system and become proficient in getting things done as well as instructing others in how to do things.

I always feel tremendously grateful to our volunteers for getting on with often quite menial tasks in an ungrumbling way. For plunging themselves into what might seem like continuous sessions of floor cleaning and pot scrubbing. And for staying fresh and hospitable to our students and short course participants and their many questions. Together, our volunteers, staff and students constitute our longer-term learning community, and close bonds of interest and care build up between them which allow them to reach out to the participants who arrive on one-week short courses without feeling drained or as if they are working in a hotel.

As well as staff, volunteers and students, we have always enjoyed visitors to our kitchen. Kitchens seem to attract certain people and offer a welcome. There is almost always time to chat while stirring a soup, chopping a carrot or shaping some bread. Looking back over the years, I remember fondly times when the wives, partners or children of scholars busy teaching have taken refuge in the kitchen, sometimes sitting on a seat in the window and chatting to us with stories, mainly about food, or sometimes joining in with the cooking.

## Diversity of Diets

The breadth of ideas infiltrating the kitchen has also been huge—and not always in agreement. Some people ask, "Why isn't the college vegan?" while other argue that we should include meat and fish for a more balanced diet. I once had a gentleman announce that he had an "o" blood group and therefore was descended from hunters and gatherers and was looking forward to going home for the weekend and eating meat, lest he fade away. Conversely, a vegan master's student once petitioned to have a dedicated week when everyone became vegan and all dairy products were banned. Interestingly, there was quite strong opposition to this, yet many people were happy to sign up individually to being vegan for a week when they felt it was truly optional and not in any way forced. People express themselves through food—and having choice around food is an important part of people's identity, a mark of free will.

When it comes to special diets, we try very hard to make sure everyone is happy; providing satisfying food underpins a stable basis for learning and enjoyment at the college generally. However, when people don't stick to their special diets, the chefs soon lose the impetus to continue with it—especially as this can result in other people without special diets not having enough to eat. Because of the potentially fickle nature of people and their diets and to guard against generating the idea that Schumacher College is a good place to "experiment" with your diet, we ask people to let us know if their diet is for medical reasons or deeply held ethical ones (in the case of vegans). We then know when we need to take the utmost care to avoid allergic reactions to foods such as dairy, nuts, gluten, sesame, etc. In the hustle and bustle of a busy kitchen with serving time fast approaching, it is not always easy to get the labeling right, but the great thing is that because of the mixed nature of the cooking groups a team consciousness shines through and there are always volunteers and students quick to be thinking of the needs of their fellows. In this way what might have been seen as an obstacle—having to prepare extra food for special diets—becomes a learning tool in the cause of team building.

## Food from the Garden

One of the biggest and most inspiring changes that I have witnessed over my time at Schumacher College is the transformation of the garden. From being a lawn and hedges, it has become a productive horticultural plot managed by the college's own garden team and is a great learning resource. The area has expanded to embrace adjoining patches of field and includes many fruit trees. As with all new enterprises, the journey from nothing to something hasn't been without difficulties. For example, there was a time when there were so many sluggy holes in the potatoes that I had to ask one of our chefs to take garden produce out of her menus because the meals were being served too late due to the extra preparation work involved. Of course, it is nonetheless a learning for students to see delicious food being created out of what would normally be considered "grade out" produce. Huge amounts of food—billions of tons—are wasted every year in our mainstream agricultural system simply because our current distribution system and "cultivation" of streamlined standards does not allow for it to be saved and sold.

I am glad to say, however, that the produce from our garden is now so much akin to shop quality that I no longer have to worry about substandard produce being brought in by our gardeners. We all really delight in the beauty and abundance of the garden produce as it comes in—glowing squashes in bronzes, greens, amber and grey; big bold beetroot, earthy on the outside and shining with concentric circles of amethyst in the middle; milky cauliflower hidden like the brains of a giant by a clasp of leaves...just to mention a few of the delights. Furthermore, the garden has provided the means and impetus for integrating seasonal cooking into our menus, which means we are more than ever walking our talk.

Looking back over the years of cooking in the Schumacher kitchen, I can see there is a thread that combines experimentation and reliability twisting together like a double helix. When the Elmhirsts first bought Dartington back in 1925, they were keen to foster experimentation in all they did. There would be no failure—only positive results and negative results (which could be learned from). Likewise, in our college kitchen, as well as turning out two wholesome meals every weekday for the last thirty years, there have been times of innovation when we have tried to do something a little different.

## The Celebration of Food and Life

We have always held celebration to be an important part of what we do at Schumacher College. This could mean making birthday cakes or reviving an ancient seasonal tradition such as wassailing. Everyone has heard of birthdays and birthday cakes, nothing surprising about that. But I will wager that not everyone has heard of wassailing, which typically involves a community walk or dance to the Dartington apple orchards in the new year to wish the trees good health and and that they be blessed with bountiful harvests. What I love is seeing how old rituals are reinvented and reinvigorated every year involving different amounts of music, storytelling, candles and ribbons—or how about burying a bean in a scone, as I have been asked to do this for this year's wassail. Typically, celebratory themes attract varying levels of creativity amongst our learning community, and this can lead to the acknowledgement of the comings and goings of both individuals, groups and the seasons being celebrated in a very beautiful way that is both poignant and joyful. So much so that these punctuating moments make moving on a little easier: they oil the wheels of life.

On a more lavishly festive scale, Lou Rainbow, when in charge of fundraising, brought in the idea of occasional large fundraising banquets that would be open to local people. This brought an extra level of creativity to the job of being a Schumacher chef as we all enjoyed thinking up three or four course meals to chime in with a theme set by Lou. One such was an Indian banquet entitled "Om Shanti." For this our chefs, Ruth Rae, Sarah Bayley and Tara Vaughan-Hughes, went to Totnes for cookery classes with an experienced Indian chef, Nita, who worked instinctively and without recourse to any standard measures. Everything was demonstrated in pinches and eyefuls, so our chefs quickly did a bit of surreptitious measuring as they made notes in order to be able to scale up the dishes easily. The banquets were spectacular, with Lou having choreographed a whole atmospheric venue for guests to enter into, as well as enlisting extra volunteers to deliver waitress service.

Less elaborate but more frequent were the community lunches which Schumacher College offered at Higher Close when we opened our second branch of the college up the hill using the old Dartington College of Arts refectory as our kitchen and dining room. These community lunches happened every fortnight and were initiated by myself and Tara and continued by Ruth and Sarah when Tara moved on to start the (immensely successful) Green Table Café. So successful and popular did these Schumacher community lunches become that they soon extended from Dartington employees to Dartington tenants and then to their friends. I kept suggesting that a ceiling should be put on the numbers, but it seemed that no chef could ever bear to turn anyone away. It was a joy to serve the wider community, and as far as I know, no one ever complained that there was a squash. It is this spirit of joyful, wholesome giving which for me epitomizes the Schumacher kitchen—and has done so since its inception.

JULIA PONSONBY is the author of *Gaia's Kitchen* and *Gaia's Feast* published by Green Books and *The Art of Mindful Baking* published by Ivy Press.

DAILY BREAD

# Simple but Not Easy!

### Voirrey Watterson

*The smell of good bread baking, like the sound of flowing water,*
*is indescribable in its evocation of innocence and delight.*
— M. F. K. Fisher

When I first arrived at Schumacher College, I found myself teetering on the edge of an exciting shift towards more holistic living that I found thoroughly engrossing. This opportunity for exploration and transformation anchored me at the college and is my main focus here.

Growing food at Schumacher College can be traced back to the arrival of Justin West in 2005 when he came to do the master's in Holistic Science. Justin was determined not to leave the college before he had made growing food an important part of the college program in practice as well as in theory. He and another master's student, Leanne Phoa, cleared the wild abundance of nettles and brambles growing on the land immediately behind the Old Postern. Inspired by Martin Crawford, a neighboring forest garden expert, they planted a forest garden, created vegetable beds and filled a polytunnel with a beautiful green forest of herbs and vegetables. Justin was still busy when I arrived in September 2007, planting more areas of forest garden around the college accommodation blocks and fruit trees in the front lawn. I was immensely excited by what he was doing and joined in his efforts outside whenever I could.

## Apple Juice

Justin had also taken on the maintenance and harvest of a large apple orchard just up the road from the college on the Dartington Estate. Whenever he could during that autumn term in 2007, he got people up there to harvest apples. He had also persuaded the college to join a local community organization, Orchard Link. Orchard Link hires out manual apple presses for community groups to turn apples into juice. Justin arranged to hire a press for a weekend in early October and invited everyone he could to come either for a good physical workout operating the press or a good mental workout in the kitchen pasteurizing the juice. There were also lots of bottles to wash which Justin had somehow saved throughout the year. We all found it very satisfying to produce hundreds of bottles of juice, and also it was tremendous fun—even washing bottles!

Every year since then, I and others have organized the apple harvest and pressing, and all things apple are now an important feature of the autumn calendar at the college. We no longer manage the orchard, but luckily those who have taken responsibility for it have continued to share the harvest with us—and, of course, we now have many of our own apple trees. Thanks to the efforts of Ella Sparks, we also do a wassailing ceremony early in the year—singing to the apple trees to encourage them to produce a good harvest!

## Wild and Fermented Food

In September 2007, Frank Cook arrived to do the master's in Holistic Science. In contrast to Justin's passion to have us grow our own food, Frank's ambition was to have us discover all the tasty herbs and vegetables growing wild throughout the landscape. That autumn term, he decided to run a series of workshops and wild food walks at the college, open to any who wanted to come, in exchange for a donation. I didn't have much money at the time, so I asked Frank if I could work in exchange instead. Thus, I found myself on many Saturday and Sunday mornings in the college kitchen, helping Frank prepare his lovely, colorful salads and huge pots of herb teas for college students. They were wonderful days. Frank's wild food walks were always interesting and thoughtful, and I went away from them keen to get better at recognizing and learning more about wild plant foods.

Frank also liked to produce wild food by fermenting it, particularly vegetables. On several evenings that term, he gathered groups of us in the kitchen to produce our own kimchi and sauerkraut. I was already a fan of sauerkraut, but it was truly a revelation to discover how simple it is to make. Many things are "simple but not easy," as Frank used to say, until we are shown how.

We made miso after a long search for the culture we needed, not readily available in the UK at the time. We even managed a public workshop making kimchi in a local art gallery—I remember cycling into town with Frank, our bike panniers loaded with vegetables, salt, spices, chopping boards, buckets, knives... It was all a real education and, like all the best education, great fun. I was totally enthused by it all and since then have continued to experiment and learn about wild fermented food. Sauerkraut and kimchi, kefir and kombucha have become regular features of the college menu. Students, volunteers and short course participants are often keen to eat them. Craft Revolution organizes workshops to show people how to make them, and I quite often do an informal workshop to show students and volunteers.

## Bread Matters

Another student still busy at the college in 2007 was Eva Bakkeslett. To complete her MA in Art and Ecology at the Dartington College of Arts, she had decided to host a Companion of Bread festival at the college. On her chosen weekend, she set up yurts on the lawn in front of the Old Postern and workshop spaces inside the building. She invited the local community, storytellers and bakers, and organized workshops and discussions. It was a wonderful weekend and gave us all lots of food for thought, both literally and metaphorically!

Eva is an ardent fan of sourdough bread, so she made sure to invite some sourdough bakers. Luckily for us, Justin had managed to do a workshop making sourdough bread with Andrew Whitley, of Bread Matters fame. Andrew has been a tireless campaigner for the revival of sourdough bread for many years and was deeply inspired by hearing E. F. Schumacher speak as a young man. He said this was his main reason for accepting Eva's invitation. At his workshops, Andrew hands out to participants some of the rye starter he brought back from Russia many years ago—"spreading the mycelial network." Justin acquired some in 2007, and this is the sourdough starter we still use today for making sourdough bread in the college kitchen. I calculate it must be forty years since our starter began in a Russian bakery in Moscow. I sometimes wonder if the microbes living in it have any sense of their heritage.

Freshly baked bread is a favorite part of the college menu. We bake at least twice almost every working day. The team of cooks love baking bread for lunch, and I spend many evenings making sourdough bread for the breakfast table. The smell of fresh bread baking throughout the Postern is surely one of the reasons why it feels so much like home. Hardly a week goes by without a master's student, volunteer or short course participant coming into the kitchen wanting to learn how to make sourdough. I often suggest they make their own bread starter (leaven) from scratch, which takes about a week. It's not difficult—the microbes needed in a bread starter are everywhere, they just need a little bit of encouragement for a few days to come together as a community in a particular place: a warm mixture of just flour and water is ideal. We also do bread workshops at the college organized by Craft Revolution.

 Voirrey Watterson is a long-term volunteer at Schumacher College. She is the Cultural-Crossing exchange mentor for Burma.

# Nature Is Here

### MATT HARVEY

Nature is there ——————→
←—————— And we are over here.
Please note: phylum, class, order, family,
genus and species. What could be more clear?
Fruit of the good tree of taxonomy

fell freely in the garden of my youth,
absorbed in bone and blood, an intravenous,
unspoken, unchallenged, accepted truth
of my class, order, family and genus.

But wilder seeds blew in on some rogue breeze
found refuge and took root—few, but enough
produced a crop of quiet epiphanies:
"It's us! Nature is us! We are such stuff

as soil is made of!" Deep inside the grower
stirs nature's urge to quicken, germinate
the seeds both within and without the sower.
But how can such truth thrive and propagate?

In South West Devon there is a raised bed
where this is known, believed in, watered, fed.

MATT HARVEY is a poet and lyricist, his latest book
is *Sit!* with artist Claudia Schmid.

# Learning by Doing

JANE GLEESON

*Gardening is an active participation*
*in the deepest mysteries of the universe.*
— THOMAS BERRY

It was 2012 when I came across a job advert looking for a horticulture teacher for a charity in Devon. I was already teaching horticulture at the time, but I wanted to move away from predominantly classroom-based learning and get my hands in the soil again. I was also seeking a community style of living with like-minded people. I had been a horticulturalist for twelve years at this point, having given up a career in psychiatry. My move into horticulture had never been planned or even dreamt of. I rather fell into it and then in love with it.

While my job as a psychiatrist had been stimulating and very rewarding, I had never felt completely at home in it and had oscillated between that and studying pastoral theology. When I did finally exit medicine, I had no plan B, but for my own sanity I started gardening in a small shared neglected garden at my London flat. I loved it. I was outdoors, tending living things and fascinated by plants and their mysteries. I started looking at and noticing plants in a new and endlessly fascinating way. A whole new vista opened up and with it a different way of looking at the world and my place in it.

I had a lucky break and was offered work in a garden center and then did the Diploma in Botanical Horticulture at Royal Botanical Gardens Kew. I have never looked back. It was during my time at Kew that I came across the shocking statistic that industrial agriculture required an average of ten kilograms of energy to grow food containing one kilogram; this is in contrast to more traditional forms of "peasant" growing that gave a 1:1 ratio.

Given the food and energy crisis, I was astounded that this was not making headline news! I became increasingly interested in how we grow our food and feed ourselves well.

So, when the opportunity to work at Schumacher College in the gardens and teach horticulture came onto my radar, I jumped at it. While I was familiar with Satish and *Resurgence*, I had not heard of the college before. On researching it a little, I was drawn to its speakers and teachers and its community-based learning, especially its "Learning by Doing" and peer-to-peer learning. I was not disappointed by what I found; in fact, the opposite. I find it an incredible place to work and learn.

The first interaction I had when I walked through the door of the Old Postern, on the day I came to scope out the college before applying, was someone offering me tea and toast. This kind, unquestioning welcome on a wet winter's day was heartwarming and indicative of the care and welcome I have felt every day I go into the college. Such a loving and hands-on community is a rich place to learn and grow whatever your field of interest. The course on sustainable food growing we have developed at the college is excellent and greatly enriched and underpinned by the college ethos and its foundational practices. I could not imagine one without the other.

What happens in the gardens is a vital part of the life, and thus the learning, of the college community, and the dynamic web of relations.

The kitchen is very much at the heart of the college, and food growing is its lifeblood that circulates around the everyday and, on multiple levels, informs and helps create the unique learning community. If you want to find your place in the world, go into the garden; if you want to learn and experience complexity, go into the garden; if you want to learn how to make the world a better place, to restore and regenerate, go look at what is happening in the garden.

Food is central to our lives, to our families and friendships, to our community and to our ecosystem's health and well-being. We all need to eat. Every time we grow, buy, prepare, cook, eat and deal with food waste, we are engaged in a complex act with political, social, spiritual, economic and ethical implications.

The opportunity the Practical Residency in Horticulture gives to sow, tend, plant out, harvest, cook with our wonderful chefs, eat and then compost the vegetables is unique. Each student gets to experience that full cycle in its complexity, in a very hands-on manner.

The students come to live and grow at the college for six months from April until September; they learn about agroecology, permaculture and organic and regenerative methods of growing food. We take sixteen students, many of whom are now working in food growing projects around the world (a good number on the Dartington Estate). In 2019 we grew sixty-four percent of all the vegetables used in the college kitchens, including a ton of onions, and our produce value came in at £30,000 (wholesale value). This is learning with a tangible and meaningful outcome.

The vast majority of our food production takes place in our five-acre agroforestry field; it is named after Henri Bortoft who taught at the college on the Holistic Science master's. We grow our vegetables in alleys flanked by widely spaced rows of apple trees and a few plums. We also have chickens foraging under sweet chestnut saplings grown from seed that we will eventually harvest on a ten-yearly coppice rotation.

We have our own edible forest garden that houses our perennial vegetables for salads, and cooking apples and cane fruit production and a very successful herbal tea garden. There are three willow and hazel coppice areas to produce our own ramial wood chips, protect our winter soils, make compost and boost fungal populations; and an insect-filled craft and cut flower garden next to one of our two large wildlife ponds. We also have our own small tree nursery providing climate-resilient food crops of fruit and nuts. Our forest garden is a diverse haven for wildlife and a productive vegetable garden designed along the principles of agroecology, where we work as best we can with the ecosystem, rebuilding and regenerating both the above- and below-ground ecology. It is a beautiful place to work.

Despite what you might sometimes read, we already possess the intelligence, capability and resources to grow all our food needs in a way that would regenerate soils worldwide, feed us with nutritious food and help repair the climate crisis we are in. We do not require agribusiness and agritech to achieve this. What we sorely need and, I believe, would greatly enjoy, is a change in food culture. The current system is fuelled by the idea that food is a commodity, like any other manufactured material, and one that needs to be made at lower and lower cost to drive production and profit. Currently in the UK, farming contributes to eleven percent of our greenhouse gas emissions and is responsible for a massive decline in wildlife species and ecological destruction, pollution and malnutrition. Yet industrial agriculture is not in fact what feeds us; seventy percent of food production world-wide is done by small-scale farmers working traditionally using methods that are aligned with ecological principles—including those of recycling resources and ensuring diversity. We are truly gardening for Gaia.

In 2017 our horticulture students produced a document detailing their vision for a healthy food system. I want to use it here since it is an eloquent explication of what the course is about:

> For each one of us, this course has meant much more than learning how to grow produce. We all came to the college with a conviction that the predominant food system is the source of many imbalances that need deep repair. We are opposed to industrial farming: it disconnects people from the land, is a source of ecological exhaustion and contributes to global warming, malnutrition and social inequality. At Schumacher College we practice farming that cares for the soil, enhances biodiversity, nourishes people with healthy food and re-roots us to the land and to each other. We have learned how to de-velop growing environments that are resilient to external changes and require very minimal fossil fuel input.
>
> This type of growing, anchored by a commitment to small-scale farming and food sovereignty, has largely disappeared in Western culture and is threatened in the rest of the world; that's why we see any practice of it as an inherently political act. Not one of us comes from a farming background, and the training we have undertaken here is a conscious step towards re-weaving the web of small-scale food producers that is so needed. What we have learned here is a practical contribution to the creation of an alternative to the predominant industrial food model.
>
> — Schumacher Horticulture students 2017: Food Manifesto

All students get to experience this type of food production first-hand with all its complexities and challenges; they get to learn and experience how food is grown, harvested, prepared, stored and cooked to a high standard of taste and nutrition. This web of relationships, this nexus of interactions is what feeds and enlivens the learning at the heart of the college.

It is a type of learning where the classroom, although important, is not confined to one room in which heady discussions around theory are held; harder to elucidate but critical is the learning that occurs within the whole community as a community—one that celebrates, cooks, cleans, gardens, reads and communicates daily. You are as likely to learn in the dinner queue or raking leaves for compost as you are from being led by an expert. This is a learning that requires movement and action, it is a learning that happens though hands-on experience, alongside others, with others. It is systems learning, not fact acquisition, and relationships are at its heart.

That is why the college feels like a home. That is why although there are the usual labels of students, teachers, office staff and volunteers these are bounded by present but porous membranes that allow flow and nutrient exchange. Each role has distinct characteristics, but all are part of the learning community, and loss of any impacts everyone's learning. The course a student takes gives their learning a distinct shape and flavor, but the foundational practices of the college are what really add depth and heart and truly educate.

Having both taught and been taught horticulture in a variety of different educational settings, I can wholeheartedly say that the college offers a learning experience with greater depth and meaning than any I have known. The actual fact of learning is much the same— sowing seeds, growing, composting, crop planning, fertility building, among others; but the substantive embodied learning out in the gardens and in the community, although far harder to pinpoint and define, is at the heart of the success of the college.

I believe everyone could enjoy growing food; it is one of the best ways to nurture a relationship to nature. Learning how to work alongside plants to feed ourselves, planting seeds, watching them grow, then harvesting, cooking and eating them changes your relationship to food and to the earth. You learn to love and respect, marvel and appreciate; learn to be actively involved in an ongoing conversation with these photosynthesizers that convert sunlight into our sustenance. This is a far cry from picking up plastic-wrapped veg in a supermarket aisle. You are less inclined to waste and more inclined to gratitude, humility and joy in abundance.

 JANE GLEESON graduated in Medical Sciences at Cambridge University and worked over ten years in the National Health Service before becoming a gardener.

VOLUNTEERING

# Learning Through Service

ELIZABETH WEBBER

*The smallest act of kindness*
*is worth more than the grandest intention.*
— OSCAR WILDE

*I Slept and Dreamt that life was joy. I awoke and*
*saw that life was service. I acted and behold service was joy.*
— RABINDRANATH TAGORE

Schumacher College hosts hundreds of people through the year, and the learning community changes week by week. You need a crew to help hold this community in constant creation—to prepare for arrivals, to take care of people in the midst of transformative learning and to clear the space for the next group coming in. The volunteer team form this crew and help the college flex to meet the different needs each course brings. They put flowers in rooms to celebrate everyone who comes, they chop extra vegetables when the numbers jump, and they lead community groups to enable participants to get their hands on the place and in so doing to feel quickly at home. These actions communicate the culture of the college—that we are all in service to each other and the world.

## Shared Purpose

Volunteers develop a deep sense of belonging through having this shared purpose; their responsibility towards the place and a simplicity of daily tasks allows them to be and become more of themselves. As Community Learning coordinator, I saw how volunteers strengthened aspects of themselves by acting in service of the learning community.

Volunteers are former students and course participants who want to give back to a place that has enriched them or people who want to learn more about how ecological learning centers work, often with the intention of developing their own projects. They learn how to organize people to work cooperatively together, to be unfazed by sudden shifts in the work at hand and to anticipate the needs of people and place. They learn to work with their own resistance and to hold steady in the kaleidoscope of living so closely among others. They develop practical skills alongside this, anything from how to facilitate group processes to building a fire in a damp climate, and they root into cycles of growing, cooking and composting.

When volunteers are in residence, our conversations tend to focus on when to soak the porridge oats and how to get people to wash up their mugs. When we reflect together at key points in their placement, we talk much more about what they have learnt about being in community. I was curious about what lives on after leaving the college and asked a group of former volunteers to talk about what their experience means to them now. This time, our conversation settled on how they felt invited to be themselves, how the relationship of reciprocity expands the space of what is possible and how they learnt to relate to themselves, others and the world with more compassion. It gave them a contrasting map of new ways of living and working together which they use now to navigate by.

The extracts below focus first on being in common and move on to this sense of invitation and the growth of reciprocity and compassion.

## Living in Common Means that Everything Is Potential Material for Learning

Evelyn Roe took the Holistic Science master's and came back first as a general volunteer and then in a teaching support role. She is currently studying Scottish Gaelic and has continued to remain involved as a short course facilitator:

> I had an idea that a community was an entity that could be defined with a boundary and you could say who is in the community and who is not. Through being at Schumacher, I got a sense of belonging to something more dynamic than that. There are so many diverse relationships among us that the whole flexibly holds together. You don't link with everybody,

you don't understand everybody, but there are enough inter-links going on that it has its own vibrant personality.

While Evelyn was support volunteer, Diana Behrens was a post-graduate student and then took on voluntary roles. After returning to Brazil, she has continued to work on community building and works with other alumni in facilitating holistic learning:

It was an amazing opportunity of learning at so many levels. The whole journey of being in so many different roles allowed me to see how when you change your perspective, your experience changes as well. How when you go away and come back again, the people change but you still feel at home. Schumacher College remains with me because it allowed me to experience something alchemical.

While Diana was helping to hold the learning community together, Samson Hart was studying for his master's in economics. He is continuing to reconnect with his Judaism, facilitating events for the diaspora, spiritual ecology groups and community gardening:

Being in a community is to be as you are and where you are in that moment in a way that is endlessly nourishing. There is a depth of relationships that is present as soon as you walk into Schumacher College grounds. Stepping into that place you tether yourself to this deep way of being amongst one another. The rhythms and continuities at Schumacher College are really true to the community spirit. Having morning meeting, you have a chance to be seen and to share together. Eating every meal together creates a bonding. These are radical acts which I experienced at Schumacher College while volunteering.

Carlota Santa Ruiz took a short course on local economies, volunteered while continuing her own work in this area and then took the Changing the Frame course, which led to her current role with the Doughnut Economics Action Lab:

I learned how to take care of and give all my love to the people and place where I am. That was something I really learned at Schumacher College, not just taking care of the place, but getting a lot of joy through taking that care.

Anja Byg took the Call of the Wild outdoor leadership course before volunteering. She has returned to her academic work focused on human-environment relationships:

> I think that care and respect is especially important in a place where the human community is always changing. It is extraordinary that there are new people coming in all the time and still you have this strong sense of connection and continuity, even though you haven't met before. It became important to me that we develop a sense of service, a sense of mutuality and the shared task that we complete together.

I was always keen to have people with embodied and imaginal practice in the team, so it was easy to say yes to poet and naturalist Anna Selby's volunteering enquiry. She led poetry courses on empathy and ecology for the college community and is continuing this work in her PhD and residencies:

> Some real lessons happen just through living and being together every day at Schumacher College, with the intention to look at how we can help this planet of ours and explore who we are as well. It changes the way you live when you see what is possible and how loving and honest people can be with one another and grow together.

Samson, Carlota, Anja and Anna were all helping to hold the learning community together at different points while Ahmed Buasallay was studying for his MA in Ecological Design thinking. He used his research about relationship to place to help the new group of postgraduates find their own connections:

> Schumacher provides different spaces for us to experience a way of being together. It is a space of asking questions and seeking to understand together. One thing I learned here is attentiveness. Now I understand what attentiveness means. I'm still learning how to do it in everyday life. While outwardly volunteering I learned inwardly how to be mindful.

## The College Invites You to Be Your Whole Self and so You Are Able to Offer More to Others

Evelyn: In all of those roles at Schumacher, it always felt like an invitation to be a volunteer. Even though I might be the one to say, "Can

I do this?" And when there, I felt safe, nourished, challenged, invited and educated. And now, I've got this benchmark. I put it alongside me, and then I navigate by it to see how I am doing now.

**Anja:** At the college I found that being of service to other people is incredibly meaningful. Because at Schumacher College you are accepted as a complete person, it is easier to offer and be in service. There is this way of being and contributing where we make use of more of us. In a lot of places, it's just a particular part of us that is wanted, whereas at Schumacher College the whole of you is accepted.

**Samson:** I loved the early morning shift, and I loved walking down the hill in the morning at dawn because the jackdaws were out, and it was just incredible. So being scheduled to volunteer for early morning shifts was an invitation to meet the dawn.

## The Creation of Reciprocity Between People Expands the Space for What Actions Are Possible

**Anna:** Being in service is sensing what is needed, what people and the place needs at any time. When it works and when everyone is in service to each other, it feels really good. Students can be shocked that lecturers are washing up because they're not used to seeing that, but everybody sharing brings this leveling where everyone fits together.

**Anja:** During the period after we closed the Old Postern, my idea of what it means to contribute changed. It's so tempting to focus on what is my unique ability and in what special way can I contribute. As a volunteer, most of the time you do very mundane things. But after the Postern closed, I saw how important those little things were, and I found more meaning in those very small things. In that situation it suddenly became quite visible that small acts of service did make a big difference. That experience has stayed with me, it changed my own perception of how I can contribute.

**Samson:** I think service is the creation of reciprocity. To be a student and then a volunteer is a very important journey. Being a volunteer allows you to just be and to give. You receive so much of good things that they are not quantifiable. The abundance of care and acceptance people have towards you is incredible. It creates this version of me that is able to be more present and to listen deeply as a form of reciprocity. Volunteering felt like a gift to me. By doing those mundane tasks, you support others in creating joy and beauty. It becomes an act of love to make porridge at Schumacher. It is an act of prayer even.

**Ahmed:** Taking care of a place gives us a greater purpose to be in it. Once we take care of the land, it recognizes us, we start feeling love from the land. It is also an inspiration to give more to it, and it becomes a reciprocation between the people and the place.

## People Relate to Themselves, Others and the World with More Compassion

**Carlota:** It's OK to be wrong. You don't have to be perfect. These are things that you know, but until you really experience them, you can find it hard to try in your daily life. Volunteering at Schumacher gave me the space to see that actually it was through making mistakes that you learn, and you grow.

**Anna:** I learned to value frugality and simplicity at Schumacher College. It's quite shocking to come back out into the world and see the level of waste. I'm feeling really spurred on by seeing how much transformation is needed. How we're going to face the reality of what's happening in the world. How are we going to make ecological lifestyle a living reality?

**Evelyn:** We had a conversation once with Satish about altruism and its implication that you may give more than you think you are able to. Satish made it clear that volunteering is an act of compassion. To look at the other and what would be a compassionate relationship in each moment. That was a really good thing for me to hold on to from then on.

**Diana:** The general agreements and some structure hold the community together and allow people to pass on this fire of passion to other people, to pass on this playfulness, this feeling of let's do it and this energy of welcoming the next group of volunteers.

**Ahmed:** The act of volunteering is teaching us how to fall in love first, to fall in love with community and the place itself, and then when you know how to fall in love, you can enter into that deeper work of building a community.

ELIZABETH WEBBER was Community Learning Coordinator at Schumacher College from 2015 to early 2020. She organized service learning and managed the volunteer team. She came to the college following a career in International Development.

# In Search of Meaning

JANE HALL

*Schumacher College has changed me in profound ways,*
*and the changes will ripple out into my life and into the world.*
— SHORT COURSE PARTICIPANT

The short course program is the crucible in which Schumacher College was formed. In 1991 when the college opened its doors to students, very few places nationally and internationally were offering courses exploring ideas of learning from nature, understanding the earth holistically and addressing the ecological and spiritual crisis of our time. Short course participants join our learning community on courses ranging from a weekend to three weeks—time enough to discover much about themselves, make deep friendships with students from around the world and start a lifelong connection with the college.

The Western world had seen decades of seemingly endless economic growth. Capitalism and globalization were the dominant paradigms. But now, thirty years later, ideas of regenerative culture that were shaped and formed within the rooms of the Old Postern have become mainstream. Many in the field of business and industry are beginning to embrace more sustainable ways of working and are keen to develop better leadership models and better relationships with the earth. Indeed, many organizations now send their staff to Schumacher College to develop and apply the holistic "head, heart, hands" model of operating in the world.

An average year sees almost eight hundred participants, lecturers and facilitators from all over the world take part in our extensive short course program, a program which is constantly morphing and adapting to incorporate the latest radical ideas, informed by highly regarded teachers. Feedback from the participants is also crucial in this process of design, and it has helped us develop as a collaborative community.

Like nature itself, the continual evolution of every course adapts to suit the particular situation. No two courses are ever identical because each will have been modified in response to the participants, environment and lecturers at that time.

But while ideas shift and evolve, there is one constant that holds: care for people and care for the earth has always been at the heart of the Schumacher College ethos. Whether it is the short course team curating and developing a course, a vase of flowers grown by our horticulture team and picked and arranged by our volunteers or whether it is the delicious fresh bread, made daily by the kitchen team—or simply somebody offering to help with the washing up.

It is that wholehearted care for the well-being of all those within our learning community that often has the most powerful effect on short course participants who join us.

They understand that a short course with us is a fully rounded experience because of the role of the learning community with whom they are invited to integrate. It offers a social experience like few other colleges. It also means the subject matter is compelling and encourages participants to return, sometimes multiple times.

That care also extends to the delivery of the courses, held by the short course team and assisted by a facilitator who acts as the still center around which others can revolve. While the lecturers share their knowledge and ideas, it is the facilitator who gathers everyone together whatever their background or ability, ensuring that all participants feel involved and included.

Holistic learning also means moving outside the classroom. The college offers a unique setting, and this is very important to many who come to study there. The medieval Dartington Estate has a rich history, and the grounds with their redwoods, riverside walks and listed gardens allow time for quiet contemplation. Of course, the Deep Time walk along the coast and day walks with picnic lunches on Dartmoor are a significant part of short course experiences. These field trips are part of the "learning from nature" ethos of the college.

People join our short course for many reasons: seeking answers to ecological and social issues of our time, wanting reflection, needing to shift their thinking. All experiences are individual—yet most leave transformed in some way.

 JANE HALL is the short course program coordinator at Schumacher College.

# PART 5

# Schumacher Worldwide

# Learning, Living and Loving

ANDREW MCAULAY

*We have a desire to connect with others. I would call this*
*a spiritual longing to be whole, interrelated, interconnected.*
— TERRY TEMPEST WILLIAMS

Over the last twenty-five years, first as executive director and then board chair, I have received many new visitors to Kadoorie Farm and Botanic Garden (KFBG) in Hong Kong, but few as remarkable as Satish Kumar. The usual protocol is for staff at the Reception to bring a visitor to the meeting room near my office, where I greet them and begin a conversation about our work as a nature conservation and education center. If all goes well and we discover a sufficient degree of affinity between our interests, then some collaboration may develop. In the case of Satish, however, he simply burst through the door of my office, hand outstretched and with a big smile on his face, as if we had known each other all our lives. And indeed, it was hard not to immediately feel connected to this man, for here was someone whose experience of life is a moment-to-moment relatedness with everyone around him. This is what it means to be "holistic."

That was in March 2010, and our relationship has proven to be one of the most enriching of my life. KFBG had invited Satish to Hong Kong to help with the development of our education program, and it was not long before I found myself at Schumacher College in England, learning about the elements that make up a holistic education centre. In fact, before I started working at KFBG, I had been living in an ashram, so I was familiar with spirituality and the idea of an intentional community, but to incorporate these themes into KFBG's science-based program still seemed like a far-off dream. Therefore, to witness the coming together of scientific learning and spiritual practice in the communal setting of Schumacher College was like having a cool dip on a hot summer's day. How refreshing to see living, learning and loving; head, heart and hands; soil, soul and society, all coming together in one place. Not to mention a ready-made network of teachers and student alumni to tap into.

## The Green Hub

KFBG has a sister organization called Partnerships for Community Development (PCD), whose core focus is training and network building for sustainable living in mainland China. PCD introduced its work to Satish, and he invited them to bring a selection of their partners for a week-long exchange with some Schumacher College teachers. This delightful event took place in September 2012 and led to, among other things, the development of a new Schumacher College course, Transitioning to an Ecological Civilization: Dialogues East and West, in collaboration with the Southwest University in China. In the meantime, Satish continued to visit Hong Kong on a near-annual basis, to give talks and teach retreats—events which we were eventually able to hold at KFBG's Green Hub, which opened in 2015 in the nearby town of Tai Po.

The Green Hub was the culmination of years of reflection and dreaming at KFBG, inspired in large part by Schumacher College. We were looking to embed our evolving sustainable living program in a local community, where we could both support the development of community resilience and also host residential retreats. The perfect opportunity arose with the government's heritage building revitalization scheme, which was offering the old abandoned police station in Tai Po, a historic Grade 1-listed building, for the use of a social enterprise. KFBG eventually won the bid from among forty organizations, thereby taking a giant leap in its evolution towards running a second site. The project has been immensely successful, winning a number of awards and inspiring an increasing number of people with its various programs, whose highlights are the residential courses with star teachers like Satish. With holistic course content, cooking together and fireside chats, you could be forgiven for thinking that you are at Schumacher College itself!

## Alumnus At Last!

Still, even with Green Hub up and running, and in spite of near-annual visits to Schumacher College, I had never actually participated in a short course there. That all changed in 2018 when I enrolled in Bones of Ritual, led by Colin Campbell and Lucy Hinton. The opportunity to let go of any work agenda and just immerse myself in the college schedule and the teachings and practices of the course, culminating in a solo night vigil in the redwood forest, was life transforming. The feelings of joy and the sense of adventure that I had experienced on previous visits reached new heights, and by the end of the course, I was both proud and deeply honored to be able to call myself a college alumnus—at last!

Not only that, but when Colin and Satish heard about my exploration of breathwork practice and my training as a breathwork facilitator, they invited me to return the following year and teach breathwork as part of the follow-up course, The Power of Ritual and the Poetry of Surrender. What an experience that was! An extended version of Bones of Ritual, combining poetry and breathwork with story and ritual, among my favorite people—and teaching breathwork for the first time outside China—it was for me one of those quantum leaps that define life's progression. I never imagined that I would have that honor... but then, that is what Schumacher College is all about: daring to imagine the unimaginable!

Now in Hong Kong another opportunity is emerging—to develop a new holistic program in a facility much larger than Green Hub. As I write, we have just concluded an initial three-day gathering with partners from around the region, including Satish, to explore options. What could not be conceived of when KFBG was first established is coming to pass. With programs and networks maturing under the guidance of the remarkable staff of KFBG, PCD and other sister organizations, we are poised for another quantum leap, in service of people and planet. These days I often find myself overwhelmed with gratitude for all the blessings life offers. Schumacher College has been foremost amongst them, and the need for such inspiration is of course greater than ever. Hats off to Satish!

ANDREW MCAULAY is a poet and chairman of Kadoorie Farm and Botanical Garden, Hong Kong (kfbg.org). He is chairman of Full Circle Foundation which supports land conservation, biodiversity and Indigenous cultures.

# Right Livelihood

YING LIANG

Schumi Learning Garden (SLG), a garden receiving its first seed from Schumacher College, is now growing into a transformative learning center for holistic seekers in China. I am so lucky and honored to be its steward and call it home. Here is the story of how it came into being.

I still remember the moment I opened and browsed the website of Schumacher College—every single word caught my attention, yet left me with only one doubt: "Is there really a college like this where you can get a master's degree?" But unconsciously I already daydreamed about myself sitting outside the Old Postern. By then I was already a second-year master's student at University of Notre Dame, USA. So the decision of jumping from one master's program straight to another was not at all an easy one, but I was convinced that I needed to learn how to lead a life that could nourish myself, my people and the earth before I could stand firm and contribute to a better world. Yet all my academic education taught me everything but this. The missing puzzles of hand and heart, soil and soul were too obvious to ignore and turn away from the opportunity to become a more holistic person.

I was in the Economics for Transition program at Schumacher College in 2015–2016, with a wonderful cohort, some of whom have become visiting teachers at SLG. I still remember all the working groups and taking care of our collective home as a community, which manifested love in action and took the grand "changing the world" slogan down to earth and into daily practice. It really gave me a strong conviction that as long as we are together, we can make change with our bare hands. And this really became an ethos of SLG, so that we can make beauty out of creativity and hard work. Talking about beauty, I won't forget how much time I had spent with the Craft Revolution program at Schumacher College, which had opened a new world of making and mending for me. Now we have a carpentry workshop at SLG, and we are working with a young carpenter whose creations are quietly at every corner nourishing the whole space.

Being so close to Totnes was something I was so grateful for during my time at the college. Besides being able to join the local rowing club and enjoy the tranquil Dart River, I experienced the Transition Town movement as a real grassroots action for strengthening the local economy, to complement with all the New Economy theory I learned in the classroom. It opened new possibilities of what a healthy economy could do, and how to do things and allow things to happen.

"Not to look for a job, create your own work," Satish's powerful statement built a courageous bridge for me to return home at ease even though without any job offer. Equipped with all the new mindsets, and the strong will and belief to act and create, I settled at a place with an allotment where I could grow vegetables not far from my hometown. During this period of being a "half farmer, half X" for a year and a half, I set up a social media platform to spread the Schumacher teachings, and meanwhile did some interpretation jobs to make a living. This period of grounding myself on the land and also building networks with ecological minds within China set a solid foundation for what emerged later as SLG.

I personally experienced in depth from Schumacher what constitutes a transformative life-changing learning experience. Yet the dream of allowing more people to have such experience wasn't realized until the summer of 2018, when I got to know the space where SLG is located, in Qixi village, nested in a mountainous natural reserve, in China's Pearl delta area, and when I met Hao, who co-founded Schumi with me and now is managing a ten-acre organic farm next to Schumi. The synergy between Schumi and Qixi farm, reminding me of Schumacher and all the growing fields and gardens, holds great potential for an eco-community to be born.

Schumi started off offering a nine-week residential program "from inner transition to outer transformation," integrating holistic science, ecological design thinking, ethnographic research and New Economy teaching into a communal living rhythm with working groups, morning circle, cooking and group meditation. Participants can find much of the learning in the kitchen and on the land and find healing in allowing all emotions such as sadness and sorrow to be witnessed and held by a safe space and a sangha. After nine weeks, people left here with strength and rootedness—albeit having to face all sorts of challenges in the real world—having experienced the true happiness and loving-kindness could always bring them back to their center.

Some participants went back to their home villages and repaired broken relationships with family, while taking up family businesses in a more sustainable way; some became mothers, wanting to raise children in nature; one participant became a vegetarian cook after finding her passion at Schumi kitchen. Magically, one participant stayed on and now is Schumi's honorable baker and cook; and another one became a partner of Schumi and the farm.

The first two long courses gave the momentum for Schumi to be more grounded in its bioregion and settled its core team.

Gradually we find new possibilities in hosting more short courses, weekend activities and evening talks and meanwhile co-designing retreat or training programs with other organizations. These make up our mainstream of incomes to be self-sufficient.

A learning center can be founded; so can a farm. A community, however, can only be grown and nurtured through decades. Schumi started off as a team of three, and now we are five, three of whom have taken various courses at Schumacher. Two other Chinese Schumacher alumni are our visiting teachers. There are around twenty community members who are residing around; some came before Schumi, others came after. Some work in the farm, some are retired parents, some are young parents raising their children in natural environment, some designers, and some practice Tai Chi and Chinese medicine.

One valuable gift I received from Schumacher is to follow the grains of all happenings and actively interact with them yet not to intervene. Schumi is realizing more and more its potential role in growing a resilient local network of people and projects that are deeply connected to Gaia, to a community of right livelihood and mutual support, and nurturing a new partnership culture. I call this Schumi 2.0.

In a time when there is no certain blueprint for tomorrow, we carefully carry the torch from our ancestors, revitalizing the forgotten wisdom, and proudly walk out on a new path that our hearts are yearning for.

You are welcome to come and visit us. We see every guest as a messenger.

YING LIANG is the executive head of Schumi Learning Garden, China. liangy712@qq.com

# Learning as Encounter

JULIANA SCHNEIDER

I arrived at Schumacher College for the first time in 2010 carrying with me the pages of a Brazilian magazine where I'd first come across "The School of the Small and the Beautiful," as the title of the story announced. I was determined to see this place that had me instantly feeling at home from just that combination of words and pictures on a page. How could I feel such a strong sense of home towards a place so distant? "It can't be home if the people there don't even know me," I told myself in the midst of a rapport that was so clear-cut and yet defied all logic.

It takes ten years from that moment to where I am now writing in celebration of the thirty years of Schumacher College, having gained an appreciation for a much wider kind of logic, a logic that I learned throughout my different involvements with this living ethos. I have gone from being a student of the Holistic Science master's (2011–12) to a resident facilitator of the postgraduate courses, a volunteer as well as short course facilitator, and finally a friend whose path has remained connected across the ocean and with the multiple seeds of this education taking roots around the world.

It was 2013 when Mari Turato (Economics for Transition 2012–13) and I invited Jon Rae, head of college at the time, and Patricia Shaw, a fellow and visiting teacher who in that year was very involved with the Holistic Science program, to come and spend ten days in Brazil. We wanted to respond to the growing interest of Brazilians (who would fly long distances for the transformative education offered at the college) by exploring how similar experiences could grow on our own soil.

We organized weekend gatherings as well as dinners in São Paulo and many meetings with alumni, getting to know projects and sharing experiences. We had no plan to create something in Brazil. We were open to the sense of reciprocity emerging between so many of us and what next steps these would open, cultivating between us an acute attention to "nextness" in the midst of very live conversations. More like the unfurling of a leaf than the building of a house, taking seriously the legacy of Brian Goodwin, Margaret Colquhoun, Henri Bortoft, David Abram, Stephan Harding, Philip Franses and so many that have taught us the ways of nature over these thirty years.

After this visit, the call was to sustain what was evoked through a continuous flow of gatherings and meetings with alumni and others. From that, a group of us came together to offer what we were calling a Schumacher Experience Week together with Toca Farm, an agroforestry project that we had connected with during Jon and Patricia's visit. It was our first open course, and although excited we were also worried that by the name "Schumacher Experience" people would immediately expect teachers from England or elsewhere in the world and then get frustrated to arrive at a group of Brazilian alumni instead.

In conversation with some Brazilian alumni, we came up with the title for the Experience that left no gaps for false expectations: "A Schumacher experience organized by Brazilians, for Brazilians, in Brazil." Our modesty "defied all logic," and we had a full course plus a waiting list of people wanting to join. By the end of the week, we learned that the ethos we recognized and cared for so much under the name Schumacher had appeared among us. We gave life to it not by following a set of practices but by carefully attending to the possibilities between us—the people and the place we were collaborating with as we drew on our varied experiences of the Schumacher education through so many years.

This experience gave us the confidence for growing a community of teachers and learners on our own grounds, of cultivating soil together. Seven years after that, and we now have over a thousand alumni who have taken our short and long courses run under the name of Escola Schumacher Brazil. Short courses have included transformative education, phenomenology of design and complexity thinking. We also offer the Schumacher Experience week, Certificate in Holistic Science and Economics for Transition which engages projects around the world.

Our soil in Brazil has also received nourishment from occasional visits from our beloved Satish Kumar, our friend Tim Crabtree and also our friend Patricia Shaw, who has become an important mentor for us in keeping one another alive to what we do. This for me has been the biggest learning through founding and leading Escola— becoming aware of the ways in which the process of organizing poses the risks of institutionalization, of turning static that which is dynamic and moving. It has been with this attention that the way we organize has also changed through these years, from having more identified leadership to being a small collective with shared responsibility for the running of the activities.

To notice these movements, these callings for change, and respond to them with openness in the midst of uncertainty has been key to the education we want to cultivate. More widely, we are seeing a world growing in challenges—with climate change having become an undeniable crisis, inequalities rising, corruption of authority revealed around the world, our Amazon and its people coming under threat. How do we respond? How can we allow our forms of organizing to continue being permeable and alive to our shifting world? This question has led to many new kinds of activities, such as bringing together voices for the Amazon in immersive dialogue, making deeper connections with the peripheries of São Paulo, opening questions around political agency and of course taking more steps into the challenge of becoming accessible to a more diverse range of participants.

This has been quite an adventure that took course after my time at the college, and although there are hundreds of other ways I could share this journey, what I happened to share here highlights what I feel lies at the heart of this education: a very particular combination of "home" and "experiment." I believe this combination is quite radical. To inhabit a home in a world where we seem to grow more and more estranged is radical. As it is to offer a learning that is genuinely rooted in simplicity—"elegant simplicity" in Satish's terms, which captures the quality of experience that the place invites—rather than in the latest technological innovations or the most sophisticated social technologies for learning. Learning as doing, as Leonard and

Dorothy Elmhirst first established in 1923 as they set the foundations for what came to be the Dartington experiment. Learning as encounter. To partake in an encounter is to be a participant in the world, to experiment by joining a process of responsive evocation. And this calling forth that so many of us experienced through the college, I've come to think, is a calling to participate more fully.

I remember William Thomas, who served the college for twenty years under the title of house manager, sitting in the snack area being approached by students giving him suggestions for things they wanted to change in the running of the college; these would range from the cleaning methods to creating sharing groups. Seeing this over and over again through the years, one day after he had been approached with yet another, I asked him how he felt about these suggestions. He looked at me with that expression that was focused yet uninvested and said, "The thing is, Juliana, this place is an experiment. There are no rules here besides what people make of it; people are always trying different things, and some try things that have already been tried many times throughout the years, and it is important that they try."

I then said, "It must be quite interesting for you, all these years, seeing people try things that you know have never worked and yet allowing them to try, and maybe for times being surprised by seeing these finally working." He smiled with the corner of his lips. "Yes, indeed."

JULIANA SCHNEIDER studied Holistic Science at Schumacher College (2011–2012). On her return to Brazil, she founded Escola Schumacher Brazil. She is also a member of the Schumacher Worldwide Research in Action community as a PhD student. escolaschumacherbrazil.com.br

# The Gaian Connection

ADRIANA PUECH

Deep in the Andes Mountains, down the Ruiz volcano, we arrived at a traditional farm where a dairy production cooperates with a forest reserve. Fierce rivers, mountain tops, hot springs, cyanobacteria were just some of the beings that were present in the land that welcomed us.

We talked about the deep time and long life of Gaia. We cooked food while exploring the Earth's composition from its nucleus to the crust. We went into a deep imagining of the tectonic plates moving under our feet and creating our ground at that very moment. We saw all sorts of creatures—algae, sweetwater insects, arboreal ferns, very ancient *arrayán* trees, wax palms, some endemic morpho butterflies that show a characteristic blue color on one side but distinct pale amber on the other, one caracara bird making its nest right in front of our eyes and, at the end of our walk, a majestic falcon that flew over our heads, flapping his wings and keeping himself at the same place for a few minutes.

We cooked, explored and related to the unseen world with awe, making kefir, cheeses and bread, exploring how those bacterial and fungi communities behaved.

We were intimate with water as we watched the stars.

We reclaimed poems

Sang beautiful songs

Told stories

And laughed with great humor.

The sense of friendship, care, adventure, ecstasy and deep experience of nature had never been so present between us. We were deeply connected with Gaia, with its own life manifesting through us…oh what a joy!

This was the recent experience from our residential Schumacher course at the Colombian Certificate Program.

It's been eight years since we started this huge adventure of co-creating a course with Schumacher College; we call it the Certificate in Holistic Science and Sustainable Life.

My experience at Schumacher College was heads- hearts- and hands-blowing! Everything was held with strong coherence and depth. It felt ancient in its legacy as if the organic, feminine, natural world presence was holding that secret place with its utmost hope and care. Before coming to Schumacher College, I felt alone in my endeavors and longings, not really knowing how to address a need for wholeness and a deep connection with nature in my life. Going to the college and belonging to that community became a support and a fertile soil for my dreams.

A two-week short course at Schumacher College provided enough impetus for me to bring forth my part in the creation of Efecto Mariposa, through which we could bring Schumacher College's philosophy and practice to Colombia. For these ten years, we have been nurtured by the core body of knowledge of Schumacher College, applying it to Efecto Mariposa's ethos. We let emergent structures appear without designing them from what might seem logical. None of us has had a fixed role, but we belong to this ecological niche. We *belong* together. In a joint way we have made sure that the whole emerges in front of us with its collective wisdom. Intuition has been core to our decision processes as well as wild imagination in the creation of our programs. We have learned to be rooted in our realities and territories. We have addressed each challenge with integrity and open heart.

Nowadays we are ten butterflies flying, enquiring, pollinating projects, weaving cocoons and creating experiences and knowledge in holistic education, understanding and making visible the relation between the territories we belong to, the food that nourishes us and the Colombian landscapes. We are a community of former students, participants, collaborators and facilitators that gives birth to many different initiatives that have impacted our country with our deepest trust in a much better world.

Attending the MSc in Holistic Science at Schumacher College for one whole year, I understood wholeness and phenomenology as the core structural challenge we are living as a global society. It gave me the possibility to be creative and free, to integrate my fragmented parts in a coherent whole. Chaos and Complexity Theory, the Gaia Theory, sacred ecology and many other key elements of my experience at the college guided me to be whole in myself. I could recognize how it meant a structural revolution in the way of seeing, thinking, feeling and addressing the issues and challenges of life and the world. And how this was important to bring the Schumacher spirit to Colombia.

Since 2012 we have had, each year, a new cycle of the Certificate in Holistic Science and Sustainable Life. It is an eight month-long Schumacher College and Efecto Mariposa process of residential intensives with online tutorials and conversations.

We start by opening our bodies to perception until little by little we embody wholeness. We practice Goethean science with plants, sunsets and sunrises, cascades and mountains. We cook and garden, exchange seeds, relate with soil in depth. We understand life cycles as we see darkness from a new perspective. We let ourselves be transformed by each new cycle, embracing chaos and letting go of what has to die in each of us, entering again and again into this liminal opportunity that allows us to gather our essence and create a new dawn of eco-consciousness.

Then we are ready to encounter with new eyes the world in all its luxurious and sensuous expressions, so Gaia can manifest throughout all its participatory beings. Almost at the end of the course, we bring together our personal inquiries, those that we have visited and streamlined all the way through the program to unfold this particular potential that each of the participants brings to the concert of life, and that meets the needs of the world.

What Schumacher College opened to us has the quality of a never-ending territory with infinite discoveries. Whatever path we decide to take, the Schumacher spirit brings us more joy, more mystery and more beauty to be contemplated. We have learned to relate with abundance from our heads, hearts and hands in this collective journey where we hold tight the questions of our times. Today we cannot be more content, satisfied and grateful for this rich, exciting livelihood and community we have created. We deeply celebrate the life of Schumacher College in our lives with profound gratitude and admiration!

ADRIANA PUECH started her life as an environmental engineer. Later she worked for UNICEF. After studying at Schumacher College, she returned to her native land, Colombia, and established a Certificate in Holistic Science in association with Schumacher College. efectomariposa.space

# Unity in Diversity

SEETHA ANANTHASIVAN

Satish Kumar wrote to me recently, saying that Bhoomi College is like the Indian expression of Schumacher College—they both share a similar philosophy and vision—so will I write an article for the 30th Anniversary commemorative book to be published by Schumacher College? I am pleased to take this opportunity to share our story.

About twenty-one years ago, we started the Prakriya Green Wisdom School, in Bangalore, India, to offer education that brought children closer to Nature and was more holistic in many ways, including the focus on head, heart and hands. About twelve years ago, we set up the Bhoomi Network for Sustainable Living, to offer short programs on a range of themes from food and farming to understanding rainforests, from intensive group participative self-exploration to holistic learning. (*Prakriya* means "process" and *Bhoomi* means "Earth" in many Indian languages.)

Schools in India—as in most countries today—mostly offer monocultural education to help children become good soldiers for the needs of the modern industrial juggernaut. We could question the Western model of education, but changing its rigid centralized structures seemed near impossible. So, we set up learning spaces that could offer new perspectives and possibilities, to help see the larger picture and encourage local action.

We could also see that there was a need to support the youth who were woken up by the enormity of climate change and ecological, social and spiritual crises, but could find no colleges to go to that would be meaningful for them. So, we planned to set up Bhoomi College to offer one-year fellowship programs in Sustainable Living and in

Holistic Education. We wished to offer a different paradigm of learning that supported process and real-life-oriented learning of ecological principles by living in a community. To support us in our work, we had begun connecting with many like-minded people in India who were pioneering activists and thinkers on sustainable living.

Later I visited Schumacher College and attended a Tagore Festival. I took in a short course that gave an overview of holistic science too. Thus, learning and living at Schumacher College influenced my thinking and experience, and I brought that experience with me. What was valuable from Schumacher for me was the way the conceptual frameworks and perspectives from holistic science, Gaia and complexity and chaos theory helped in understanding many of the principles and processes that we worked with in Bhoomi College.

For example, a focus area for us has been to mobilize Indian roots of sustainable living, to learn from our own farmers, tribal people, artisans and others. Indian culture is known for its underpinnings of *unity in diversity* as a strongly holistic theme, which is being trampled upon in the eagerness to embrace the globalized economic system. Rationalistic and reductionist education has made most Indians undervalue the intuitive philosophy of holism of Indian culture. Hence, using scientific frames of thinking about holism that Schumacher is known for, helped us to better articulate and own our holistic processes to address the problems of sustainability in India.

India has also evolved a very large number of traditions of fostering spiritual growth through meditation, yoga, Ayurveda, pilgrimages, chanting and other practices—all with the same aim of finding oneness with a larger reality or universal consciousness. As a culture that evolved over five thousand years or more, India is an amazing manifestation of the part and the whole, emerging and growing together. It is inspiring to see this reality through the lens of holistic science as taught at Schumacher College.

Another example of how the learnings from Schumacher helped us look at our own work with new insights is regarding the core processes some of us have invested in over the last forty years—self-exploration in groups, based essentially on tenets from the Indian *Sankhya* philosophy, including significant work with our emotive selves. These core processes have helped a large number of us co-hold a holistic philosophy but remain individuals in our interests and approaches. Again, we could see that these core processes, rooted in Indian philosophy, can be applied as holistic science.

While there is much that is common in the philosophy of Schumacher College and Bhoomi College, many areas of concern have to be necessarily different for us in India. About seventy percent of the Indian population—over 800 million people—live in rural areas, with most farmers holding less than two acres of land. We have the same problems as in many parts of the world, but on a larger scale—farmer distress and suicides, water famines, great disparities of income, energy- and resource-gobbling unwieldy cities and more. There is now a strong and heartening response to these crises in India, mostly through local and regional initiatives concerning food and farming. We have felt the need to join in and have set up a Learning Center for youth in a rural area.

India also has rich biodiversity which is getting eroded, and some NGOs and educational institutions have been working to conserve rainforests, grasslands, etc. in various regions. We have again felt the need to do our bit and are setting up a research station in the Sharavathi Rainforests in the Western Ghats of India.

Today we need radical systemic change in our economic, political, educational and other institutions. We need more sharing of ideas and working together between the East and the West. In these extremely challenging times that we live in, it feels good to know that Schumacher College exists—a brave and vibrant learning community which is an embodiment of *Unity in Diversity* that integrates much that is valuable in the East and the West.

 SEETHA ANANTHASIVAN is the founder of Aastha Foundation and the editor of *Bhoomi* magazine.

PEACE AND PERMACULTURE DOJO, JAPAN

# Moved by Love

KAI SAWYER

The seeds of Schumacher College were first sown in my mind when I met Satish Kumar at a student-organized educational initiative called The Education for Sustainable Living Program at the University of California Santa Cruz in 2005. This was a time when many young people in the United States were struggling to reconcile the realities of the wars in Iraq and Afghanistan, climate change, racism and inequality against their daily academic lectures which seemed disconnected and irrelevant to our daily human experience.

Satish inspired us, a group of highly motivated University of California students, to reimagine higher education and integrate soil, soul and society into our academic life and activism. We organized a weekly lecture series that was open to the public on important ecological, social and spiritual topics. There was also an activism component called Action Research Teams where students organized projects that aimed to make institutional change in areas like university-wide composting, biofuels for campus shuttles, encouraging the university to go one hundred percent renewable energy and raising awareness about environmental justice. This program had such a profound impact on my life that I dedicated the next two years of my life to being an organizer of the program. As I write this, I now realize that we were a sprout from a seed that had come from the Schumacher College tree.

After two years of busy organizing, I went on a journey into the jungle of Costa Rica to relearn how to live. Living life simply with monkeys, harvesting fruits from the forest, chopping wood, carrying water and cooking with the sun, it was the first time I actually felt the presence of our precious planet and that I was part of nature. From there I spent time at Plum Village Zen monastery and various permaculture farms in Europe to learn how to live in harmony with the earth and myself. I felt like I found what I was looking for and all was good. Then in 2011, a massive earthquake happened that triggered the Fukushima nuclear meltdown in my home country Japan.

I left my permaculture oasis and returned to Japan as I felt I had a mission to do something about this catastrophe. As we say in permaculture circles, "the problem is the solution," but this problem seemed extraordinary. This was a life-changing event for many as they struggled to assess the dangers of living life in nuclear fallout, where the air you breathe, the water you drink and the food you eat contains radiation. Many quit their jobs, moved as far from Fukushima as possible and began to examine their lives more earnestly. In the midst of the confusion, there were a few prominent activists who shined a light for a new ecological and humane vision for society. One of these activists is an anthropologist and university professor, Keibo Oiwa, who has been at the center of the environmental movement in Japan, and it was through getting to know Keibo that I reconnected to Schumacher College.

Keibo had been taking his students to Schumacher College. In 2015, I participated in the Tender Loving Care Japan tour that Keibo and his close collaborator Ueno organized for Satish. During that tour I realized how much of my life journey had been deeply influenced by his teachings. What resonated most were my efforts to integrate sustainable agriculture with social activism and spiritual practice: "soil, soul, society."

It was after this tour that Keibo asked me if I would like to organize a trip to Schumacher College for Japanese people to learn about deep ecology and holistic science and go on the Deep Time walk with Stephan Harding. In 2016, we did our first all-Japanese five-day Schumacher College experience. We were aiming for fifteen participants, but we had so many applicants that we ended up with a group of about twenty-five. Every year we have had over twenty participants, and slowly we have increased the number of days at Schumacher College to seven days at present. There is so much to learn, to experience, to reflect on life and envision how to proceed on each of our pilgrimages.

For me, it is a real treat to spend time at Schumacher College and immerse myself in a community that gracefully engages with the massive challenges we face as humanity. The friendly community in a fairy-tale setting, the creative and holistic pedagogy, the community of like-minded people growing in an ecosystem of hope is truly a refuge for me.

Modern Japan's pursuit of efficiency and speed have made it impossible for us to take time even when we get sick. More and more people sense something is not right, but it's hard to see beyond the symptoms and walk a different path. The people who come with us to Schumacher College are looking for hope, for personal healing, for a change in their lives. To go on an adventure of consciousness and to deepen their "being." It's been an honor to witness people go through a deep healing process during our trips to Schumacher College. For some, it is a completely new experience, sometimes disorienting and emotionally stimulating; for others, it's a remembering. Remembering that we are not alone on this pilgrimage for peace. For me, I see Schumacher College as a mecca for those who love the planet and want to serve life.

Schumacher College is a foundational inspiration for the Peace and Permaculture Dojo that I co-founded in Isumi City, Japan. We wanted to create a refuge, a place for cultural experimentation and a training *dojo* ("a place for the path") for the more beautiful world our hearts know is possible. It is our living tangible vision for the culture of reverential ecology and an education center to explore the holistic trinity of soil, soul, society. Other inspirations include communities like Plum Village monastery and the Bullocks Permaculture Homestead. We are currently renovating an abandoned traditional Japanese farmhouse, learning how to build dwellings, *daichinosaisei* (bamboo charcoal earth regeneration), practicing natural farming and forest gardening, training in nonviolent communication and mindfulness and learning how to grow sustainable culture. Most of those involved have been inspired by Satish, and many have been to Schumacher College on the Japanese tour. I like to think of the Dojo as the Japanese grandchild of Schumacher College, firmly rooted in the earth, traditional Japanese culture and a spirituality that guides us to be moved by love not fear.

 KAI SAWYER is the co-founder of Tokyo Urban Permaculture and the Peace and Permaculture Dojo in Japan. His website is tokyourbanperma culture.com and English blog is livingpermaculture.blogspot.com. His favorite phrase is "moved by love."

THE SCHUMACHER SPROUTS, BELGIUM

# Ne me Quitte Pas…

SABINE DENIS

A couple of years ago, we left the Schumacher College to the sound of the tune "Ne me quitte pas" by the Belgian artist Jacques Brel. The college will "never leave us" (*ne me quitte pas*), no more than we will leave the college. Forever changed by our Schumacher experience at Dartington, we remain deeply grateful to the cosmic forces that brought us there.

Upon our return in Belgium, we interpreted the lyrics of the song literally: "Laisse-moi devenir/L'ombre de ton ombre" ("Let me become/The shadow of your shadow") and began our journey of spreading the Schumacher ecosophy throughout mainland Europe, as it had left a profound mark on us. We planted its first seed in the fruitful soil of the Froidefontaine Farm in Belgium, in the shadow of the college across the Channel.

SABINE DENIS is a visiting professor at Louvain School of Management and a board member of World Wildlife Fund Belgium.

# PART 6

# Schumacher
# Alumni Experiences

# Shaping Sustainability

SARAH BUTLER-SLOSS

After attending an inspirational Schumacher Lecture in London given by Amory Lovins back in 2000 and meeting the wonderful Satish Kumar, I booked myself onto a weeklong course at Schumacher College. It was my first week away from my very young children and felt a big deal at the time. It proved to be a transformational week and an inspirational course, despite the fact that Amory Lovins, the key lecturer, was stuck in the USA, as 9/11 had struck three days previously! I was back the following year and the year after.

Why? The learning approach of Schumacher College inspired an appetite to learn and understand subjects at a deep level, enhanced by the fact that it successfully nurtured the mind, body and spirit at the same time, which is so rare.

As a result, in those three weeks, spread over three years, I learned and developed my thinking hugely, and it inspired a change in my life. Not only did I learn from lectures given by the leading thinkers and players in the sustainability space, such as Janine Benyus, Gunter Pauli, Hardin Tibbs and Amory Lovins, but I spent a week with them, as well as a group of fascinating fellow students. We talked, discussed and debated thoughts and ideas over delicious vegetarian meals, on long walks on Dartmoor, while cutting vegetables for the evening meal or even when cleaning the toilets!

Thus, we delved deeper into issues, exchanged thoughts as equals, had a laugh and experienced some great landscapes, food and drink and music together. From meditating at dawn, lectures in the morning, walking on Dartmoor in the afternoon and playing or dancing to drums in the evening, the Schumacher experience was a wonderful and enriching one. Getting up close and spending time with the leaders in the environmental space also gave one the confidence and appetite to increase one's own contribution to the space.

The Ashden Awards to promote clean, green and sustainable energy systems was just beginning as a small seed of an idea when I started the first course, and thanks to the courses, it took shape and became a more ambitious and exciting organization. I'm one of many other students who was immensely impacted by Schumacher. Many have gone on to significantly shape the sustainability agenda in this country and globally, thanks to the amazing and excellent approach to learning that Schumacher takes. It is certainly the best learning experience I've had. Thank you, Schumacher and all the great people involved with it. Long may it thrive.

SARAH BUTLER-SLOSS created the Ashden Awards. ashden.org

# East and West

NANCY LAN LIU

I first heard of Schumacher College from the Gross National Happiness (GNH) Center in Bhutan and took five courses from late 2015 to mid-2019. The names are the Right Livelihood Program UK and Bhutan—Finding Deeper Purpose; Transitioning to an Ecological Civilization: Dialogues East and West; Nourishing the Soul; the GNH Bridge Program; and lastly the Power of Ritual and the Poetry of Surrender.

Pangolin became my soul animal. The soul vigil connected me with my parents' spirits. My office in Central Hong Kong became Commune 2338, a hub for positive change makers, impact managers and Gaia's guardians.

In a nutshell, Schumacher College has led me to right livelihood, and I've found my comrades. Together we shall construct Indra's Net and achieve harmony at all levels.

 NANCY LAN LIU is a student of spiritual ecology. She has established Commune 2338 as a hub for ecological and spiritual seekers. lan@com mune2338.com

# A New Worldview

TOM RIVETT-CARNAC

When the annals of the great transformation from a world of exploitation and overconsumption to one of regeneration come to be written, as I believe they will, Schumacher College will be revealed as having played an outsized role. But even among the august company of people whose lives and paths have been transformed by the place, I believe there will be few who have benefited as much by its touch as me. Schumacher College not only gave me a new worldview, it gave me a career that has constantly surprised and delighted me and, most importantly, a wonderful wife and later a family. I have traveled a long way since I left the magical place but have always been clear about what I owe to it. It is a debt that can never be repaid.

Apart from a brief visit to attend a course in 2001, I first arrived at the college in 2004 with a beaten-up truck and a few cases of woodworking tools. Anne, Satish, Stephan and Brian generously consented to allow me to live at the college, sleeping usually in North Woods, and I took over a disused studio space. Each day I would cut ash, hazel and elm from the estate and shape it where it lay with knives to create the components of chairs. It was slow, satisfying work, and something about the tactile, mesmeric nature of steel on fresh wood began to attract those that were visiting or teaching at the college to come and spend a few hours or days with me in the woods and we would talk and work together.

Thus, began one of the greatest periods of education in my life. I learned about complexity theory from Brian Goodwin while sitting together in the pouring rain and carving an old oak. I debated the nature of the energy transition with Amory Lovins while selecting hazel stems. I learned more from Wendell Berry about the woods and how to be quiet in them than I have ever been really able to express. And of course, spent many joyful hours in discussion with Satish about love, renunciation and transformation.

And it was not just the teachers. I began to get to know the students on short and long courses, and over time and through many hours of conversation, I began to understand the world in a different way. Like all the best learning, the experience of Goethean observation, emergence, complexity theory and systems thinking felt more like a remembering than something new, but once they had rooted, they changed the way I experienced the world.

They say that change happens in two ways—first very slowly and then very fast. I was at Schumacher College for over two years before the changes that were happening in me began to have a major visible manifestation. This happened first through a partnership with Antony Turner who astonishingly offered me a job as a consultant advising corporations in their transition to the clean economy. He made this offer intuitively, since I clearly had none of the skills or experience needed, but it opened a new vista for me. After some years with him, I was offered another job by Nigel Topping, a fellow participant in the MSc in Holistic Science (in the end I stopped living vicariously through others and did the course myself). Nigel hired me to work with him at Carbon Discloser Project (CDP). For seven years, I learned from him how to engage with the world and push for change without compromising what we had both learned at Schumacher College.

In 2013, my life changed again as I was approached to join the United Nations and to lead political strategy for the UN Climate Convention in the process that eventually led to the Paris Agreement. Working at the highest levels of business and government, the learning about systems thinking and complexity theory were highly valuable as I developed strategies to try to intervene in a broken process. In the end, the Paris Agreement was adopted, and as the gavel came down, I was sitting in the front row, flanked by Nigel Topping and Paul Dickinson, both of whose paths had also been profoundly altered by Schumacher College (and indeed are featured in this book).

Since 2015, I have continued to try to bring together the worldly work of averting the climate crisis with the principles of transformation that I learned years ago at the college. In 2020, I published a book called *The Future We Choose*, together with Christiana Figueres, and continue to run our podcast *Outrage and Optimism*. The footprint of the college, or perhaps its spirit, has never left me, and I hope I have played a role in spreading its message further. For all the years of experience that it now has, the message that it has projected for so long is more relevant now than ever.

I also cannot end this comment without expressing the single transformation for which I am most grateful to the college. When I led a morning chores group to do the laundry one morning in 2006, I was aware that my group contained an exceptionally beautiful young woman, but I never could have known that Natasha Walter, as she was then, would have such an impact on the course of my life. We have now been married for twelve years and have two children, Zoë and Arthur. Schumacher College is the genesis of our origin story and will always be a part of us. I sincerely hope it continues to flourish long into the future.

 TOM RIVETT-CARNAC is the founding Director, with Christiana Figueres, of Global Optimism and co-author of *The Future We Choose: Surviving the Climate Crisis*. globaloptimism.org

# Taking the Tree Trunk
# from Our Eye

NIGEL TOPPING

I arrived at Schumacher College in the summer of 2006, very much a factory manager with an interest in how the world works, a growing awareness of the looming climate and ecological crisis and a thirst for learning. The first lesson I remember was how to significantly upgrade my abilities to see. Of course, the lesson wasn't described as "Improve your seeing capabilities 101" but as a simple drawing lesson. Well, I am no artist, so this was a real challenge. But I am competitive and always eager to please teacher, so I gave it my best shot, determined to produce some beautiful, accurate, evocative drawings of the grand horse chestnut tree at the entrance to the college. We were given a mere thirty seconds to draw, first with pencil, then charcoal, then ink. Week one, back to school, totally out of my comfort zone.

The first two sketches went badly. I looked intently, captured the shape of the tree, noticing some of the gaps which showed patches of sky, the jag of major branches. "Five seconds left!" Thirty seconds go very fast. Determined to produce something which at least looked like the tree, I quickly added a sturdy trunk. Disappointment. Somehow, despite my keenness and attention, my sketch was rubbish. Try again, charcoal this time. More attention to shade and light, impression of the shape. "Five seconds left!" Wow, that went fast. Again, a quick two lines to show the trunk and I was done. Again, disappointment at my childish attempt to represent such a simple object, one we all know how to draw—a tree. One trunk, lots of branches diminishing in size as they spread fractally from the centre and masses of rich green leaves against a clear sky.

241

And suddenly I could see clearly—actually look at the whole tree before me for the first time and realize that I could not see the trunk, so dense was the foliage all around. The trunk was in my eye, my mind's eye, so firmly that I had not been able to draw the real tree. Third attempt lucky, and while by no means did it put me on the path to becoming an artist, it was, at last, recognizably a picture of the actual tree before me—with no trunk visible!

And so now, as I work with a beautiful community of activists, thinkers, policymakers, business leaders, investors, scientists and young people working to address the climate crisis, I am always on the lookout for the tree trunks which block our vision of the true system of the world in which we are embedded. Our blindspots are manifold—the most common being the assumption that somehow, *we* are part of the solution and *others* are part of the problem! This desire to split the world in two, to be right, to be good and for others to be wrong and bad is, I believe, the single biggest barrier to us coming together to implement the solutions at hand. And the corollary is the single biggest lesson I took from my time at the college—we are all connected to everything, we cannot choose to be connected to the trees but not the banks, to organic farms but not to oil. We are all responsible, we must all work together, to build the future we dream of. The pointed finger of blame always finds its way back to us, disempowers us, highlighting our fear rather than inspiring our hope. In demonizing, we play to our weakest instincts, preferring the smug feeling of being right to the scary possibility that we might be wrong and that the other, like us, might just care about our home, our future generations and that together we have the power to change. In opening up to this possibility, we take the tree trunk from our eye and learn to see. We open up our hearts and risk falling in love with the world, the whole world, all over again.

After twenty years working in the manufacturing industry, NIGEL TOPPING used his year at Schumacher College to pivot to working on how to harness the power of business to address global problems. This led him to work at the Carbon Disclosure Project and to leading the We Mean Business coalition in support of a successful Paris Agreement. He acts as the High Level Climate Action Champion for COP26.

# Community Spirit

PAUL DICKINSON

I first visited Schumacher College in 1997 as part of an MSc in Responsibility and Business Practice run by the University of Bath. The cofounder of this course was Anita Roddick, a great humanitarian and visionary founder of the Body Shop. I recall we spent a week at the college, and I found the experience to be completely transformative in a variety of different ways. It may indeed be the combination of experiences that was so powerful.

The first thing I noticed was a community spirit. We lived, cooked and cleaned together, and this forged deep bonds between the students and the faculty, such that we all became participants. This equality created a very nurturing learning environment. The second thing I noticed was that we were consciously exposed to nature and invited to spend time experiencing the natural world as a part of our educational experience. This was a somewhat subversive yet powerful force directing our development. We encounter nature in many forms every day, but to have the experience of nature elevated to a formal component in the educational environment was novel yet transformative. The third thing I noticed was the level of expertise of the teaching staff, either in terms of holistic considerations like morality and ethics, through to holistic science like Gaia theory and the comprehension of geological time.

The impact on me of these experiences was profound. I sought community in many ways, becoming a trustee of the Findhorn Foundation in Scotland a decade later. I became aware of the vast power of nature in terms of processing the energy from the sun, and the fragility of humanity when exposed to changes in earth system conditions. In response to the science I learnt at Schumacher College, I established a non-governmental organization called CDP (formerly Carbon Disclosure Project), with the specific goal of utilizing the power of the global business system to avoid dangerous climate change. For the last ten years, half the management team of CDP have been alumni of Schumacher College through some form of participation. The college exists as a beacon of hope and light in a dangerous time. It has touched me deeply, and I believe it undertakes some of the most important work in the world. It helps people put their inner house in order, better to be able to rearrange the world, for our common good.

PAUL DICKINSON is the executive chair of CDP, and co-founder of Mitchell and Dickinson.

# A Well-Being Economy

JULIA KIM

As the program director of the GNH Centre Bhutan, it has been a powerful and delightful experience to lead programs that have immersed students on a learning journey spanning the vibrant community of Schumacher College and the vast Himalayan mountains of Bhutan. Since 2015, the GNH Centre has collaborated with the college to offer transformative educational programs that blend Bhutan's unique development philosophy of Gross National Happiness (GNH) with the holistic "head, heart and hands" approach embodied by the college. Together with Julie Richardson and Satish Kumar, the Right Livelihood Program and the GNH Practitioner Program have focused on the dynamic interface between the inner transformation of individuals and broader systems change in service of a Well-Being Economy. Together with students from around the world, we have explored how the economy is not a static and immovable structure, but is rather created by our own values, intentions and the systems we choose to create. It is fitting that E. F. Schumacher's notion that "small is beautiful" is reflected, both in the intimacy and deep connection I experienced at the college as well as the bold innovation and experience made possible by the country of Bhutan, partly *because* it is a modest Himalayan kingdom charting its own development path.

From the start, I have been struck by how students have been able to relate to and experience key dimensions of GNH (such as community vitality, time use and psychological well-being) simply by participating in the daily tasks and rhythms of community life in the Old Postern. Moreover, our institutional collaboration has been marked by a natural synergy and alignment of vision, which in turn has enabled the kind of trust, creative freedom and boldness in education that I have seldom encountered elsewhere. It is a testimony to this alchemy that many students have gone on to stay warmly connected with one another, and to share their inspirations, challenges and ongoing efforts in the world, long after the courses have finished. It has been an honor to be a part of this shared journey, which has in turn shaped my own growth and evolution, as well as that of the GNH Centre in Bhutan. At a time of deepening spiritual, social and environmental crisis, I believe that this kind of holistic, action-oriented and transformative education will be of increasing value and importance in the world.

Dr. Julia Kim is the program director, GNH Centre, Bhutan.

# Lasting Gifts

EMILY RYAN

Being a member of the Schumacher College community is one of the great joys of my life. My time at the college began as an MSc Holistic Science student in 2007–2008 and continued after graduation as short course facilitator, and then program director of Cultivating an Ecoliterate Worldview: Person, Place and Practice, from 2010–2014.

As master's students living at the Old Postern, we lived what we learned, digesting the intellectual fare at every turn of our lives together. We were thirteen students, ages 22–62, from eleven countries. When not engaged in studies, we harvested, fermented and cooked wild foods, walked for miles along the River Dart and in the North woods and celebrated around the fire and at the Postern's tiny bar, aptly named the Edge of Chaos. Our conversations lasted long into the night and included everything we'd absorbed during the day: Goethe's dynamic way of seeing and his revolutionary scientific methodology; deep ecology and Gaian systems; and healing the wounds left by reductionist science and corporate capitalism. Over time, an intellectual intimacy grew between us, and we began to dare personal growth and vulnerability.

As an educator, I draw upon what I learned during my tenure at the college in every aspect of my work. After a decade of teaching at the graduate level, I have shifted my attention to teaching science to urban, underserved middle and high school students. These young people are hungry for inspiration and information they can rely on. There are three core lasting gifts I harvested from my experience that inform my work most significantly. They are:

- A grounded, scientifically supported understanding that we are Earth, and as such, we can recreate a role for (young) scientists, one where human beings act in solidarity with all life, rather than in control of it.

- The unwavering belief that, regardless of circumstance, all humanity shares in the birthright of knowing their true nature, and that this vital knowledge is what must take us through the complex crisis we are now facing.
- Because of what we achieved as an MSc cohort, I am seized by a calling to have others experience what a learning community can truly be: a place of reciprocity, where mutual respect and care create the conditions for this true nature to emerge and flourish.

We must learn how to teach our children, *all* our children, that they have intrinsic value as a unique part of the web of life, and as such, they each play an essential role in the healing of our world. Creating a learning environment where children are safe enough to stretch themselves into these new areas of growth, to be vulnerable enough to champion their own experience, and the experience of their peers, is critical to the success of this endeavor.

Attending a year-long residential master's program is an enormous privilege. Schumacher College made me stronger, more focused and better trained to stand on this unwavering ground. If someone had asked me what I was looking for in a college, as the real estate agent did with the Elmhirsts the day they went shopping for an estate, in addition to it being "beautiful," I would have said, "I want it to be brave." Schumacher College is both.

EMILY RYAN, MSc, is a transformative educator who teaches ecological awareness and the shift to a planetary identity to students all over the world, ranging from inner-city youth to adult communities. Emily@ emilyryan.net

# A Home and a Community

EVE ANNECKE *and* FIONA TILLEY

We first came to the college as short course participants. We have since returned many times as teachers, facilitators and participants. Our first time working together was in February 2013 on a course titled Beyond Development. Since then, we have taught on Becoming Indigenous, the MA in Ecology and Spirituality and facilitated numerous short courses. We share a passion for process-led teaching. Its introduction more formally into the college pedagogy further supports the integration and deeper learning provided by the transformational context of the Schumacher community. In a nod to being sometime facilitators, we have chosen to meander through our memories of life at Schumacher College using the practice of a virtual dialogue. Imagine, as we have done often, stepping into the snack room of the Old Postern, where you meet old friends and catch up over a cup of herbal tea.

*Tell me again, what was it that called you to walk up the
driveway past the horse chestnut tree to the college for the first time?*
**Tilley:** Passing the horse chestnut, her conkers were scattered everywhere across the driveway. It was mid-October 2008, and I was here for a course on Mythodrama being led by Richard Olivier and supported by Emily Ryan. In fairness, I knew little to nothing about either. It was more the course title, Sustainable Leadership, and the college's reputation that had called me. Or at least that is what I thought then. I was a lecturer in Environment and Business at the University of Leeds. After over twelve years of teaching, it was slowly dawning on me that I was making very little difference to the lives of my students or having much impact on sustainable development. I was in need of the educational reminder that it was possible to make a difference.

**Eve:** I came to participate in Fritjof Capra's five-week short course on systems theory in the summer of 1993. Seven months pregnant with my second-born and South Africa on the brink of our first democratic elections. I received a message about this strange and new place for studies in ecology and spirituality via an ancient technology: word of mouth. No World Wide Web, email or social media back then. Not sure how word had traveled that fast to the southern tip of the African continent, but that's what happened.

*What happened as a consequence of that brush with community learning?*
**Eve:** I've come to see the horse chestnut as a kind of portal. I became vegetarian, for one. A lifelong friend of the college for another. Along with a visit to the Gorée Institute, Senegal, I was indelibly inspired by the role of place in transformative learning. So much so, that it seemed I was pregnant not only for my second-born, but the Sustainability Institute and Lynedoch EcoVillage, Stellenbosch, South Africa, were seeded too. These became an articulation of post-apartheid, democratic values through ecology, community and the human spirit.
**Tilley:** Twelve months later, I was back at the college to wrap up the Certificate in Education for Sustainable Development. I had just completed my notice and had walked away from my tenured lectureship into an unknown future. I honestly believed at the time that within six months I would have found a new career and be on my way again. Little did I know that I was fundamentally changed by my time at the college. The unlearning was about to commence. Thankfully I was well held by the college community, and I had been invited to volunteer. I have so many people to be utterly grateful to for the kindness they showed me during this time of unfolding and changing. The college is the perfect place to be in a liminal state. No one questions this state of being. A rare experience, I have found.

*You are one of those who have found themselves returning again and again, can you describe what the college has come to represent for you?*
**Tilley:** This is the easiest of all questions to answer. The college to me is home. As Ram Das says, we are all walking each other home. Schumacher has been one of those places where my heart has felt most open. I feel truly blessed to have found it.
**Eve:** Coming home. Joy in participating in so many different groups

in various roles, at times, too, of great personal trauma and struggle, I have somehow found myself in the spaciousness of the ancient yew tree, walking with the River Dart, sweeping the floor, cooking, being held by the buzz of community living and riveting intellectual engagement simultaneously woven into my own inner gaze. This joyous, messy grittiness in the exquisiteness that is Dartington is for me quite unique.

*What does the college represent for you now?*
**Tilley:** A very good friend and fellow Schumacher College facilitator, Richenda MacGregor, once described the college to me as a living organism. It is a being that is ever changing, never the same from one day to the next. Every time I step into its environs after a break of a few weeks or more, I have noticed changes. People have left or arrived. Ways of doing things have subtly altered. The nuance of the community culture has evolved. Do you gong before sessions or not? Is there still a whiteboard in the reception area for orientation? Is the cooking led or un-led at the weekends? Are there planning meetings on Tuesday and Friday mornings?

   In spite of all these necessary procedural activities, the college remains for me at its core a home and the community a family. It is a place that I find acceptance and belonging. Unfortunately, in the modern world these are ever-diminishing qualities. I therefore cherish the college community deeply for the safe harbor it has offered me over the last thirteen years.
**Eve:** A place where Rauiri showed me I can sing. A home brew of creative imaginations that expand and contract, like breath. Friendship. Stories.

*Can you share a memory that rests in*
*your travel bag like a much-cherished gift?*
**Eve:** It is winter, midnight and raining. A group of us have gathered in the Postern courtyard with our teachers Loretta Afraid of Bear Cook and Karonhienhawe "Linda" Delormier. It is the first of four midnight sweat lodges in Redwoods. To end, they assure us, by 2:30 a.m. each night. Loretta is in her seventies, her hair long, grey and beautiful. They are in pink dressing gowns, nighties and gumboots. We arrive at the sweat lodge in nerves covered by general hilarity—Schumacher

mayhem. The fire is really hot. The rocks arrive, and somehow we are so busy settling that there is no welcoming prayer to the ancestors. Pray, I urge, pray! And suddenly there is a loud crack as a rock splits. In that strange crack, we fall into the abyss, and our night lodges delve into the universe, to places long forgotten. And then, as suddenly, it's over and we are muddily making our way back to bed. A bedraggled array of wide-eyed humans.

**Tilley:** There are so many and I keep adding to them (thankfully). I could say watching William Thomas making his classic chai for those attending an Earth Talk when they used to be held in the Old Postern. Or the time the same William gave me a boiler suit to wear while I clamber on top of the ovens to clean the fan above (a gem of a volunteer afternoon task).

Then there was the evening I could hear Martin Shaw and participants playing the drums in the time leading up to an evening session. I also hold a special place for a time I sat around a fire in Brian's garden listening to one of my poetry heroes, Drew Dellinger.

My overriding go-to memory is from May 2011, Iain McGilchrist had just delivered a lecture on the short course Divided Brain; not being on the course, I was waiting in the dining room for the group to arrive for lunch. As people began to trickle in, there was a palpable feeling that something quite extraordinary had just happened. Eventually I saw Philip Francis, eyes sparkling and a wry smile. All he said was, "That's one of the best lectures I've heard." High praise indeed. Some of us rushed to the facilitator to grab the recorder and quickly copied the audio onto a computer upstairs in the student common room. Later that afternoon we lay in hammocks and sofas listening to Ian's groundbreaking discourse from his book *The Master and the Emissary*.

It was moments like that when I could pinch myself for how lucky I was to be a part of such a place as Schumacher College.

*You described earlier the college as a living dynamic organism with a life of its own, ever changing and evolving. If you could describe one quality of this living being that most allures you, what would it be?*
**Tilley:** The college is a learning community with a regular turnover of students, volunteers and staff. This brings with it newness and vitality. This sits within a solid container that acts like a backbone to

each week. The container is the rhythm of the day made up of shared moments when the entire community is invited to gather for morning meetings and mealtimes, fireside chats with Satish and Monday night open lectures, not to mention soirees on a Thursday at the end of a course. At these regular beats of togetherness, I get to experience the inbreath and outbreath of the college community's collective learning. This is often when the most spontaneous and anarchic moments occur. The care for one another, and our bigger ecological self—Gaia—can palpably be felt.

**Eve:** Mystery. Something happens every single time. I have thought that all that is needed is an open heart. But it doesn't mean everyone leaves happy. When a thing happens, it is often the crunchy one that walks alongside one for the longest time afterwards. Doing its transforming kind of work.

*If you found yourself standing on the front lawn of the Postern*
*with a magic wand in your hand, what one wish would you make*
*for the college going forward into its next thirty years?*

**Tilley:** If I had a Harry Potter moment and could point my hazel wand at the college, I would ask for the Postern to grow legs so that we could move it around the world and many more people could experience what it is like to live and learn here. Or instead of growing legs, the college could become more like a rhizome sending out subterranean roots and shoots connecting past, present and future alumni, enabling them to establish their own Schumacher-inspired projects in their own places. Thereby expanding the reach of this amazing home of ecological transformation much further.

**Eve:** I'd magic a message from the land that wove an invisible cloak that whispered "sanctuary" over Dartington, and then spread gently and fast across the world carrying community, myth, laughter and connection.

EVE ANNECKE is a Bertha Fellow exploring the power in retreat. She is a co-founder of Sustainability Institute, Stellenbosch, South Africa.

FIONA TILLEY stepped away from her academic career and university life, and she is now an eco-facilitator.

# PART 7

# The Future

# Regenerative Learning

PAVEL CENKL

*What is, is now, must have the quivering intensity*
*of an arrow thudding into a tree.*
—J. A. BAKER, THE PEREGRINE

## Foundations

I arrived at Schumacher College on a rainy Sunday afternoon in early October 2019, and after being given a ride to campus by Stephan Harding and Julia Ponsonby and being shepherded into my temporary lodging in the Postern Cottage for some much needed jetlag-induced rest, I found my way to the dining room for a delicious supper of leftovers assembled and warmed by students and volunteers. Thanks to the welcoming community of staff, students and volunteers, I found my footing in a few weeks and felt I had truly found my place as a part of this new family.

As the new Head of College, I was asked almost immediately after arriving about my ideas and vision for the future Schumacher—a college with a thirty-year history of progressive education, nearly 20,000 alumni around the world, and with Satish Kumar's continuing presence as the community's spiritual leader.

Humility. Patience. Listening. Learning. Living.

These words were the touchstones I reached for in my answers nearly every time.

Clearly, as the many voices in this book have shared, the legacy of education at Schumacher College is deep and expansive, and I continue to learn each day about the profound relationships that make this place what it is. Over three decades, the college has built an international reputation for holistic and progressive education with an emphasis on community, ecology and the strength of shared work to build meaningful and generative relationships.

What we have come to call *community learning* is a foundational practice of Schumacher's ethos. This deep weave of living, learning and working together is the fabric of every day and is the rhythm by which everything else at the college grows. Days begin with porridge and a creative array of fruits, nuts, yoghurts and milks to make an entirely different breakfast experience each day. Prepared each day by one of the college's volunteers, breakfast is simple, the soaking of the oats overnight linking one day to the next.

Morning meeting is the foundation of every day. We meet for only thirty minutes, but the meeting is a chance to share readings, ideas and announcements and set the tone for the day. With more than two hundred morning meetings each year, everyone has many chances to facilitate, participate and shape the day as they choose.

To ask, "What does the future of Schumacher College look like?" is really to ask, "What is the future of higher education?" When I came to Schumacher in 2019, the college was on the cusp of a substantial revisioning of many of its systems. Further, by dint of a failing centuries-old slate roof, the college had been forced to leave its spiritual home, the Old Postern, for the first time since 1991. By October, the community was still coming to terms with what it meant to be connected to place and had found creative ways to work in new surroundings.

What struck me then, and what continues to encourage my thinking about the college, is that the students, staff and volunteers came to realize that Schumacher College was not a thing, and not a building, but a set of ideas and a way of life that could hold a community of learners together with a shared ethos and approach to living, learning and working in a shared community of practice.

The core of Schumacher College has always been the dynamic interweaving of rhythms of experience, ecological systems and learning. As we celebrate the college's first thirty years, I am reminded of all the work done to foster, support and celebrate community learning before my arrival—from prior heads of college, administrators, and faculty to learning community coordinators and volunteers all helping to create the space for learning as a continuum across students' lived experience in the community and to the thousands of students who each added their own timbre to the songs we sing at morning meeting that ground us at the start of every day.

The key to maintaining successful communities, as we have learned through the years, is to embrace and encourage their dynamism, vibrancy and passion—as we must in order to continue the evolution of the Schumacher community into the future.

In writing this chapter about Schumacher's future, I am reminded of the work of Donella Meadows, who wrote in 1997 about finding leverage points at which to maximize our ability to change complex systems. She explained that "ideas, cultures, community norms and paradigms are the sources of systems. From them, from shared social agreements about the nature of reality, come system goals and information flows, feedbacks, stocks, flows and everything else about systems." If we can address our global challenges at the level of cultural paradigms and worry less about making incremental changes in our daily behavior, she suggested, we can have far greater success in making meaningful change.

Dr. Meadows was right, of course, and although she never taught at Schumacher College, her work underlies much of what we do. I firmly believe that by identifying community learning and daily rhythms of practice as the core of learning, the college has built a solid foundation for a flourishing learning environment whose participants are empowered to leave the college and go out into the world and make meaningful change in their own communities.

## A Crisis of Form

> *Every nation and every man instantly surround themselves*
> *with a material apparatus which exactly corresponds*
> *to their moral state, or their state of thought...It follows,*
> *of course, that the least enlargement of ideas...would cause*
> *the most striking changes of external things.*

—RALPH WALDO EMERSON

This epigraph, from an 1838 lecture, entitled "War," Mr. Emerson gave on nonviolent resistance is a foundational statement on how the social construction of ideologies reifies ideological spaces which then reinforce cultural conventions. Of the many subsequent thinkers, writers and activists who have engaged with this idea, I am most often inspired by the striking visual work of Neri Oxman of the MIT

MediaLAB as a means to make tangible many of the questions inherent in Mr. Emerson's lecture.

Dr. Oxman, an influential designer and scientist, has worked for many years at the intersection of art, science and design and has spoken and written widely about the need for more multiscale systems that are interdisciplinary in both their nature and structure. I could think of few examples more salient for the development of a resilient, adaptive and multiscale curriculum.

In her engagement with material design, Dr. Oxman explores the power of gradients—suggesting that an increased resolution (in modeling, 3D printing and computation) can help us to make objects with gradients so fine they challenge our notion of boundary and of materiality entirely. She continues to interrogate the privileging of form over the use of materials we have readily to hand; she asked in her 2010 doctoral thesis ("Material-Based Design Computation"), "How can a material first approach, prioritizing environmental performance and material behavior over form, be accommodated by design, and in what stages of the design process can such an approach be implemented?"

We find ourselves in a similar "crisis of form" in education today, wherein even the best-intentioned programs in ecological thinking and sustainability are effectively locked in a staid paradigm of learning that emphasizes traditional modes of engagement with ideas. Imagine if we could ground every program by meditating on the idea that nature does not first set out thinking, "I need to make a tree; what should I make it out of?" But, rather, we would recognize that trees grow in intimate relationship with their ecosystem, in concert with the soil and sun and soaking rains, and entwined with the spirit and substance they derive from the seed from which they began.

In a reflection on John Dewey and Ralph Waldo Emerson, Richard Rorty writes, "One should stop worrying about whether what one believes is well grounded and start worrying about whether one has been imaginative enough to think up interesting alternatives to one's present beliefs." At Schumacher, this imagination stems from the delicate balance between individual learning and working with the community and the creative problem solving that is born of our engagement with one another as we move through the rhythms of learning every day.

It is in this reflective nature of learning, where community support enables an open and collaborative engagement with creative, integrative, codesigned and often transgressive ideas that we can find the most potential for a new revolution in regenerative learning.

## A Regenerative Revolution

> *Sustainability is not deliverable. Sustainability is not a thing.*
> *Sustainability is not simply about efficient technologies*
> *and techniques. It is about life…it is a process of reciprocal*
> *relationship—a process by which living things support*
> *and are supported by a larger whole.*
>
> — BILL REED

In the 1980s, Robert Rodale helped to popularize the term *regenerative* with respect to agriculture when he coined the term *regenerative organic agriculture*, noting that we need to think and act "beyond sustainability, to renew and to regenerate our agricultural resources." Regenerative organic agriculture, he wrote, "takes advantage of the natural tendencies of ecosystems to regenerate when disturbed. In that primary sense, it is distinguished from other types of agriculture that either oppose or ignore the value of those natural tendencies."

Since then, the term *regenerative* has found its way into many disciplines, from architectural design to medicine and technology to leadership design and community development to braking systems on hybrid automobiles. Although varied in its approach in different disciplines, this *regenerative turn* has helped to reinforce the reinvestment of energy, capital and resources into building new systems that are more socially, economically and ecologically resilient, and which begin to reintegrate separate systems toward the goal of a single unified socioecological system.

*Learning* in a regenerative fashion, specifically, underlies all of these practices, and as such, learning can be both the foundation and the catalyst for further developing regenerative thinking across many different industries. Particularly as regenerative thinking acknowledges that humans are themselves "nature," and there is greater hope of evolutionary potential in a state of intentional interrelationship.

According to Bill Reed and Pamela Mang, regenerative design is co-evolutionary and is entwined in the "development of a whole system of interrelated living consciousness—a new mind." Regenerative learning must be dynamic and must leave space for what might be described as a "continuous re-patterning." Take the pattern of a graduate seminar, for example. If you have been in higher education long enough, whether as a student or a teacher, you have a nearly instinctive sense of what that experience might be like: students seated around a table, notebooks or laptops open before them as they prepare for a discussion on the day's topic. After some opening pleasantries, the professor will deliver an opening statement to help frame the day and then ask some general questions. Discussion carries on with students bringing examples, challenging one another, asking questions, with the professor guiding and inserting themselves only to help keep the class headed in the right direction.

What would be different if, instead of in the classroom, students met the professor in an open field, or in a woodland or by the river? What if they stood or walked, without notebooks or laptops in hand? What if it began to rain? Would the class retreat into a classroom? Why?

What if each day in class was different, with the class dynamic responsive and "classroom" space being distinctly aligned with topic, season, weather and student engagement? Why should field trips be an exception rather than a daily practice? These are practices already interwoven into the daily practice of learning at Schumacher.

Christopher Alexander, who taught at Schumacher College for an extended period, writes in his wildly influential book, *A Pattern Language*, "When you build a thing, you cannot merely build that thing in isolation, but must also repair the world around it, and within it, so that the large world at that one place becomes more coherent, and more whole; and the thing which you make takes its place in the web of nature, as you make it."

Regenerative learning enfolds, refolds, reintegrates, generates, regenerates and spirals both inwards and outwards in an energetic dance that supports the whole while expanding outward to create new community clusters wherever tendrils of learning reach into new places, take root and flourish.

Regenerative learning is rooted in the everyday, entwined with the infinite and reaches toward the yet to be imagined. It embraces adaptation, is nourished by feedback loops and fosters the dynamic emergence of resilient systems.

It is tied to ecological systems at every level—from sharing time in the gardens sowing seeds, weeding or harvesting produce—to co-creating meaningful course assignments, from program development to governance across the institution.

Regenerative learning insists that we rethink education at every scale and in every instance.

Regenerative learning:

- Is always an emergent choreography of integrative practices.
- Actively creates space for uncertainty and ambiguity.
- Nurtures creative, compassionate, critical, playful and contemplative practitioners.
- Flourishes in a network of learning communities grounded in ensemble methodologies.
- Incites a lifelong hunger and yearning for learning, curiosity, search, inquiry and wonder.

To be part of an evolving model of regenerative learning is one of the main reasons I came to Schumacher College. The future of the college, in concert with Dartington Hall Trust, is one tied to the future of learning across the globe—a model of learning that helps us to rebuild community, reconnect with ecological systems, create roadmaps for new social, artistic and economic approaches to our world's challenges—in short, regenerate at every scale.

However, without every aspect of this system communicating with every other, without the soil in the garden or the water in the River Dart straining at its banks in springtime informing the decisions made around the conference tables at the college, regenerative learning is incomplete.

Without the college encouraging its alumni around the world to continue building on what they have learned—about economics, or science, or design, but also about *learning* itself—regenerative learning is incomplete.

Without understanding and responding to inputs and feedback from all stakeholders and constituencies, regenerative learning is incomplete.

The challenges are great, but the blueprint is here, even if as yet incomplete, laid out before us on the table, surrounded by our cups of mid-morning tea, a jar of dried apples perched on the corner and a cozy fire in the nearby woodburner.

It starts here, with us, now.

## Flourishing

> We are not lacking in the dynamic forces needed
> to create the future. We live immersed in a sea of energy
> beyond all comprehension.
>
> — THOMAS BERRY

We may be in a time of profound ecological and social challenges, but we cannot let that limit our thinking to being reactive and only focusing on resistance. Institutions like Schumacher College are essential—as beacons of hope, as places of animated regeneration—to help us rebuild learning from the ground up and guide us toward engaging with the richness of cultures and ecologies that seems always to envelop us.

We must always soak the oats for tomorrow's porridge.

Thomas Berry, former Schumacher College teacher and self-proclaimed *geologian* (an earth-rooted theologian), would no doubt have embraced the idea, one which draws together many threads of this chapter, of "designing to evoke aliveness." In their important work on *Cultivating Communities of Practice*, Etienne Wenger et al. have coined this phrase to describe the many ways that communities can be helped to develop a vibrancy and forward momentum to develop into communities like the one at Schumacher College, to keep planting the seeds to cultivate an entwined sense of aliveness—a way for us to continue leading the way toward a fully immersive learning community at the forefront of ecologically focused *thinking, making and being*.

We can and must do better, and I can think of no more progressive and energetic and just and magical place than Schumacher College to lead the way.

I am fortunate to be here at the college and see these ideas in practice every single day. Sometimes when I walk through the campus, perhaps to Craft Ed for a cup of afternoon tea, I might pass our garden team as they make their way up the lane from Henri's Field, wheelbarrows and tools in hand, sodden and muddy from the late winter fields, and talking, already, about tomorrow's plans.

When I bring my cup or porridge bowl to wash it in the kitchen, I often talk with the cooks about their plan for the day—whether that's about installing a new oven or making pavlova for a special dessert.

On Wednesday mornings when I make my way to breakfast, the Chicken Shed is practically vibrating with the sounds and movement of students and volunteers engaged in "morning glory"—a weekly hour of dance to celebrate the very act of being alive in this magnificent place.

And when I join students at mealtimes (my favorite thing to do at the college), I nearly always hear something about what they are studying that day, where they are heading for class that week and how it is their shared practice as a community of learners—nearly as much as the time spent in the classroom—that they feel most connected with.

Wherever I go, I am reminded that Schumacher always resonates with the entwined rhythms of thinking, making and being in every aspect of what we do.

Head, Heart and Hands must be the foundation for the next thirty years of Schumacher College to redefine learning around the world. With our global network of nearly 20,000 alumni, with active alumni clusters in over a dozen different countries, together we have sown the seeds; we have cultivated the terrain; and now more than ever we need to come together to help this future flourish.

Much work lies ahead.

Join us.

You are always welcome.

Before becoming the Head of Schumacher College, DR. PAVEL CENKL was the Dean of Sterling College, Vermont. He is working on a new book titled *Resilience in the North: Adventure, Endurance and the Limits of the Human.*

# Acknowledgments

Good projects are always a consequence of co-creation. This book is no exception.

First of all, thank you Rob West and your team at New Society Publishers, including the editor Murray Reiss, for your most enthusiastic and inspiring collaboration in the making of this book. It has been a pure pleasure to work with you all.

Thanks to my colleagues at Schumacher College, particularly Pavel Cenkl, Julia Ponsonby and Stephan Harding for your advice, help and support in contacting contributors and conceptualizing the book.

I would like to express my deep gratitude to Jenny Routley at the Resurgence Trust. I am a techno novice and without your skillful, efficient and loving involvement, corresponding and communicating with more than fifty contributors, this book would not have come to fruition. We worked during the lockdown of COVID-19. So, while maintaining the social distance, we managed to work efficiently and intimately! So, thank you very much, Jenny, for your marvelous help.

Mark Gough and Elaine Green also gave their time, attention and assistance in the realization of this book. I am most grateful to you both.

My thanks go to Angéline Bichon and Delia Spatareanu for your delightful illustrations and outstanding photography which make the book visually pleasing and inspiring.

Last but not least, my heartfelt gratitude and thanks go to all the contributors who have offered their articles as a labor of love. Without your generosity, the book would not have been possible. This book is a product of the gift economy. Thank you all.

# About the Editors

SATISH KUMAR, long-time peace and environment activist and former Jain monk, has been quietly setting the global agenda of change for over 50 years. He settled in the United Kingdom after an 8,000-mile peace pilgrimage and took the editorial helm of *Resurgence* magazine in 1973, a post he held until 2016. Over the decades, he has been the guiding spirit behind a number of internationally respected ecological and educational ventures, including founding Devon's Schumacher College, authoring several books, including *Elegant Simplicity*, and presented the documentary *Earth Pilgrim*. Satish was awarded an Honorary Doctorate in Education from the University of Plymouth, an Honorary Doctorate in Literature from the University of Lancaster and the Jamnalal Bajaj International Award for Promoting Gandhian Values Abroad. He appears regularly in the media, is on the Advisory Board of Our Future Planet, and he continues to teach and run workshops as a sought-after speaker in the UK and abroad. He lives in Devon, UK.

PAVEL CENKL, PhD, is Head of Schumacher College and Director of Learning at Dartington Trust. Formerly Dean at Sterling College in Vermont, Pavel has spent decades weaving together expertise in ecologically minded curriculum development, environmental philosophy and experiential learning. An avid endurance and adventure runner, through a project called Climate Run, Pavel has covered hundreds of miles in the Arctic and subarctic on foot in order to bring attention to the connections between our bodies and the more-than-human world in the face of a rapidly changing climate. He is author of *Nature and Culture in the Northern Forest* and *This Vast Book of Nature*. Pavel lives in Devon, UK.

## ABOUT NEW SOCIETY PUBLISHERS

New Society Publishers is an activist, solutions-oriented publisher focused on publishing books for a world of change. Our books offer tips, tools, and insights from leading experts in sustainable building, homesteading, climate change, environment, conscientious commerce, renewable energy, and more—positive solutions for troubled times.

We're proud to hold to the highest environmental and social standards of any publisher in North America. When you buy New Society books, you are part of the solution!

- We print all our books in North America, never overseas
- All our books are printed on **100% post-consumer recycled paper**, processed chlorine-free, with low-VOC vegetable-based inks (since 2002)
- Our corporate structure is an innovative employee shareholder agreement, so we're one-third employee-owned (since 2015)
- We're carbon-neutral (since 2006)
- We're certified as a B Corporation (since 2016)

At New Society Publishers, we care deeply about *what* we publish—but also about *how* we do business.

Download our catalog at https://newsociety.com/Our-Catalog or for a printed copy please email info@newsocietypub.com or call 1-800-567-6772 ext 111.

## ENVIRONMENTAL BENEFITS STATEMENT

**New Society Publishers** saved the following resources by printing the pages of this book on chlorine free paper made with 100% post-consumer waste.

| TREES | WATER | ENERGY | SOLID WASTE | GREENHOUSE GASES |
|---|---|---|---|---|
| **42** | **3,400** | **18** | **150** | **18,100** |
| FULLY GROWN | GALLONS | MILLION BTUs | POUNDS | POUNDS |

Environmental impact estimates were made using the Environmental Paper Network Paper Calculator 4.0. For more information visit www.papercalculator.org.

Certified

**B** Corporation

MIX

Paper from responsible sources

FSC® C016245

www.fsc.org

new society
PUBLISHERS
www.newsociety.com